TOY STORIES

Toy Stories

ANALYZING THE CHILD IN NINETEENTH-CENTURY LITERATURE

Vanessa Smith

FORDHAM UNIVERSITY PRESS   NEW YORK 2023

Fordham University Press has no responsibility for the persistence or
accuracy of URLs for external or third-party Internet websites referred
to in this publication and does not guarantee that any content on such
websites is, or will remain, accurate or appropriate.

Fordham University Press also publishes its books in a variety of electronic
formats. Some content that appears in print may not be available in
electronic books.

Visit us online at www.fordhampress.com.

Library of Congress Cataloging-in-Publication Data
available online at https://catalog.loc.gov.

Printed in the United States of America
25 24 23   5 4 3 2 1
First edition

for Leo and Georg

Contents

Preface: A Toy Is Being Beaten

Maria Edgeworth introduces a tract on children's education with the problem of the child's will to destroy its playthings. The Brontë siblings begin their literary lives scripting antagonistic games with toy soldiers in tiny books. Esther Summerson, departing the scenes of her early childhood, buries her beloved "Dolly" in the garden. Agnes Grey's young pupil mercilessly beats a rocking horse. Maggie Tulliver batters the torso of a wooden doll to soothe her wounded feelings. Over the course of the nineteenth century, and across the variety of genres through which that century represented its children, we find example after example of infantile rage, shame, and distress made manifest through the brutalized toy. Not quite domesticated or socialized by the educational treatises, juvenilia, marriage plots, and Bildungsromane that contain them, scenes of sabotage enacted in play offer glimpses of un-Romantic nineteenth-century childhoods overwhelmed by a visceral anxiety that seeks relief in the domain of first possessions. Children repeatedly thwart the hopes of the object lesson. They willfully break their toys. Moreover this destructiveness is registered as a mode of communication, disclosing levels of emotion that the child cannot yet otherwise articulate. Toy damaging may manifest a perverse cherishing, or comfort-seeking, but the interiority it addresses is psychic before it is domestic. It parlays with negative feeling: anger, envy, frustration, and then grief and guilt. It is transgressive but typical, crossing genders, classes, and races and displaying itself in heroes and villains, "good" children and "bad," the spoiled and the deprived, the otherwise responsible and the irredeemably delinquent. It can be co-opted by enlightened commentators or reminiscing adults as creatively formative, but its spirit of refusal must also be acknowledged.

    Broken toys do not feature in the accepted history of Euro-American child-
hood. By that account, the late eighteenth century sees the emergence of an
individuated child subject in the educational treatises of Locke and Rousseau,
both of whom begin to formulate a fundamental qualitative separation between
childish and adult capacities and apprehensions. For Locke, the child is a proto-
rational subject, and the territory of play is preserved for the articulation of
minor childish difference: "I consider them as children that must be tenderly
used, that must play and have playthings."[1] Rousseau argues more broadly that
"nature wants children to be children before being men," and proposes that
"childhood has its ways of seeing, thinking, and feeling which are proper to
it."[2] The Romantics expanded Rousseau's notion of a distinct childish discernment, privileging the innocent child as a touchstone of moral integrity. Virginia
Blum briskly follows this narrative across the nineteenth century:

> While the eighteenth century began to formulate childhood as a trope
> in antagonism to perceived incursions of industrialization, the nine-
> teenth century promoted the child to a subject in its own right. Thus
> the Romantics created the "child" as a potential space for the adult
> imagination, a figure for the recuperation of a pre-industrial attune-
> ment with nature; as the nineteenth century progressed, this imagina-
> tive space was increasingly legitimated as lived experience. The child's
> relationship to the adult was reshaped from one of dominance and
> subordination, as well as the distinction between the inchoate and the
> achieved subject, into a futile encounter between the nostalgic imagi-
> nation (the bliss of childhood innocence) and a progressive evolution-
> ary mythology. [. . .] The site called "childhood" was isolated as an
> extrasocial haven from a growing sense of anxiety attendant on adult-
> level experience.[3]

The overwrought or furious child wreaking havoc with its objects can, with
effort, be recuperated to this notion of pre-industrial nostalgia. But the child
saboteur's protest, with its surplus of psychic ambivalence, represents an irre-
futable manifestation of childhood anxiety, rather than of exemption from a
yet to be unlocked "adult-level experience."
    As with histories of the child, stories of damage do not feature in histories
of the toy, which tend to be either material- or consumer-culture focused. In
both cases a parallel trajectory to the child's is adumbrated, with mini-adult
toy artifacts giving way to independent childish playthings. Teresa Michals
argues that the violence that characterized the lives of Medieval and early
modern children was "fence[d] out of child-safe spaces, the physical and

cultural spaces in which children were encouraged to play" during the eighteenth and nineteenth centuries.[4] Michals claims that a reduction in the aggression of child's play was a corollary of this development of a "child-safe"
ethos: "The open violence of earlier children's play is perhaps its most dramatic
difference from later ideals."[5] Antonia Fraser suggests that "with the dawn of
the eighteenth century, one is immediately conscious of a change of atmosphere
in the world of toys. [. . .] It is as though the eighteenth-century children at last
relax."[6] In Fraser's and many other toy histories, the evolution of play is conflated
with purported cultural evolution, with the primitive cultural artifact being
shown to "grow up" into the complex or benign modern toy of which it is the
progenitor.[7] However eighteenth-century child's play appears in a more aggressive light, both domestic and political, in literary texts such as Cowper's "Hope,"
where

> From infancy through childhood's giddy maze,
> Froward at school, and fretful in his plays,
> The puny tyrant burns to subjugate
> The free republic of the whip-gig state.[8]

The nineteenth-century children's literary archive divulges numerous such
puny infant tyrants engaging in openly violent play. Though the plots of children's tales work hard to chastise and school destructive behaviors, the naughty
child's come-uppance often fails to undo the damage it inflicts upon narratives
of proper developmental conduct. The literary examples that this book uncovers
attest neither to childhood as an innocent, extrasocial haven nor to the toy as
repository of increasingly benign affect.[9] Yet precisely because those narratives
of infancy and play are so firmly entrenched, scenes of toy damaging, which
provide glimpses of the child not repressed but regressed, stand out in the
nineteenth-century archive. They render a child full of rage and woe visible
through its objects.

    This book proposes that to understand nineteenth-century depictions of the
child and its surprisingly fractious play we need to think forward rather than
backward. Instead of tracing instances of nostalgia for lost innocence across
the literary archive, I read the tremors of a violent modernity in those narratives
of object-focused damage and regret that I term "toy stories," and posit that the
inauguration of object relations psychoanalysis in the play therapy of Melanie
Klein would eventually make sense of their premature spasms. Toy stories are
effectively portals: not only do they look forward to a version of the child that
was as-yet psychoanalytically unconceived, but they demand new methods of
reading, reconfiguring the literary forms in which they startlingly appear.

Instances of children's object-focused violence perturb their narratives, introducing a countervailing regressive momentum to developmental plots, troubling
distinctions between artifice and authentic interiority, confusing character and
thing, and exposing realism's objects to odd fracture.

There has been extensive critical discussion of nineteenth-century childhood
and its literary representations. Key interventions have queried the child-concept
per se, focused on the kinds of citizen modeling and child surveillance managed in the pages of children's books, or highlighted the conditions of real-world
social and political deprivation that accompanied and made a mockery of
Romantic versions of childhood.[10] However, despite the broad acceptance that
Freud, at least, is a nineteenth-century subject whose insights can validly be
applied to nineteenth-century sociability, there remains a reluctance to apply
psychoanalysis retroactively to the realm of childhood.[11] Let me very briefly
consider two rightly influential examples of such hesitation. The first is Sally
Shuttleworth's *The Mind of the Child* (2010), a study that scrupulously maps
the influence of developments in psychology, sociology, and physiology on
nineteenth-century literary representation, as manifest in the conceptualization
of the child. In arguing for such attunement, Shuttleworth positions her approach against "studies of the figure of the child in nineteenth-century literature
[that] have been [. . .] prone to draw on Freudian analysis as an interpretative
tool," claiming that "in cultural and psychoanalytic accounts of childhood,
the dominance of Freudian theory has tended to create a revolutionary, or
originary, moment around 1900 which has obscured earlier work in the field."[12]
Her research into the nineteenth-century childhood psyche sits within a larger
"literature and science" subfield focused on the co-responsiveness of literary
writing and pre-institutionalized nineteenth-century psychology, of which she
is an inaugural figure.[13] But her reference to Freud's impact as "obscuring"
work that predates it hints at an assumption underpinning the resistance to
psychoanalytic hermeneutics within what is understood to be properly historicist scholarship: that Freudian analysis is fundamentally obscurantist, working
with a veiling virtuosity to occlude the labor of predecessors. This objection is
articulated more explicitly by Sharon Marcus, to whose trenchant critique of
psychoanalytically inspired "symptomatic reading" this introduction will return.
In *Between Women: Friendship, Desire, and Marriage in Victorian England*
(2007), Marcus discloses previously overlooked female intimacies hidden in
plain sight in the literary and historical archives of Victorian Britain. She locates
in, among other topics, the nineteenth-century girl-child's often willfully destructive play with her dolls, a new way of understanding novelistic depictions
of women's friendship and fetishism. Her approach yields virtuosic readings,
as when, for example, she convincingly recasts *Great Expectations'* (1861) Pip as,

effectively, a dildo passed between women. But Marcus defends the chronology of her intuitions, rejecting the application of Freudian paradigms to Dickens's perverse threesome, and asserting that "the eroticism of Estella's relationship with Miss Havisham [. . .] cannot be understood using twentieth-century frameworks as out of joint with the historical moment of *Great Expectations* as the spectral Miss Havisham is herself out of joint with time."[14] Marcus's sleight of hand here is to conflate anticipation with nostalgia. Miss Havisham's present actions are dictated by a riveted backward glance; to think about Dickens with psychoanalysis, however, would involve not simply critically anachronistic hindsight, but a willingness to allow that Dickens may have foreseen something Freud and his inheritors came to express.

If Sigmund Freud is a cipher for purported anachronism within such synchronist critical studies, in the realm of the child psyche he is something of a straw man. His contribution to analyzing the "mind of the child," as opposed to the regressed adult, was in fact a minimal one: his single foray into child analysis, the case-study of "Little Hans," was mediated by the boy's father, Freud claiming that "the technical difficulties in the way of conducting a psychoanalysis upon so young a child would have been [otherwise] insuperable."[15] Nonetheless, his assertion in the "Analysis of a Phobia in a Five-Year-Old Boy" that "there must be a possibility of observing in children at first hand and in all the freshness of life the sexual impulses and wishes which we dig out so laboriously from under their own debris," provided the impetus for both his daughter Anna and Melanie Klein—female, émigré analysts who were themselves nineteenth-century children—to pioneer more direct techniques of infant observation and therapeutic intervention.[16] In turning to the meticulous and extended praxes of these child analysts to think about nineteenth-century toy stories, this book embraces anachronism as provocation rather than anathema. It seizes on prescience as a feature of literary writing that requires a reciprocal forward-oriented critical practice, not fenced by the chronological boundaries of an "ambient culture" whose pervasive influence can only be conjectured.[17] The readings ventured here are receptive to the discerning capacities of literary form. *Toy Stories* proposes that both the work of Klein, and the ways in which it was vigorously contested in the alternative account of child analysis advanced by Anna Freud, articulated an understanding of the cathexis between child and toy that had been adumbrated in fiction. A reciprocal implication, though not one pursued within this book, is that the novel's proto-psychoanalytic intuitions about child's play might be understood to have provided a deep context for developments in child analytic practice, readying educated audiences for the ambivalent, fraught child both analysts' work would disclose.

What he was in toys, he was (as most men are) in other things.

CHARLES DICKENS, "THE CRICKET ON THE HEARTH"

Introduction: Child's Play

Melanie Klein was born Melanie Reizes in 1882. Her father was a doctor, and she aspired to medical training but never received a university education. Instead, she married early and had three children over the course of her twenties. In 1910 she moved to Budapest (where her marriage eventually broke down) and became interested in psychoanalysis, entering therapy with Sandor Ferenczi, one of Freud's key interlocutors. With his support she began to analyze the learning difficulties of her four-year-old son, Erich, interpreting his questions about the world, his dreams and stories, and his play with "little figures," including chess pieces. This work formed the basis of her first paper, "The Development of a Child," which she read to gain admission to the Hungarian Psycho-analytic Society in 1919.[1] Klein moved to Berlin in 1921 where she commenced an analysis with Karl Abraham, who further encouraged her work with children. In a key early paper, "The Psychological Principles of Early Analysis" (1926), Klein introduced her *"play-technique,"* a combination of participation in child-directed games, careful observation of the child at play, and freely articulated symbolic interpretation. Her earliest sessions, conducted in her home or those of her patients, depended on materials to hand: the child's own objects and toys. As her practice in Berlin widened, she established a particular set of telling play objects to use in her analysis:

> On a low table in my analytic room there are laid out a number of small and simple toys—little wooden men and women, carts, carriages, motor-cars, trains, animals, bricks and houses, as well as paper, scissors and pencils. Even a child that is usually inhibited in its play will at least glance at the toys or touch them, and will soon give me a

1

first glimpse into its complexes by the way in which it begins to play
with them or lays them aside, or by its general attitude towards them.[2]

Later she would provide dedicated sets of toys, housed in individual drawers,
for each child patient. It was Klein's contention that "in their play children
represent symbolically phantasies, wishes and experiences"; that is, that play
might be understood as a mode of free association.[3] Hers was a version of the
"talking cure" tailored to pre- or early-linguistic interlocutors. Arguing that
children playing employ the same "language"—the same "archaic, phyloge-
netically acquired mode of expression" as that of the dream—she suggested
that play be approached using the analytic method Freud had established in
The Interpretation of Dreams (1900).[4] *Spielzeugwerk*, as it were, replaced *Traumwerk*: play with toys or drawing or acting out substituted for the child's words
as the content of the analysis, providing access to attitudes toward the primary
love object, the parent. The privacy of the toy drawer in turn analogized the
confidentiality assured the adult patient by the Hippocratic oath: "Each child's
playthings are kept locked in one particular drawer, and he therefore knows
that his toys and his play with them, which is the equivalent of the adult's associations, are only known to the analyst and to himself."[5]

"It is when the child plays with the small toys that we can see the expression
of opposing emotions most distinctly," Klein argued.[6] She took up the Freudian
concepts of projection and introjection, refiguring these as "mechanisms"
through which the child negotiates between reality and emotional life. In the
former case, "internal" or psychic relationships, particularly conflictual relationships or aggression, are projected onto external objects, so that things in
the world become charged with feeling. Reciprocally, introjection involves the
child's reincorporation of these "good and bad objects" so that they are understood to be present in the internal world or ego.[7] Klein then reconceptualized
these processes as a synthesized experience of "projective identification,"
whereby the child projects repudiated parts of itself (its aggression and envy)
outward, eventually reaching a stage where its own ambivalence can be tolerated and these parts can be accepted and reassimilated. In both Klein's and
wider object relations theory, "object" tends to be person before thing: the
internalized or repudiated parent; the self that rejects or repairs; the part-object
(breast, genital) that focalizes the infant's greed or envy. However, in Klein's
early work with children, the term object becomes complicated by the physical
presence of the toy. Even as it does the work of language in the child-analytic
scenario, the toy has an intractable materiality that anchors the slippery term
"object" irrefutably to a thing in the world. The more robust a toy—the more
effectively it can *withstand*—the more effectively it might *stand for* internal

Figure 1. Family figures. Toys used by Melanie Klein in her psychoanalytic work with children. One of a set of cards produced by the Child Psychotherapy Trust. Reproduced by permission of the Wellcome Collection (wellcomecollection.org.) Scan: Nicholas Keyzer. [Attribution-NonCommercial 4.0 International (CC BY-NC 4.0)]

conflict. To put it in terms she did not, Klein recognizes child's play as a psychic forcefield in which freewheeling unconscious symbolization encounters the provocation, but also the inertia offered by the object's material solidity.

Within Klein's therapy space of articulate play, toy damaging had a special significance. "I have found the child's attitude towards a toy he has damaged is very revealing," she wrote.[8] "Aggressiveness is expressed various ways in the child's play, either directly or indirectly. Often a toy is broken or, when the child is more aggressive, attacks are made with knife or scissors on the table or on pieces of wood [. . .]. It is essential to enable the child to bring out his aggressiveness."[9] Freud's formulation of his theory of the death drive (*Beyond the Pleasure Principle* [1920]) at the time Klein began her work had a fundamental impact on her understanding of the internal life that manifests in such play.

She would come to regard the infant as besieged by huge anxiety caused by "the death instinct within," and suggested that this was managed by a phantasy of "splitting," and the projection outward of loving and hating feelings (life and death instincts) into the maternal body. Klein interpreted the child's toy damaging as an attack on disarticulated body parts, most often of the mother, and termed this anxious infantile state the "paranoid-schizoid position."[10] In this play dynamic, aggression was quickly followed by feelings of remorse: "Feelings of guilt may very soon follow after the child has broken, for instance, a little figure. Such guilt refers not only to the actual damage done but to what the toy stands for in the child's unconscious, *e.g.* a little brother or sister, or a parent."[11] Guilt, Klein argued, in turn leads to the impulse to make reparation, which includes "the variety of processes by which the ego feels it undoes harm done in phantasy, restores, preserves and revives objects."[12] Klein would later come to see the tension between a primary envy, which seeks to attack, cannibalize, and spoil the object, and a reparative gratitude as the key manifestation of this iterative process. The paranoid-schizoid position gives way, sequentially rather than in any final sense, to a "depressive position" in which anxiety manifests not just on behalf of the infant self, but also on behalf of the aggressed object, resulting in an urge toward repair.

Klein's analysis was from the outset dialogic. She presented her interpretations immediately to the child and noted the way it responded in its ensuing play, never underestimating infant ability to comprehend her bluntly anatomical associations. Indeed, she found in "even very young children a capacity for insight which is often far greater than that of adults."[13] They appeared ready and able to receive the analyst's interpretation (toy-like, it clicked). Klein's explanations were registered within the play world over time, rather than immediately and verbally. The analyst translated the play into concepts that were then reciprocally interpreted or acted out in the fellowship of continued play. She made manifestations of infant destructiveness and rage, and the child's corresponding sense of deep anxiety at its own sadistic impulses, explicit. Klein repeatedly observed in her patients "the relief obtained from the interpretation of very frightening and painful material."[14] The child appeared next session to have been soothed by analytic recognition and its symptoms—as registered in the continuation of the game—alleviated. While in this sense Klein's patients evinced gradual psychological progress, this was registered primarily through the increasing ease of their play. A successful Kleinian analysis allows the child, not to grow up, but to show "a more childlike nature."[15] Klein's toy work made the child's negative affect representable, and her interpretation made it speakable. The child experienced toy story becoming word, and found that punishment had not ensued, and the intense anxiety expended in repression was no longer required.

Klein's willingness to engage with "negative material and aggressive impulses" that showed up in child's play, and her recognition of "the intense anxiety that aggressive thoughts and actions aroused in patients and which she found had to be verbalized for work to continue" met with resistance from her colleagues in the Berlin Psychoanalytic Society, to which she had been admitted as a full member in 1924.[16] As Meira Likierman suggests, "such accounts were the first of their kind, and the handful of earlier accounts of direct work with small children were docile by comparison."[17] But while Klein's early theories were contested in Berlin, they were received with enthusiasm in Britain. Klein was invited to give six lectures to British Psychoanalytical Society members in 1925, the society's president Ernest Jones reporting in a letter to Sigmund Freud that "she made an extraordinarily deep impression on all of us and won the highest praise both by her personality and her work."[18] After the death of Abraham in 1926, Jones proposed that she come to London, inviting her to practice her methods on his own children and to join the British Psychoanalytical Society. From the time of her move there until her death in 1960, she presented numerous papers and published widely, developing an increasingly complex theory of object negotiated unconscious phantasy, subsequently extended to the analysis of adult psychoses, from her initial observations of children's play.[19]

Meanwhile during the 1920s Sigmund Freud's daughter Anna was also establishing a practice and publishing reputation in the field of child analysis, following a brief career as a teacher. From 1918–21 and then from 1924–29, she was in analysis with her father. She was one of the unnamed subjects of Sigmund Freud's "Ein Kind Wird Geschlagen" ("A Child Is Being Beaten" [1919]), in which he explored the sadomasochistic implications of beating fantasies in children, adolescents, and adults. The paper Anna Freud presented to gain membership of the Vienna Psychoanalytical Society, "Beating Fantasies and Daydreams" (1922) responded to and developed her father's analysis, implicitly drawing on her own memories and experience as patient.[20] Both her early commitment to education and her self- and publicly appointed role as the bearer of the Freudian legacy must be borne in mind when considering her approach to child analysis. Her practice with children commenced in 1923, and she began teaching child analysis at the Vienna Psychoanalytical Training Institute in 1925. She promoted a scientifically formulated model of infant observation, insisting on the differences between child and adult subjects and the ways in which these limited the possibility of conducting a transference-based psychoanalysis with children. In the "Introduction to the Technique of the Analysis of Children," first presented as a series of lectures to the Vienna Psychoanalytical Society in 1926 and published in German in 1927, she took aim at several aspects of Klein's child therapy.[21] Referencing her own work with ten child patients, which eschewed analysis of play with toys and focused purely on material from dreams and daydreams, she rejected Klein's fundamental thesis that children's play could be equated with adult free association, and the further implication that the child could form a transference with the analyst, despite their still dominant attachment to the parent. Only in dream interpretation, she argued, does there exist "a field in which we can apply unchanged to children the methods of analysis of adults" (18). In May 1927 the British Psychoanalytical Society held a symposium to discuss Anna Freud's approach. Klein responded robustly both to what she saw as Anna Freud's misunderstanding of her own theories and to the alternative approach she had outlined.[22]

Anna Freud shared with Klein an ability to recognize the astuteness and flexibility of both children's phantasying and capacities for interpretation. Her description of an analytic session is itself play-like: analyst and child "set off together" in search of the dream's origins; "the child amuses itself with the pursuit of individual dream elements as with a jigsaw puzzle, and follows up the separate elements or words into real life situations with great satisfaction" (19). Perhaps, she muses, in a sentence worthy of R. L. Stevenson or J. M. Barrie, this is "because the child still stands nearer to dreams than the adult" (19). Or it may be that it simply has not assimilated the commonplace understanding that dreams have no meaning. Either way, it is proud when, together, child and analyst construct a successful dream interpretation. This notion of co-assemblage only collapses at the end of Anna Freud's discussion of the *Traumwerk*, when she returns to tutorial mode to assess the child on its interpretative performance: "I have often found that even unintelligent children, who in all other points were as inapt as possible for analysis, did not fail in dream interpretation" (19). Her work was, in a broad sense, educative and communitarian in its aims.[23] Following the "Analysis of Children," one of her next projects was a series of four lectures delivered to the Vienna "Hort," the working-class daycare system, which was later published as *Psychoanalysis for Teachers and Parents* (1928). She continued to engage with educational institutions throughout her career. Melanie Klein regarded what she termed Anna Freud's "pedagogic admixture" as a fundamental flaw in the latter's version of child analysis: "If the analyst, even only temporarily, becomes the representative of the educative agencies [. . .] he becomes the representative of the repressing faculties."[24] In 1937, shortly before she and her family were to leave Vienna, Anna Freud was involved in establishing the Jackson Nursery, offering care to infants selected from the poorest Viennese families. Here she began practicing methods of infant observation that were further advanced at the Hampstead War Nursery that she set up in London with Dorothy Burlingham, catering to the needs of war-displaced children from, again, the poorest East End homes.[25] As Elisabeth Young-Bruehl describes her practice: "The children's adult companions took notes on small cards about their behavior. These notes were recopied and filed thematically in a wooden file box at the end of the day, and then they were used as the source material for discussions."[26] Anna Freud's focus on real-world change meant that relief was provided as much through proper hygiene and food as through a modeling of positive attachment.

Her careful scientism, manifest in the emphasis on observation and recordation, has seen Anna Freud consistently cast as the plodding technician to Klein's virtuoso theoretician.[27] Yet in *The Ego and the Mechanisms of Defence* (1936), her major contribution to psychoanalytic theory, Anna Freud also set out a complex theory of childish aggression, referencing mechanisms of introjection and projection. She proposed two models of how children defend against their extreme aggression and the anxiety it generates: identification with an antagonist, whereby "a child introjects some characteristic of an anxiety-object" and "by impersonating the aggressor, assuming his attributes or imitating his aggression [. . .] transforms himself from the person threatened to the person who makes the threat," and a version of projection she termed "altruistic surrender," where the gratification of others' instincts substitutes for the fulfillment of one's own instinctual wishes.[28] While Anna Freud's emphasis was on how the child's ego develops to protect it from the assaults of negative affect, she, like Klein, recognized the intensity of anxiety generated by aggressive feeling, providing numerous illustrations of the ways in which both aggression and defense were acted out in children's play with their own toys or real-world objects. However Anna Freud continued adamantly to resist Melanie Klein's play-technique: both her establishment of a dedicated set of illustrative play objects in her consulting rooms (rather than using the child's own toys) and her assumption that children's play with such toys analogized adult free association. The initial barbed exchanges between these two pioneers of child analysis in 1927 set the scene for later controversies that split the British Psychoanalytical Society after Sigmund Freud and his family and a further group of Viennese Jewish psychoanalysts, including Klein's daughter Melitta, moved to London in the wake of the Anschluss.[29] Early disagreement focused not just on Klein's technique, but on her consonant insistence that very young children without advanced language skills might be analyzed, and, with that, her increasing focus on the role of attachment to the mother. Her privileging of the breast as exemplary part-object challenged the "phallo-centric view of female development" established by Sigmund Freud's version of the Oedipus complex.[30] Between 1940 and 1945, following Freud's death, and as war raged and subsided across the globe, tensions erupted within the British Psychoanalytical Society in a series of debates, retrospectively dubbed the "Controversial Discussions." These exposed and reified a fundamental split within the society between Kleinians and Anna Freudians, centered around Klein's evolving conception of whole, part, and internal objects, and on her conception of development as an oscillation between extreme psychic states (paranoia, depression).[31] Eventually a further "middle group" assembled, which sought to reconcile and build upon the strengths of the two analytic models.

Donald Winnicott has subsequently emerged as the most influential of this group for child analysis, and his absence as a key psychoanalytic interlocutor for this project may come as a surprise. Winnicott took up Klein's toy-therapeutic prototype, reframing it to privilege what he called the "transitional object." Like Klein, he argued that the toy is capable of sustaining the onslaught of the child's most intense feelings. Such object relating becomes, in Winnicott's terminology, "object use": the toy's endurance of childish assault trains the child to understand that neither its hatred nor its love is capable of destroying its object. In his 1951 essay "Transitional Objects and Transitional Phenomena," Winnicott emphasized the object's suitability to "survive instinctual loving, and also hating and, if it be a feature, pure aggression."[32] However, Winnicott, like Anna Freud, resisted Klein's theory of projective identification, insisting that "[t]he analyst must take into account the nature of the object, not as a projection, but as a thing in itself."[33] Klein had conceived of the toy as allowing the child to give expression to both aggression and the huge burden of anxiety that aggression generated, in a play realm whose analytic explication did not lead to punishment: this freedom alone would enable it to come to an understanding of the distinction between play and reality. Winnicott's transitional toy, on the other hand (typically a soft object such as a security blanket or teddy bear, rather than a robustly anthropomorphic figurine of the kind that Klein used) was understood as a quite literal mediator between "the child and the outside world" (to use a phrase he adopted from Anna Freud, whose educative emphasis his work shares), which might enable the infant to relinquish their sense of omnipotence and establish a relationship with an objective reality. Where for Klein children's play was a primarily communicative activity, at once material and symbolic, for Winnicott the transitional object was the toy through which the child first learns to symbolize. While both his and Klein's methods lead the child by means of the object to an acceptance of the reality principle, damage and the recurrently regressive anxiety and aggression to which it attests

are more effectively grown out of in the Winnicottian Bildung. I shall address
the prevailing literary critical preference for the work of Winnicott, and my
sense of the importance of holding on to Klein and Anna Freud's foundational
insights, later in this chapter. First, I want to elaborate aspects of their antipa-
thetic work that seem to me important for a reconsideration of both literary
form and critical practice.

Domestic Realism

Klein's therapy with children translated play with objects into a form of symbolic communication: "In interpreting not only the child's words but also his
activities with his toys, I applied this basic principle to the mind of the child,
whose play and varied activities—in fact his whole behavior—are means of
expressing what the adult expresses predominately by words."[34] Introducing
"the parameter of the toy" allowed Klein's work to develop significantly from
the model established by Freud in the case study of Little Hans, and to encompass a nuanced account of the child's "drive to relate to objects in the external
world from a very early age," its "need to gain relief from the externalization
of inner conflict," and its "epistemophilic instinct to seek out new objects, toys
and playmates as part of a process of symbolisation that enabled the child to
develop means of relating to the external world."[35] In her "Analysis of Children,"
Anna Freud acknowledged the expediency of this method:

> The play technique worked out by Mrs. Melanie Klein is certainly
> valuable for observing the child. Instead of taking the time and trouble
> to pursue it into its domestic environment we establish at one stroke
> the whole of the known world in the analyst's room, and let it move
> about in it under the analyst's eye [. . .]. There is this advantage over
> the observation of real conditions, that the toy environment is manage-
> able and amenable to the child's will, so that it can carry out in it all
> the actions which in the real world, so much bigger and stronger than
> itself, remain confined to a phantasy-existence. (28)

Anna Freud is prepared to concede that Klein's approach has benefits if it is
restricted to a participant-observation model. Her own method, which confines
itself to the child's established domestic environment, involves a lengthy process
of preparation for engagement with the analyst, which she refers to as "dressage"
(a term with resonances of "grooming" [5]).[36] It is in relation to her comments
on her own "preparation of the child" within its home that we may understand,
perhaps, the somewhat double-edged allusions to the lack of "time and trouble"
involved in Klein's method ("she is saved the necessity of such a preparation"

[28–29]). Anna Freud was concerned that the child lacks agency in entering the analytic situation: "the decision for analysis never comes from the child who is to be the patient, but always from the parents or other persons round it. The child is not asked for its consent" (5). Her preparatory efforts are therefore to "induce in the child in some way the missing readiness and willingness" (5). In addition to methods that range from "creeping into a confidence" to direct "attack," Anna Freud insinuates herself into the domestic scene by rendering herself indispensable (9, 6). She is ready to type out a little boy patient's "daydreams and self-invented stories of which he was proud [. . .]. In the case of a little girl who was undergoing her preparation at the same time I zealously crocheted and knitted during her appointments, and gradually clothed all her dolls and teddy bears" (10).

Against Klein's creation of a dedicated, extramural domestic play space, then, Anna Freud posits her infiltration of an existing domestic environment using tactics ranging from threat to demonstrated usefulness. She is troubled by the diminished influence of the domestic sphere in the Kleinian play scenario. Klein's toy models, her therapy room dollhouse of miniature wooden figures, animals, and cars, enshrined a further order of substitution: the displacing of parental authority through the transference. Anna Freud's objections to Klein's claim that transference can be established between analyst and child patient are grounded in the notion of the quotidian precedence of the family unit.

> The child is not, like the adult, ready to produce a new edition of its love-relationships, because, as one might say, the old edition is not yet exhausted. Its original objects, the parents, are still real and present as love-objects [. . .]; between them and the child exist all the relations of everyday life, and all its gratifications and disappointments still in reality depend on them. (34)

Anna Freud is resistant to divorcing domestic objects from the realm, and with that the authority, of the parent. Yet as Klein points out in her response, this objection bespeaks a fundamental misreading of the relation of the symbolic to the real. For Klein the toy "bridges the gulf to reality": it is not a sample of the intractable domestic real, an item over which the parent and analyst fight to gain possession, nor is the play-technique something that can itself substitute for the relationships of home.[37] The work of the analyst is to help the child begin to discriminate between its phantasy and reality. An indication that Klein has delivered an accurate interpretation is, first, that "children begin to distinguish between the 'pretence' mother and the real mother and between the wooden baby-doll and the live baby brother. They then firmly insist that they wanted to do this or that injury to the toy-baby only—the real baby, they say, of course they love."[38] In the next stage of the analysis, and "only when very powerful resistances have been overcome," children come to "realize that their aggressive acts were directed against the *real* objects. When this admission is made, however, the result, even in quite little children, is generally a notable step forward in adaptation to reality."[39] In contrast to Anna Freud's positing of a competitive relationship between parent and analyst, acted out in domestic spaces with everyday objects, Klein argues for the instantiation of an accurate understanding of the difference between representation and reality through analytic interpretation. She urges that "we must on no account identify the real objects with those the children introject." The child uses the play space to articulate what it finds unspeakable: it uses "dolls and other playthings" found in the "box of toys" in Klein's rooms to depict associations, with the analyst "follow[ing] up the child's symbolic mode of representation."[40] Klein counters Anna Freud's literalism with a symbolic materialism, working in the language of metaphor.[41]

The analytic case studies that Anna Freud draws upon in the "Analysis of Children" are, in fact, interlarded with toy stories. One little girl daydreams:

> "Sometimes I pretend I do die, and then come back into the world as an animal or a doll. But if I do come back into the world as a doll, I know who I mean to belong to—a little girl that my nurse was with before, who is specially nice and good. I want to be her doll and I would not mind at all being treated like they treat dolls. [. . .] Perhaps she would get another doll for Christmas but I would still be her favourite. She would never prefer any doll to the baby doll." (21)

Another, who sleeps with a toy rabbit, recalls the following dream:

> "Once upon a time there was a little rabbit, whose family were not at all nice to him. They were going to send him to the slaughterhouse and have him slaughtered. But he found it out. He had a car which was very old but could still be driven. He went for it at night and got in and drove away. He came to a dear little house in which a little girl (here she used her own name) lived. She heard him crying downstairs and came down and let him in. Then he stayed to live with her." (22)

The ideational content of these toy dreams is not dissimilar to that of the toy stories Klein recounts in the 1926 paper on the play-technique to which Anna Freud is responding ("The Psychological Principles of Early Analysis"), though Klein's more confronting examples disclose "rage and anxiety" where Anna Freud offers more benign representations of infantile envy. (Six-year-old

Erna, for example, "placed a little doll on a stone, pretended that it was defae-
cating and stood other dolls round it which were supposed to be admiring it";
she then asked Klein to play the baby that soils itself: "this was followed by a
reaction of rage in Erna, and she played the part of a cruel teacher who knocked
the child about.")[42] Yet whereas Klein enters into and interprets the play activities dictated by the child in order to "*relieve* the child, to establish a fundamentally more favourable relation to the parents and thus to increase its power
of social adaptation"—that is, to facilitate its relationship to a real understood
to be outside of and referenced within the world of play—Anna Freud appears
to understand the toy as a piece of the domestic real confiscated from the domestic setting, unlawfully appropriated from the true love-objects, the parents.[43]
Hence her own limited and competitively framed interventions in the toy world,
explicitly aimed at seducing the child into analysis using demonstrations of
superior dexterity: the knitting and crocheting of clothes for dolls and teddy
bears, the willingness to act as amanuensis, or the performance of "much
cleverer tricks with a piece of string" than the child can manage itself (16). In
a subsequent paper, "The Theory of Child Analysis" (1928), in which she reiterated her opposition to the Kleinian method, Anna Freud insisted that
anxiety is generated in the young child by immediate domestic scenarios involving "real, living parents, and not [. . .] their internalized images."[44] She
concluded,

> Since we have found that the forces with which we have to contend in
> the cure of an infantile neurosis are not only internal, but linked to
> external sources as well, we have a right to require that the child ana-
> lyst should also assess the child's external situation, not only the inter-
> nal one. For this part of his task, however, the child analyst needs some
> basic knowledge of the upbringing of children in general. This will en-
> able him to assess and criticize the influences which have an impact
> on the child's development; and, if it should prove necessary, to take
> the child's upbringing out of the hands of those in authority, and for
> the period of the analysis be in charge of it himself.[45]

Here the hesitancy to intrude on the domestic authority of the parent has given
way to an assertion of the right of the analyst to act as substitute parent or
teacher, inducing "direct modifications" in the child's behavior through active
intercession in its home or school environment.[46] In both formulations there
remains fundamental resistance to understanding intervention as interpretative
rather than educative, and the therapeutic environment as best constituted by
an extramural rather than domestic space.

This debate about the relationship between the playroom and wider domesticity, and the further contest it reveals over the nature of the real and its relationship to the symbolic, are starting to sound similar to those played out in literature over the course of the nineteenth century. What connected fictional worlds to the real world; should objects speak for themselves; with what authority might authorship take solid things and charge them with metaphor? Jacqueline Rose has pointed out that the child and the realist genre are often coupled, each serving as guarantor for the other, ratified by the trope of innocence. Discussing the tendency of children's fiction "to inherit a very specific aesthetic theory, in which showing is better than telling," she argues that children's literature's "'realist' aesthetic," which manifests as a rejection of overt narration, the gradual retirement of the storyteller behind the tale, reflects the development of the larger novel form.[47] The emergence of realism as a dominant literary genre, Rose implies, involves the retreat of authorship behind objects, a disguise of the shaping hand behind the replicant everyday. Peter Brooks has made explicit an analogy between play and realist form, arguing that the childhood desire "to play with toys that reproduce in miniature the objects amid which we live" constitutes a mode "of repetition of the world with this difference that the world has become manageable."[48] Realist fiction equally, he suggests, is "adult play," that "desires to be maximally reproductive of that world it is modeling for play purposes."[49] Although he takes the Freudian *fort/da* game, which proved a significant point of departure for Klein's theories of play, as "a basic scenario in mastering reality through play," Brooks shies away from any acknowledgment of the aggression nested in that psychoanalytic scenario, arguing that the novel evolves as "serious" rather than violent play.[50] Realism is, in his reading, "a kind of literature and art committed to a form of play that uses carefully wrought and detailed toys, ones that attempt as much as possible to reproduce the look and feel of the real thing."[51] His toy models are enlightenment educative playthings of the kind I discuss in Chapter 1, participating in the object lesson's fantasy of rational, modular play.

Anna Freud was an early devotee of novelistic realism in both her choice of reading and her writing. Her biographer Elisabeth Young-Bruehl notes that from an early age, she "liked only stories that excluded the fantastic, the totally unreal."[52] She quotes Anna Freud: "At an age before independent reading, when children are read to or told stories my interest was restricted to those that 'might be true.' This did not mean that they had to be true stories in the ordinary sense of the word, but they were supposed not to contain elements which precluded their happening in reality."[53] Anna started writing poetry during her analysis with her father, and in 1919 began work on a series of short prose pieces, which by 1921 she was expanding into a projected novel, *Heinrich Mühsam* (Heinrich Laborious), whose title suggests something between Bildungsroman and cautionary tale.[54] She also continued to experiment with shorter (two to three sentence) prose pieces.[55] Klein, on the other hand, produced a body of "expressionist erotic" poetry and stream-of-consciousness prose works, compared by Phyllis Grosskurth to the narratives of James Joyce or Arthur Schnitzler, in the years before she entered analysis.[56] By drawing attention to both the realist sympathies of Anna Freud's theories and the ways in which Kleinian toy stories served to disrupt traditional narratives of the child, I do not, however, intend to characterize these two theorists as old-fashioned realist and proto-modernist, Arnold Bennet to Virginia Woolf. Both, as we have seen, were signed up to a complex psychoanalytic version of reality, focused on psychic accommodation and founded on Freud's articulation of the reality principle. For both, objects are first and foremost the human subjects of primary attachment; in Klein's case analogized by and in Anna Freud's case constituted through a quite separate realm of quotidian things. However, to think of their competing models of the relationship between psychic resolution and the object world as generic as much as theoretical is to begin to understand why the nineteenth-century novel may harbor inklings of their versions of the child, the world, and interior life.

Blunt Criticism, Wild Analysis

In the "Analysis of Children" Anna Freud equates her own analytic technique with literary production. She compares preparing the child for analysis by "becom[ing] useful" with the seduction of the reader in the opening pages of a novel: "my way was rather like that of a film or novel which has no other intention than to attract the audience or reader to itself, and with this aim concentrates on the interests and needs of its public. My first aim was in fact nothing else but to make myself interesting to the boy" (10). In her later retranslation of the text, she makes clear that what she is imitating here is lowbrow or commercially oriented writing: "My attitude was like that of a film or novel meant to attract the audience or reader by catering to their baser interests."[57] This is dishonest seduction, manifest in this specific case in the willingness to act as secretary to an author-child in "the writing down of his daydreams and self-invented stories of which he was proud" (10). Yet if we return to her first paper, "Beating Fantasies and Daydreams," we find a very serious engagement with the notion of fictional authorship, played out in a context in which she herself figures as the child proud of her "daydreams and self-invented stories." Anna Freud's essay develops from her father's 1919 essay "A Child Is Being

Beaten," one of a number of occasions on which he referenced her younger self as anonymous case study. In his essay, Freud focuses on the masochistic fantasies of children as they evolve across three stages, the first and third of which "are consciously remembered" and in which the child being beaten is someone other than the child phantasying, and the second of which remains unconscious and in which the child itself is being beaten.[58] He mentions in particular "two of my four female cases" in which "an elaborate structure of day-dreams, which was of great significance for the life of the person concerned, had grown up over the masochistic beating-phantasy."[59] One of these cases of daydreaming, Freud suggests, "almost rose to the level of a work of art."[60]

Anna Freud's essay, which speaks to Freud's paper while continuing to withhold her own identity as focal case study, instates herself, under the cloak of anonymity, as this creative genius among Freud's daydreaming children. She records the evolution of her beating fantasy from something whose "content was quite monotonous" into a master narrative subject "to a great variety of alterations and elaborations."[61] Yet the paper also goes on to tell a further story: the story of telling another story. Between the ages of eight and ten, we are told, "the girl initiated a new kind of fantasy which she herself called 'nice stories' in contrast to the ugly beating fantasy."[62] As she explains,

> These "nice stories" seemed at first sight at least to depict nothing but pleasant, cheery scenes that all exemplify instances of kind, considerate, and affectionate behavior. All the figures in these nice stories had names, individual faces, external appearances that were detailed with great exactness, and personal histories which frequently reached far back into their fantasied past. The family circumstances of these figures, their friendships and acquaintances, and their relationship to each other were precisely specified and all incidents in their daily life were fashioned as true to reality as possible. The setting of the story readily changed with every change in the life of the daydreamer, just as she incorporated bits and pieces of events she had read about.[63]

Anna Freud here models a type of realist storytelling that, alternately, perfectly mimics or interpolates the everyday. Yet as she goes on to make clear, the nice stories and the beating fantasy are libidinally correlated: "each occurrence of the beating fantasy—which on occasion did break through—had to be punished by temporary renunciation of the nice stories."[64] The stories evolve in a serial format ("'continued stories'"), but, rejecting the idea that they as a whole constituted a version of "a novel published in installments," Anna Freud instead claims that "each completed tale" is a novel in itself: "entirely independent of the others, and formed exactly like a real novel, containing an introduction, the development of a plot which leads to heightened tension and ultimately a climax."[65] In this version of herself as author, a carefully networked domestic narrative is shadowed, in a pattern Klein would elucidate in her child therapy, by phantasies of sadistic violence and anxious guilt.

If Anna Freud identifies with the novelist narrator, she figures Klein as the overzealous critic. Sigmund Freud had qualified his advocacy for the significant potential of child analysis with the comment that "it cannot be very rich in material; too many words and thoughts have to be lent to the child."[66] When Klein responded to this provocation with virtuoso hermeneutics, Anna Freud amplified her father's objections, suggesting that Klein engaged in a risible level of hyperinterpretation: "she tries to find beneath everything done in play its underlying symbolic function. If the child overturns a lamp-post or a toy figure she interprets it as something of an aggressive impulse against the father; a deliberate collision between two cars is evidence of the sexual union between the parents" (29).[67] Klein saw symbolic interpretation as the key to understanding the child's relationship to the real: "In play," she wrote, "the child's attitude to reality reveals itself."[68] Anna Freud, on the other hand, was insistent that the everyday offered a wealth of non-symbolic contexts, which outweighed the probability of transferred psychic associations:

> Instead of being invested with symbolic meaning [child's play] may sometimes admit of a harmless explanation. The child who upsets a toy lamp-post may on its walk the day before have come across some incident in connection with such an object; the car collision may be reproducing something happening in the street; and the child who runs towards a lady visitor and opens her handbag is not necessarily, as Mrs. Klein maintains, thereby symbolically expressing its curiosity as to whether its mother's womb conceals another little brother or sister, but may be connecting some experiences of the previous day when someone brought it a little present in a similar receptacle. (29–30)

Anna Freud seeks to replace what she sees as an over-reading of the quotidian thing with rational, context-focused explanation: "upsets" may be material rather than emotional. Yet her choice of the word "harmless" to describe her own explanatory principle is telling. The implication is that interpretation itself has the potential to injure, even as it seeks to clarify negative affect.[69]

Where does this harm hit home? One implication of Anna Freud's critique is that interpretation can be too intellectually heavy for its object, placing a weight on innocent actions that equates to an overburdening of the child. The daughter of the psychoanalyst who introduced the notion of infantile sexuality nonetheless finds herself, in the arena of the toy, asserting a cigar to be just a

cigar.[70] The toy stories embedded in the "Analysis of Children" are left declaratively unanalyzed: of the girl who daydreams of becoming a doll, Anna Freud
claims "It is *superfluous to add* that of her brothers and sisters the two of whom
she was particularly jealous were younger than her. Her current situation could
not find clearer expression in any account or association" (21; my emphasis); of
the dream of the little rabbit toy she simply states that its meaning "shows itself
quite transparently" (22). Anna Freud's refusal to understand her own mediation
as operating transferentially (let alone counter-transferentially) means that she
ends up depicting the work of interpretation as redundant in the case of the
child, or at best subordinate to a pedagogic imperative.[71] Repeatedly the es-
chewal of interpretation, the statement that meaning is self-evident, is linked
to a conflation of the "real" (in Klein's terms the real object of the feelings
elicited in the play-situation) with the domestic. Klein's argument, on the other
hand, is that symbolic interpretation is the key to therapeutic amelioration: the
opposite of harm. Her recognition of the work of transference, and in particular
negative transference, in child analysis allowed her to understand the therapeutic process as involving internalization of the therapist as good object. In
practice, an often apparently heavy-handed exegesis takes place within and
finds legitimacy as part of a broader trajectory of empirical alleviation.

If Anna Freud was critical of what she regarded as Klein's top-heavy hermeneutics, she nonetheless anticipated that her own combination of the educative
and analytic might be seen as simply ad hoc by adherents of classic Freudian
psychoanalysis. She concludes the "Analysis of Children," "I am prepared for
the practising analysts among you to say, after what they have heard here, that
my methods with children are so different that they cannot be called real
analysis at all, but a form of 'wild' analysis which has borrowed all its expedients
from analysis but nowise confirms to strict analytical principles" (51).[72] Bearing
her sense of her own analytic unorthodoxy in mind, Anna Freud's dispute with
Klein may readily be conceived in terms of differences in critical, as much as
authorial, practice. In a benign reading, Klein's interpretations render a level
of symbolism visible that becomes enabling for understanding character and
for allowing narrative, which had appeared stymied, to progress. In Anna
Freud's unsympathetic reading, Kleinian analysis is at once crude and overly
intricate: a heavy-handed, superfluous supplement to straightforward and self-
explanatory stories. In a benign reading, Anna Freud's accrual of carefully
observed data allows for an attentive, historically attuned and therefore robust
representation of child psychology. Unsympathetically, she is "Heinrich Laborious," peddling a "pedagogic admixture," unable to sustain the distinction
between phantasy and reality upon which psychoanalytic technique depends.
These differences are played out in an anecdote Anna Freud relayed regarding

her 1927 treatment of a boy who had previously been seen by Klein. While he had initially improved under Klein's care, a relapse manifested in increased nervousness and weight loss, and he was recommended to Anna Freud for further analysis. In a letter to the boy's father, Anna Freud claimed that her task had been complicated by the fact that "Frau Klein has revealed to him the deepest layer of his problems; the surface area was not even touched, so I have to work with him in a remarkably roundabout way, detouring from bottom to top, to end where I usually start out. The trump card, which I usually play to persuade a patient, is in his hand already."[73]

Anna Freud referred to this unusual case of doubled therapy as "an illustration of the English controversy": that is, a perfect enactment of the positions assumed by Klein and herself over that same year regarding the technique of child analysis.[74] But its terms also anticipate, with a curious exactness, those of recent literary critical debates about the value of symptomatic or "suspicious" reading versus "surface" or descriptive reading. In an influential article, Stephen Best and Sharon Marcus advocate a critical practice that attends to manifest rather than latent meaning. Best and Marcus link the acceptance of psychoanalysis as a metalanguage to the literary critical privileging of a "hermeneutics of suspicion" that locates the meaningful in what is "hidden, repressed, deep, and in need of detection and disclosure."[75] In Anna Freud's anecdote of distributed and stymied child therapy Klein, like Freud's present-day literary critical inheritor, the classic symptomatic reader, goes immediately for depth analysis, forcing Anna Freud in turn to work back from interior to surface in a "roundabout way," and to surrender the glory of the critical reveal, or as Heather Love has framed it in her work on descriptive reading, to "give [. . .] up [the] role of interpreting divine messages to take up a position as humble analyst and observer."[76] Rejecting the purported "charisma" of symptomatic hermeneutics, Love and other devotees of descriptive reading promote a critical practice borrowed from the social sciences "grounded in documentation and description rather than empathy and witness," and which evinces an Anna Freud–like "lack of interest in questions of interpretation and symbolic meaning."[77] Yet descriptive readers are also newly interested in the object world, in ways that recall Klein's focus on the toy. They question "the distinction between a meaningful world of human actions and intentions on the one hand, and an inert and insignificant world of material objects on the other."[78] The hard divide between the manifest and the symbolic, the surface and the interior, the worlds of the human and the inert that these critical turns have underlined is, however, one that Kleinian object relations had long resolved. Klein would show that objects need to be hard-surfaced *and* symbolically resonant in order to be therapeutic. Her toy therapy looks to material things and descriptive processes as a means of articulating a complex vision of human interiority, which none-theless categorically disrupts humanist narratives of the child.

Novel Children

These examples of the two analysts working with alternative versions of literary narrative and preempting opposing forms of critical reading are only the most obvious signposts of the relevance of their methods for literary studies. Yet Anna Freud's work has suffered an almost wholesale neglect from literary scholars. And while Klein's theories have received important attention, partic-ularly from Eve Kosofsky Sedgwick, Jacqueline Rose, Mary Jacobus, Caroline Dever, and Adam Frank, they have also encountered increasing critical resis-tance. Jacobus's and Rose's brilliant readings focus, following Lacan, on the content of Klein's symbolic interpretation rather than on her child-therapeutic praxis.[79] Rose sets the stage for a number of critics who have linked Klein's theories to those modernist writings produced at or since the time she was working as a child analyst.[80] Jacobus's and Dever's projects align more imme-diately with this book's interest in noticing correspondences between nineteenth-century literary formations and representations and Klein's insights. Jacobus's engagement with Klein over three significant publications is situated within a wider project to connect object relations theory with early nineteenth-century aesthetics. However, she remains concerned with Romantic paradigms of childhood from which the current study departs, while her telos is "the version of object relations associated with contemporary post-Kleinian thinking."[81] Dever tracks the disappearance of the mother as prerequisite to identity for-mation across nineteenth-century literary and twentieth-century psychoanalytic texts.[82] Klein figures alongside Lacan, Kristeva, and Winnicott, as analysts involved in a consecutive revision of the Freudian representation of maternity. Dever is concerned with unpacking conceptual apparatus and their relationship to plot, rather than attending to therapeutic practice and its implications for literary form. Frank deploys Kleinian thought in deft readings of nineteenth-century performative poetics. His work differs significantly from the current project in its focus on the theatrical: he only makes passing reference to Klein's play-technique (that is, to play in the ludic sense).[83]

These critics are all deeply attentive to Klein's own writings. Sedgwick, on the other hand, whose impact in making connections between Klein's work and later affect studies was the furthest reaching, admitted that "encounters with other writers' persuasive paraphrase" rather than direct confrontation with Klein's knotty prose impelled her engagement with Kleinian theory. Despite this disambiguated approach, Sedgwick, in trying to come to grips with Klein's style, implicitly invoked Klein's toy work. Connecting her own personal child-hood preference for chunky dolls to her adult comfort with Klein's thinking, Sedgwick suggested that

> the invitingly chunky affordances of Klein's thought probably have most to do with a thematic aspect of her view of psychology: it's she who put the objects in object relations. In her concept of phantasy-with-a-ph, human mental life becomes populated, not with ideas, representations, knowledges, urges, and repressions, but with things, things with physical properties, including people and hacked-off bits of people.[84]

Sedgwick's most influential intervention in relation to Klein was her champi-oning of reparation as a model for literary interpretation.[85] She famously de-ployed the concept of the reparative to strengthen the purchase of positive affect—joy, surprise—upon a critical practice understood to be in the grip of a hermeneutics of suspicion (in Sedgwick's terms, of "paranoid" reading). As Robyn Wiegman has pointed out, Sedgwick's "salvific" reformulation of rep-aration as equatable with critical generosity destabilizes the concept's delicate positioning by Klein within a cycle of phantasying that also productively engages with the paranoid. Wiegman convincingly argues that "the current attraction to reparative reading is about repairing the value and agency of interpretative practice itself."[86]

It is the post-Kleinians that have more recently occupied critical attention, with Donald Winnicott emerging as object relations theorist of choice for discussions of both the child and literature, and of their intersection. Barbara Johnson in *Persons and Things* (2008), Carol Mavor in *Reading Boyishly* (2008), and Amanda Anderson in *Psyche and Ethos* (2018) all provide exegeses of Winnicott's theories alongside discussion of literary authors, as part of, alter-nately, a rethinking of the subject-object relationship, an analysis of the aes-thetics of maternal attachment, and a polemic against the alleged psychoanalytic erosion of literary critical attention to moral agency.[87] Naomi Morgenstern, David Russell, and Alicia Christoff find Winnicott and other middle-group post-Kleinians useful as a way into reading contemporary and nineteenth-century texts, while Alison Bechdel's academically and more widely popular graphic novels, particularly *Are You My Mother?*, deploy and translate Winn-icottian terminology.[88] Lois Kuznets's influential study of the the figure of the "come to life" toy in children's literature glances over Klein's contributions to the practical study and theoretical analysis of toy-play, instead using Winnicott's transitional object to inform her analysis.[89] Martha Nussbaum's claim that Winnicott "has never had a secure home in the academy" seems less and less true.[90] Yet Winnicott's tendency to serve in work on object relations as a figure of resolution, moderating the scratchy quarrels of Klein and Anna Freud and synthesizing their opposing theories, obscures the degree of his indebtedness to both predecessors. Amanda Anderson, for example, in elevating Winnicott as figurehead for a "healthy" model of infant development that is environment- rather than drive-centric, repeatedly reduces Klein to a "hinge figure between Freud and British object relations."[91] Anderson regards Winnicott, rather than Anna Freud, whom she ignores, as responsible for insisting on the "dynamic and environmentally contingent condition in which infants and children develop."[92] Carol Mavor, on the other hand, mistakenly places Winnicott and Klein together as 1920s cofounders of object relations theory; in a lengthy chapter on Winnicott she then looks briefly at a single essay of Klein's, "taking Klein's analysis to task" for "her mistake of not positively recognizing the maternal (the mother) in the child."[93] Klein's true theoretical contemporary, Anna Freud, is given even shorter shrift: dismissed in a footnote as "an early 'analyst' of children, though principally guided by her father's own views."[94] Rebuking Klein for her purported failure to accept messiness and privileging of "hate in her analysis," Mavor, following Adam Phillips, instates Winnicott as founder of "a welcome and new theology of mothering."[95]

Mavor's criticisms echo term for term Nussbaum's "Winnicott on the Surprises of the Self," an essay that misunderstands Klein as an insistently orthodox theorist, afraid of the messy and hatred-focused, in order to elevate Winnicott as conceptualist of an ethically engaged play. Nussbaum attributes to Winnicott all the subtleties of Klein's theory of reparation. While acknowledging that Winnicott's recognition that the child seeks to reconcile feelings of love and hatred for the mother follows Klein, she refuses to grant the ethical complexity of Klein's version of this synthesis, the depressive position, referring to it as "forbidding and philosophically obscure."[96] Instead she champions what she believes is Winnicott's original formulation, the "capacity for concern" (terminology in fact derived from Klein's formulation of the depressive position). Nussbaum claims that Winnicott's "insight" endows Klein's "psychoanalytic category [with] a distinctively ethical heart."[97] She further praises Winnicott's replacement of Klein's "object relating" with the concept of "object use"; a substitution that transforms the Kleinian object into something experientially useful rather than expressively damaged. However, Winnicott's distinction between object use and object relating, again, reiterates the earliest disputes between Klein and Anna Freud, parlaying Anna Freud's emphasis on understanding objects as "part of shared reality, not a bundle of projections."[98] Most recently, Alicia Christoff simply erases Klein in favor of Winnicott in her reading of Sedgwick reading Klein. Christoff hears Winnicott's soothing tones in

Sedgwick's rendition of Klein's theory: "In my view [. . .] the description of Kleinian theory in this essay sounds more like Winnicott and other followers in the Independent tradition than like Klein herself."[99] I would argue that Klein sounds like Winnicott because, chronologically and foundationally, Winnicott sounds like Klein. Yet Winnicott's echoing of Klein's thinking in comforting, accessible form, further mediated through Sedgwick, is registered here as original formulation. Christoff's inability to hear Klein's doubly elided voice enacts the fact that, as J. B. Pontalis astutely observes, "In the work of Winnicott [. . .] repetitions are turned into findings."[100]

Nussbaum's Wizard of Oz image of Winnicott as the magician who enables the tin-eared Klein to finally find a heart, and the widespread neglect of Anna Freud within the literary critical version of object relations history, are symptomatic of a broad consensus that Anna Freud remains too father-fixated, Klein too negative and "unmaternal," to represent the child. Why does this matter? Since the turn to twentieth-century psychoanalysis as a lens for reading nineteenth-century literature was always going to upset received notions of chronological precedence, why is an order of influence important when it comes to theory? It is in such acknowledgment that the politics of this book's argument inheres. Repeatedly, these pioneering women analysts figure as belated invitees to what should be a celebration of their foundational work, inheritors of a tradition they inaugurated. By handing Klein and Anna Freud's rebarbative, entangled and conflicted insights over to the reconciliatory formulations of male synthesizers who often conceal their debts, recent critics eclipse a very significant instance of wholly female-led paradigm shift. Moreover, the discourse around this preference barely conceals a misogynist subtext. Winnicott, by endorsing the "good enough mother," trumps Klein in maternal understanding; Anna is forever consigned to a masochistic servitude in relation to the father Freud. Yet in attempting to reconcile the domestic-pedagogical method of Anna Freud with Klein's ability to recognize and soothe negative affect, Winnicott's soft toys lose the edge of either foremother's, particularly for analyzing the unanticipated toy work of narrative fiction.

Across the nineteenth century, literature negotiates a course, with swerving bias, between inner life and outer things. And literary criticism repeats that swerve, shifting allegiance between subjects and objects, depths and surfaces. In the chapters that follow, I shall focus analysis of that generic and critical tension through the model of children's therapeutic play with toys. While this book engages with a variety of prescient representations of toy work, including educational tracts and juvenile fragments, it is primarily interested in the dominant nineteenth-century genre of the novel. Hence, two of its chapters focus on topics central to novel studies: characterological realism and the trajectory of the Bildungsroman. Two others, devoted alternately to theories of child-rearing and education, and to sibling miniature book-crafting, adolescent journaling, and the eulogistic preface, nonetheless turn in conclusion to a work of fiction. Moving between Anna Freudian surface and Kleinian depth, between close domestic observation and ludic simulacrum, between narratives of development and of regression, the novel does not unproblematically evolve over the course of the century into an increasingly interiorized, increasingly "psychological" form. Rather, it debates how subjects are fictionally constructed, formulating, testing, rejecting and returning, and reflexively encapsulating this process in emblematic representations of child's play. As this book tracks the toy through its denotative and connotative appearances in nineteenth-century literary texts, locating the enraged, envious, or disturbed infant among the archives of senti-mental realism, it asks, what can the toys of the Kleinian playroom, that sat so uneasily with Anna Freud's version of psychoanalysis—wooden and anthropo-morphic, puppet and doll, the building blocks of houses that were not homes—tell us about how fiction worked to conceive the child through increasingly fleshed-out character, life-like domesticity, and a teleology of development? Reading with the child's exemplary ludic capacity to protest and recover and protest again at the forefront of our minds can help us to understand, not only what the novel's little figures and objects are deployed to express, but also the kinds of therapeutic effects they might generate in their readers.

Chapter 1, "Proper Objects," investigates the toy as it shows up in the edu-cational theories of Jean-Jacques Rousseau and Richard and Maria Edgeworth. Despite their pedagogic agenda, these writers acknowledge the child's aggres-sion, attempting to manage its relationship with its toys both through the formulation of the object lesson, and by figuring this childish violence as a mode of enlightened investigation. I reevaluate Rousseau's hypothesizing, in the final book of *Émile* (1762), of the girl Sophie, created for the needs of the youth, in terms of his depiction of the female child as doll who plays with dolls. I then turn to the Edgeworths' coauthored educational treatise *Practical Edu-cation* (1798), excavating the family romance behind its construction. In that book's opening chapter, "Toys," Maria invokes Rousseau as "able champion" of the object lesson. I recast her chapter as an intricate riposte to Rousseau's version of the education of the female child, and argue that this explicit "attack" was carried on in her first novel, *Belinda* (1801). In *Belinda*'s far-from-conventional marriage plot, characters seek to determine the degree of the other's artifice, while eschewing that most artificial of constructs, the child of nature. The novel's love tests are, in my reading, examples of projective identification, whereby characters become thing-like, objects animated, and resolution occurs through both damage and reparation.

The second chapter, "Possible Persons," brings together Klein's play-technique and the work of Charles Dickens to think through recent theories of character and its relation to self- or personhood. It begins with a reading of *The Cricket on the Hearth* (1845), the most explicit toy story of Dickens's *oeuvre*. Where Dickens here offers an Anna Freudian version of object relationships that instates the values of the hearth, the figure of Tackleton the toy-merchant, hawker of grim-faced, demoniacal toys, manifests an alternative vision of brutal play that cannot quite be swept under the domestic rug. The chapter then moves to *The Old Curiosity Shop* (1841), and particularly the figure of Daniel Quilp, angry puppet counterpart to Little Nell's waxwork doll. Where previous readings have tended to highlight the counterintuitive and contradictory appeal of these two characters, frequently declaring allegiance with the more animated Quilp, I propose that they be understood as a therapeutic pair, symbiotically manifesting the unstable dynamics of aggression and reparation. Finally, I compare Caleb Plummer's "Blind Daughter" Bertha in *Cricket on the Hearth* and *Our Mutual Friend*'s (1865) Jenny Wren: two "doll's dressmakers" whose overtly reparative work is susceptible to convulsions of aggression and guilt. My reading of these characters draws attention to the affinities and tensions between Kleinian reparation and Anna Freud's model of altruistic surrender.

Chapter 3, "Our Plays," engages with the juvenile fiction of the Brontës, whose writing careers originated in perhaps the most famous of Victorian literary toy stories. A gift of twelve toy soldiers prompted the Brontë siblings to commence what they referred to as a series of "plays," set in the imaginary worlds of Glasstown, Angria, and Gondal, which were eventually transcribed in tiny print into tiny books. Whereas the miniature books have been traditionally interpreted as objects of mourning, this chapter asks that we return to their foundation in games with toy objects, and to consider the juvenilia as play therapy. It then looks at journal entries that disclose Charlotte Brontë's increasingly anguished sense of the disruption of her "plays" as she commences a pedagogic career, and at her eventual repudiation of fantasy writing in favor of the "homely materials" of novelistic realism across a series of valedictory pieces. These texts pre-enact the conflict between Klein and Anna Freud over the relative developmental merits of play versus domesticity and the pedagogic. Turning briefly to Charlotte's perplexingly unlikeable first novel *The Professor* (1857), I offer a reading of the protagonist Crimsworth as sadistic avatar, which seeks to reconcile Kleinian toy therapy with ideas set out in Anna Freud's "Beating Fantasies and Daydreams."

The final chapter, "Bildung Blocks," explores the Bildungsroman, the novel of development, and itself the purportedly evolved nineteenth-century novel: a union of educational narrative with achieved psychological characterization.

Commencing with a discussion of the figure of the puppet in the originary Bildungsroman, Goethe's *Wilhelm Meister's Apprenticeship* (1795–96), it foregrounds violent play as fundamental to the representation of childhood within this genre. It argues that the Bildungsroman's toy stories encapsulate a counter-imperative of regression working against its developmental propulsion: one that exposes the thesis of the novel's maturation—from sentiment to realism, from the depiction of flat to rounded character, from the picaresque to the Bildungsroman—as comparably marked by formal reversion and compromised interiority. I pursue this insight through two female Bildungsromane: Charlotte Brontë's *Villette* (1853; considered her mature masterpiece), and George Eliot's *The Mill on the Floss* (1860; considered to linger too long in scenes of childhood). I read the first-person narrative of Lucy Snowe, the most intransigent of Brontë's "little, poor and plain" heroines, not, as has been more often proposed, as a record of traumatized affect, but as a tale of Kleinian envy, wrought in a character landscape that is as much toy world as the achieved realism to which Brontë claimed to aspire. And in Maggie Tulliver's "grinding and beating" of her broken wooden doll in Dorlcote Mill's attic, I find a toy model for understanding the larger scale and insistent ways in which undercurrents of rage and remorse damage beloved objects in this backward-glancing Bildungsroman.

There might have been other ways to think through the presence of the toy in nineteenth-century literature. Julie Park has used eighteenth-century versions of some of the classic play objects whose nineteenth-century descendants I discuss here—doll, automaton, puppet—to think through the construction and workings of the eighteenth-century novel.[101] Susan Stewart's focus on toys as part of a study of scale and literary form, Peter Brooks's discussion of realism as a version of toy-modeling, or Daniel Tiffany's use of the "toy medium" to connect lyric poetry with discourses of materialism are also adroit applications of toy prototypes to literary study.[102] Thing theory has directed attention to the (non-relational) object; Matthew Kaiser has parsed play as both practice and privileged metaphor of a Victorian world in flux, bracing itself for modernity.[103] One might find numerous toy comparisons across the nineteenth-century archive to confirm that authors were thinking of the novel in toy-like terms, and that the toy was in turn serving to represent the working of a proto-Unconscious. Thackeray prefaces *Vanity Fair* (1848) in the role of puppet-master, "proud to think that his Puppets have given satisfaction to the very best company in this empire," especially "the famous little Becky Puppet [. . .] pronounced to be uncommonly flexible in joints, and lively on the wire," "the Amelia Doll [. . .] carved and dressed with the greatest care" and the "Dobbin Figure," which "though apparently clumsy, yet dances in a very amusing and natural manner."[104] Thomas Hardy sought to demolish "the doll of fiction" by forcing readers of *Tess of the D'Urbervilles* to confront the existence and consequences of female sexuality.[105] However, this book strives to push beyond analogy in its discussion of literary toy stories, to think about the work that such formal playfulness and violence performs. Toy stories divulge an anti-developmental counter-history of the novel, in which character is flattened, Bildung regresses, realist objects are warped by the psyche. In the pages that follow, I argue that this anti-maturational imperative would, surprisingly, find its clearest articulation in early child analysis. Nineteenth-century novels continue to agitate and comfort their readers because of the ability of their narratives to damage and soothe character objects, just as nineteenth-century children, it turns out, broke their toys to express their feelings.

1
Proper Objects

Tucked into the early pages of *Beyond the Pleasure Principle* (1920), the thought experiment that would fuel Melanie Klein's bold theorization of child's play, is a rare Freudian toy story. Freud reports his observation of "the first game played by a little boy of one and a half and invented by himself."[1] Though not intellectually precocious, the child (in actuality Freud's grandson Ernst) was well behaved. "This good little boy, however, had an occasional disturbing habit of taking any small objects he could get hold of and throwing them away from him into a corner, under the bed, and so on, so that hunting for his toys and picking them up was often quite a business" (14). The action is accompanied by "a loud, long-drawn-out 'o-o-o-o,'" and "an expression of interest and satisfaction" (14). Freud and the child's mother interpret this as an attempt to articulate the German word "fort," meaning "gone." Freud writes, "I eventually realized that it was a game and that the only use he made of any of his toys was to play 'gone' with them" (15). This displacement of the toys' proper "use" with more troublesome yet emotionally satisfying play is reiterated in the boy's subsequently observed behavior.

> The child had a wooden reel with a piece of string tied round it. It never occurred to him to pull it along the floor behind him, for instance, and play at its being a carriage. What he did was to hold the reel by the string and very skillfully throw it over the edge of his curtained cot, so that it disappeared into it, at the same time uttering his expressive "o-o-o-o." He then pulled the reel out of the cot again by the string and hailed its reappearance with a joyful "*da*" ["there"]. This then was the complete game—disappearance and return. (15)

While Freud says it was often only the "fort" part of the game that was witnessed, he claims that the return was attended by greater pleasure. In this way he puts a gentle spin on his interpretation of the child's play, which he sees as enabling it to manage the renunciation it had made "in allowing his mother to go away without protesting. He compensated himself for this, as it were, by himself staging the disappearance and return of the objects within his reach" (15). The child converts its own passive objecthood, forced to endure separation at its mother's whim, into active control of objects to hand. Yet while, in this light, positive affect—joy, pleasure—is generated by play, Freud also hazards a less benign interpretation, supported by a further toy story:

> Throwing away the object so that it was "gone" might satisfy an impulse of the child's, which was suppressed in his actual life, to revenge himself on his mother for going away from him. In that case it would have a defiant meaning: "All right, then, go away! I don't need you. I'm sending you away myself." A year later, the same boy whom I had observed at his first game used to take a toy, if he was angry with it, and throw it on the floor, exclaiming: "Go to the fwont!" He had heard at that time that his absent father was "at the front," and was far from regretting his absence; on the contrary he made it quite clear that he had no desire to be disturbed in his sole possession of his mother. We know of other children who liked to express similar hostile impulses by throwing away objects instead of persons. (16)

The paired scenarios indicate how aggression and hostility are "staged" to return a "yield of pleasure" (16). As Freud notes, "the unpleasurable nature of an experience does not always unsuit it for play" (17). Child's play becomes a key example, in this paper, of a compulsion to repeat and work through experience in the interest of gaining mastery over powerful and destabilizing feeling.

With its incorporation of early twentieth-century political upheaval, the fort/da game, like the play technique that Klein developed in part from it, has tended to be read as historically situated. Indeed it is mobilized in as a benign "*normal*" example of a repetition compulsion that manifests in "the dark and dismal subject of the traumatic neurosis" of soldiers returned from the recent Great War (14). Psychoanalysis announces the appearance of ludic hostility in what had been understood to be the successfully disciplined child: the "good little boy" produced by nineteenth-century education and domestic management, even as World War I was being taken to mark a parallel literary turning point away from nineteenth-century domestic realism toward the formal free play of modernist experimentation. Yet the literary archive tells a different story.

Rejection and aggression show up in the earliest depictions of children's play. "A child does not attack persons but things" writes Rousseau in *Émile* (1762), preempting Freud's recognition that the object serves as substitute for the interpersonal.[2] Maria and Richard Edgeworth's *Practical Education* (1798) commences with the child's "hostile impulses," figuring it "idle and miserable, surrounded by disjointed dolls, maimed horses, coaches and one-horse chairs without wheels, and a nameless wreck of gilded lumber," while its mother plaintively asks "'Why don't you play with your playthings, my dear? I am sure that I have bought toys enough for you; why can't you divert yourself with them, instead of breaking them to pieces?'"[3] Baudelaire, in his essay "The Philosophy of Toys" (1853) speaks of "desire" that "plant[s] itself in the child's cerebral marrow, it fills his fingers and nails with an extraordinary agility and strength. He twists and turns the toy, scratches it, shakes it, bangs it against the wall, hurls it on the ground."[4] Far from abhorring such toy damaging, Baudelaire warns that if the child exhibits a care that inhibits violent play: if "only rarely do they show them to their little friends, all the while imploring them *not to touch*," it is prematurely socialized and deeply suspect: "I would be instinctively on my guard against these *men-children*."[5] The toy artifacts unearthed in these pre-psychoanalytic accounts of child's play may be unfamiliar, but their treatment is uncannily recognizable. Though often adduced to educative theses, such shattered playthings anticipate modernity's articulation of object relations.

Literary scholars have for some time now followed the fate of the object across eighteenth- and nineteenth-century texts. Querying the twentieth-century emphasis of Bill Brown's seminal collection *Things* (2004), which heralded a shift toward object orientation in literary and cultural studies, Mark Blackwell frames his *The Secret Life of Things* (2007) around the question "where was 'thing theory' in the English eighteenth century?" Blackwell's contributors, who focus on what are variously termed "'it-narratives,' 'novels of circulation,' 'object tales,' and 'spy novels,'" trace (referencing Brown) "'a particular subject-object relations'" across the eighteenth century, concluding with its nineteenth-century aftermath in children's literature and the novel.[6] Lynn Festa contrasts eighteenth-century it-narratives, which "endeavour to inculcate virtue through satiric discipline," ridiculing the shallow materialism of luxury-oriented acquisition, with nineteenth-century children's morality tales, which instill an ethos of good proprietorship in the middle-class child by endowing quotidian objects with tender feelings and memories that render them requisite of proper care.[7] However, this chapter will argue that the broken toys of long-nineteenth-century educational theory attest to a less resolved relationship between the object and childish affect, manifesting an undercurrent of anxiety

and antagonism in the schooled child. The eruptions of uncontained hostility
to which damaged playthings bear witness in turn fissure debate across both
educational treatises and novels about what constitutes the "proper object" of
child's play. If the furious distress anticipates that of the infant analysands of
early child therapy, the debate in turn offers a line of continuity with the concerns of its divided foremothers. As I noted in the introduction, Melanie Klein
"found the child's attitude to a toy he has damaged very revealing."[8] She interpreted both aggressive and reparative impulses in little children, as they manifested in destructive play with toys. Anna Freud contested what she saw as
Klein's attempt to establish an impossible transference with children still
immediately involved in primary familial relationships, preferring to use toys
in a more reserved way, motivated by an educative as well as analytic imperative. The nub of their disagreement was the value of the toy object. Where
Klein came to employ bespoke toys in a segregated analytic space as objects
of play and its interpretation, Anna Freud's child analytic case studies, which
privilege the preexisting domestic scene, come closer to Festa's description of
the nineteenth-century moral tale: they "endeavor to harness the imagination
to prosaic ends, ensuring that even fanciful narratives be put to household
use."[9] Klein and Anna Freud's tussle was in this sense also one over "proper
objects."

"Things, Things!"

If Rousseau acknowledges the destructive propensities of children's interactions
with objects, the aim of *Émile* is to channel these and other "natural" childish
impulses toward effective education. Rousseau explicitly understands the infantile world to be filled with bad objects: the child's enraged projections. "As
he extends his relations, his needs, and his active or passive dependencies," he
writes, "the sentiment of his connections with others is awakened," and "the
child becomes imperious, jealous, deceitful, and vindictive. If he is bent to
obedience, [. . .] he attributes it to caprice, to the intention of tormenting him;
and he revolts. If he is obeyed, as soon as something resists him, he sees in it
a rebellion, an intention to resist him. He beats the chair or the table for having
disobeyed him" (213). This is the very child, compound of intense feeling and
limited and material modes of expression, that will later send its toys "to the
fwont," and whose communications would eventually find articulation in
Klein's playroom. For Rousseau, committed to education rather than analysis,
maturation is nonetheless conceptualized as object relating: to understand
childhood is to study the self "in his relations with things" (214). In the first
book of *Émile*, which focuses on the infant, Rousseau writes:

Children's first sensations are purely affective; they perceive only pleasure and pain. Able neither to walk nor to grasp, they need a great deal
of time to come little by little into possession of the representative sensations which show them objects outside of themselves. But, while
waiting for these objects to gain extension, to move, so to speak, farther
away from their eyes, to take on dimensions and shapes for them, the
recurrence of the affective sensations begins to submit them to the
empire of habit. (62)

"Affective sensations" are understood here to rule the earliest impressions of
external objects, even before sensory data are properly apprehensible—before
the infant can clutch or focus. To guide the child from response to reason via
objects and to steer it clear of what Freud would call "disturbing habit" is the
aim of Rousseau's treatise. Yet he makes quite clear that this is a battle of wills:
"Either we do what pleases him, or we exact from him what pleases us. Either
we submit to his whims, or we submit him to ours. No middle ground; he must
give orders and receive them" (48). The contest proceeds via a fort/da logic:

When the child stretches out his hand without saying anything, he
believes he will reach the object because he does not estimate the
distance. [. . .] But when he complains and screams in reaching out
his hand, he is no longer deceived as to the distance; he is ordering
the object to approach or you to bring it to him. [. . .] The more he
screams, the less you should listen to him. It is important to accustom
him early not to give orders either to men, for he is not their master, or
to things, for they do not hear him. Thus, when a child desires something that he sees and one wants to give it to him, it is better to carry
the child to the object than the object to the child. (66)

Rousseau turns his enlightenment version of the fort/da game to a different
end, designed to decouple external and internal objects and install a modulat-
ing principle of reason, yet he cannot avoid demonstrating that in the compe-
tition for hold over the object, the authority of the parent/preceptor is equally
at stake.

The echoes of Rousseau's unsentimental yet tender observation of the
infant are audible in a number of Melanie Klein's papers. As noted in the
introduction, Klein's willingness to recognize capacities for phantasying in
very young children was one major source of contention with Anna Freud.
The infant nonetheless provided Klein with subject matter for some of her
most original and discerning theoretical work, offering key developmental
scenarios through which to articulate her complex evolving understanding

of projection, introjection and part and whole objects. As with Rousseau, this involves a highly creative attempt imaginatively to enter the perspective and sensorium of the baby. In "Weaning" (1936), she too speaks of the infant measuring the world and its objects in relation to its own body and drives: "The earliest feelings are experienced in connection with external and internal stimuli." She too observes that "the child's focusing on and attachment to a part of the person is characteristic of this early stage of development, and accounts in great measure for the phantastic and unrealistic nature of his relation to everything, for example, to parts of his own body, to people and to inanimate objects, all of which are at first of course only dimly perceived"; and she too spells out, in her own terminology, the battle between gratification and "hostile impulses" played out in relation to what are necessarily part (because only partially perceived) objects: "The object world of the child in the first two or three months of its life could be described as consisting of gratifying or of hostile and persecuting parts or portions of the real world."[10]

Both Rousseau and Klein acknowledge the importance of the breast as initial focal object for the infant. "The moment he knows his nurse, he has already acquired a great deal," writes Rousseau (62). Klein sees the breast as the part object that channels the gamut of childish affect: "In the earliest stage of mental development every unpleasant stimulus is apparently related in the baby's phantasy to the 'hostile' or denying breasts, every pleasant stimulus on the other hand to the 'good' gratifying breasts."[11] In Rousseau's treatise, however, breast and mother are not interchangeable part and whole objects: he addresses a class and a period for which sending the child out to wet-nurse was common practice, and this combined with his commitment to a pedagogic imperative that he regards as a purely masculine prerogative means that Rousseau represents the breast/woman as functional rather than libidinal object. Like Klein, he acknowledges the early receptivity and intellectual curiosity of the infant: "Why, then, should a child's education not begin before he speaks and understands [. . .]?" (63), but is resistant to the potential precedence this accords the nursing woman.[12] His version of the "bad" or "hostile breast" is not a phenomenon of infantile projection but of social fact. He proposes a relationship between female character and quality of milk: "Imbalance of the passions, like that of the humors, can cause the milk to deteriorate. [. . .] If she is a glutton, an intemperate, she will soon have spoiled her milk" (57). Recommending a peasant nurse who has been raised on a largely vegetable diet he opines that "the milk of herbivorous females is sweeter and healthier than that of carnivores" (58).[13] While Rousseau implicitly recognizes the importance of the breast in early phantasy, and explicitly acknowledges the nurse's role as initial educator of the sucking child, the breast is effectively consigned in his scheme from site of potential tuition to source of animal nourishment.

In "Weaning" Klein outlines the infant's progress from perceiving the mother as part-object, represented solely by the breast, which can be seen as gratifying or withholding, and in the latter case is subject to aggressive and sadistic phantasy, to the perception of the mother as "a whole person and a loving being."[14] Once this happens, the guilt induced by the memory of these aggressive phantasies is managed by reparative, creative acts that are evident in a new kind of play: "We find [these reparative tendencies] at work in the first play-activities and at the basis of the child's satisfaction in his achievements, even those of the most simple kind for example, in putting one brick on top of another, or making a brick stand upright after it had been knocked down."[15] Rousseau too traces a shift from aggressive to constructive play; one he seeks to claim pedagogically. Acutely aware of the destructive impulses manifest in children's play—"a child wants to upset everything he sees; he smashes, breaks everything he can reach"—he outlines numerous techniques by which objects, including toys, and activities of play can be maneuvered away from expressions of "attack" toward the domestic and social education of the child (97). *Émile* models what would become known as the "object lesson": a "science [. . .] of things" designed to be "truly useful" to the child (108). The object lesson employs the material article—a piece of coal, an apple, a handkerchief—as prop: elaborating outward from this aid, the teacher may draw practical, economic and historical lessons, and segue seamlessly into moral symbolism. Sarah Anne Carter notes that such pedagogy taught children to "think with things"; the object lesson was devised on the assumption "that material things had the potential, at least in part, to convey information."[16] Rousseau proposes that the child that "breaks everything he can reach" can be educated by stealth; its toys and games co-opted into lesson format. Cultivating a few beans leads to a sermon on property; a walk to see the horizon and stars, rather than a classroom globe, teaches it about the world; "a round top turning on its tip represents the heavens turning on their axis; the top's two tips are the two poles" (170). Night games are devised to deprivilege sight and keep pedagogy firmly within the tactile domain of the object. "Really, what will they play with that I cannot turn into an object of instruction for them?" Rousseau confidently queries (148).

Rousseau's appropriation of things to hand encompasses a further claim that childhood objects should eschew luxury. He rails against the valuable infant toy: "One no longer knows how to be simple in anything, not even with children: rattles of silver and gold, and coral, cut crystal glasses, teething rings of every price and kind. What useless and pernicious affectations!" (69). Instead, he adapts both found and self-fashioned things to his games. A treasure hunt discloses a box containing, instead of sweets, "very nicely set out on moss or cotton, a June bug, a snail, a piece of coal, an acorn, a turnip or some other similar foodstuff" (137); he suggests immersing the child in a manufacturing workshop rather than in books (177). Yet while Rousseau seems to be advocating for the simplest of toys, his fundamental recognition of the child as one who attacks "not persons but things" must also be factored into this object choice. Valuable ornamented rattles are to be replaced by teething toys of "wood, leather, rags, soft matter which give and in which the tooth leaves an imprint" (69); there is no cost incurred in the damaging of an acorn; to place a child in a workshop for a day is to incur less expense than in the purchase of a defecating duck.[17] Rousseau's useful toys are ways of protecting property from destruction and disciplining the unruly child, of winning what he has identified as a battle of wills with the wayward infant.

Rousseau's discourse on the object in *Émile* inaugurates, in the pedagogic realm, a critique of the primacy of the sign; one which became foundational for the later twentieth-century interrogation of logocentrism inaugurated by Derridean deconstruction.[18] "Never substitute the sign for the thing except when it is impossible for you to show the latter, for the sign absorbs the child's attention and makes him forget the thing represented," Rousseau writes, enshrining the educative potential of the thing itself over the "dangerous supplement" of speech (170). Deploring the pedagogic tendency to employ "Words, more words, always words" (108), Rousseau asserts instead the communicative power of "Things, things!" (180)—his two exclamatory sentences enacting the displacement of logophobia by pragmaphilia.[19] If speech is superfluous, modes of representation—painting, and above all writing—are his anathema. "I want [Émile] to have no other master than nature and no other model than objects. I want him to have before his eyes the original itself and not the paper representing it," he claims, devising his ideal drawing lesson. Equally, he advocates "no book other than the world" (168). Reading is "the plague of childhood"; books are children's "greatest misery" (116); tossing them from his ideal playpen Rousseau exclaims petulantly "I hate books" (184). Famously, his single exception is *Robinson Crusoe* (1719), now the favored candidate for the first novel of the English canon.[20] He recasts *Crusoe* as a novel of "instruction," proposing a redaction "disencumbered of all its rigmarole, beginning with Robinson's shipwreck near his island and ending with the arrival of the ship which comes to take him from it" (a clipped version of the novel that indeed emerged as the children's *Crusoe* across the century to come). As Rousseau makes clear, this is the novel recast as object lesson:

I want [Émile] constantly to be busy with his mansion, his goats, his plantations; I want him to learn in detail, not from books but from things, all that must be known in such a situation; I want him to think he is Robinson himself, to see himself dressed in skins, wearing a large cap, carrying a large saber and all the rest of the character's grotesque equipment, with the exception of the parasol, which he will not need. I want him to worry about the measures to take if this or that were lacking to him; to examine his hero's conduct; to investigate whether he omitted anything, whether there was nothing to do better; to note Robinson's failings attentively; and to profit from them so as not to fall into them himself in such a situation. (185)

Here the child is understood to be both mimic and interlocutor of the text. While it is encouraged imaginatively to identify with "Robinson himself," it is also envisaged as carefully investigating the novel's scenes of self-tuition, in order to profit not only by example but from "his hero's" failings.[21]

In her study of *Robinson Crusoe*'s shifting status as adult and children's book, Teresa Michals argues that what Rousseau recommends is a very literal disencumberment of Defoe's protagonist. She proposes that Rousseau intended his child's version to commence after the shipwreck, thereby depriving "his Crusoe of the wealth of tools and goods with which Defoe so generously supplies him."[22] Michals then turns to Joachim Heinrich Campe's *Robinson der Jüngere* (1779), published in London as *The New Robinson Crusoe: An Instructive and Entertaining History, for the Use of Children of Both Sexes* (1788), drawing attention to Campe's "attacks" on what she calls the "awkward warehouse of tools and other goods" that Crusoe brings from the ship (46). Campe wrote that "'The Old Robinson Crusoe . . . is erroneous in one particular sufficient to destroy every advantage that this history might produce, which is, that Robinson Crusoe is provided with all sorts of European tools and instruments necessary to procure him many of those conveniences that belong to society'."[23] Michals in turn claims that the things Campe arraigns, "Rousseau simply wishes away," arguing that both authors seek to limit Crusoe's capacity to appropriate items brought from the wreck to shore as his first island objects.[24] However Rousseau's plan to begin his version of the novel with the "shipwreck near his island" suggests no such deprivation: the new uses to which Crusoe puts things from home and the new values he accords them are as vital to Rousseau's object lesson pedagogy as the items he fashions from local materials. In both cases objects decontextualized become expressive; their functionality is interrogated or reappropriated.[25] Michals's discussion of versions of the Crusoe tale from

Rousseau's onwards is informed by her interest in changing notions of age-appropriate reading. She argues that an emphasis on psychological interiority that accompanied the late-nineteenth-century development of the field of literary criticism clinched the relegation of *Crusoe* to the realm of childhood, with critics from Dickens to Leslie Stephen commenting on the "deficit of psychological complexity in the novel," and the adult reading experience henceforward figured as a purely nostalgic reengagement with a "scene of immature play."[26] However, Rousseau's circumscribed Crusoe offers, precisely, a "scene of immature play" as space of a psychologically complex understanding of childhood feeling. The concern about which of Crusoe's objects might be most useful to the developing child: should domestic items be jettisoned or included in solitary self-fashioning?—again recalls the conflict between Anna Freud and Melanie Klein over the use of domestic versus specifically fashioned toys in child therapy, and the further argument over whether their primary purpose lies in symbolizing internal relationships or in therapeutically educating the child. If Rousseau's *Robinson Crusoe* is a book object exempted from the mantra "not from books but from things" by being reconfigured as a child *bricoleur*'s manual, its protagonist's umbilical attachment to the shipwreck by a line that eventually breaks, but which allows him to secure objects that can be cherished or abandoned, cloned or rejected, is an essential part of *Robinson Crusoe*'s maturational subtext.

Rousseau's object lessons were taken up as practice in the innovations of his protégé, the Swiss educator Johann Heinrich Pestalozzi (1746–1827), whose *How Gertrude Teaches Her Children* (1801), an epistolary text expanding the pedagogical model established in his popular *Leonard and Gertrude* novels (1781–87), notably figures a female educator rather than Rousseau's insistently masculine preceptor. They were further developed in the pedagogy of Friederich Fröbel (1782–1852), who eventually gave the name *Kindergarten* to the Play and Activity Institute he founded in 1837 at Bad Blankenberg. Fröbel developed a philosophy of infant education that blurred the distinction between work and play. He designed boxes of block-like wooden toys known as "Spielgabe" (play gifts) or "Fröbelgabe" (Fröbel gifts), which were to be used in specific games (Spiele) envisaged so that the child's play might evolve in tactile and conceptual complexity from the simple balls of Box I through to the connecting wooden cubes, oblongs, and prisms of Box VI.[27] Later still Maria Montessori (1870–1952), whose principles influenced Anna Freud's pedagogy, would use colored objects to train children to count. If Fröbel's "Gabe" and Montessori's objects, freighted with an educative agenda, instance Marcel Mauss's later insight that there are "no free gifts," the toy we find across nineteenth-century literature, repeatedly attacked in hostile play, comes closer to Georges Bataille's notion of *la part maudite*: "his majesty the baby" is figured wasting and spoiling gifts and their logic of reciprocity and gratitude. Unlike his followers, Rousseau offers the object lesson complicated by semiosis, and understood to be at the mercy of the willful child. His desire to substitute "Things, things!" for "words, more words": objects for signs, returns us to Klein's insistence on interpreting "not only the child's words but also his activities with his toys"; to her fundamental "principle" that play is a "means of expressing what the adult expresses predominately by words"; and to her assertion that "in its play, the child acts instead of speaking."[28]

Once Rousseau has substituted everyday things for costly or intricate toys, there are in fact few conventionally designated toy objects to be found in the early books of *Émile*: a shuttlecock, a kite, a wax duck. The exception comes, not at any point in Émile's childhood education, but in the final book of the treatise, with the discussion of the education of Sophie, the ideal female companion who "has to be given to him" (357). In the toy-language of *Émile*, woman represents a contradiction. Arguing that a husband should not make his wife a servant, confined to housekeeping tasks, Rousseau suggests that this would be to render her "a veritable automaton" (364). Yet if this is consistent with his rejection of the mechanized model throughout the treatise, when speaking of the purported female capacity for emotional manipulation he nonetheless presents woman as natural automaton: "Woman, who is weak and who sees nothing outside the house, estimates and judges the forces she can put to work to make up for her weakness [. . .]. Her science of mechanics is more powerful than ours; all her levers unsettle the human heart" (387). It is in relation to this latter version of femininity—at once domestic and artificial, that the toy comes to the fore, as mirror and metaphor. The doll is the girl's "special entertainment," he writes: "boys seek movement and noise: drums, boots, little carriages. Girls prefer what presents itself to sight and is useful for ornamentation: mirrors, jewels, dresses, particularly dolls" (367). Having characterized feminine play as inherently self-regarding, Rousseau then figures the doll as the toy the female child grows *into* rather than outgrows:

> Observe a little girl spending the day around her doll, constantly
> changing its clothes, dressing and undressing it hundreds and hun-
> dreds of times, continuously seeking new combinations of orna-
> ments—well or ill matched, it makes no difference. Her fingers lack
> adroitness, her taste is not yet formed, but already the inclination
> reveals itself. In this eternal occupation time flows without her think-
> ing of it; the hours pass, and she knows nothing of it. She even forgets
> meals. She is hungrier for adornment than for food. But, you will say,

she adorns her doll and not her person. Doubtless. She sees her doll and does not see herself. She can do nothing for herself. She is not yet formed; she has neither talent nor strength; she is still nothing. She is entirely in her doll, and puts all her coquetry into it. She will not always leave it there. She awaits the moment when she will be her own doll. (367)

The female child's toy trains her to develop from "nothing" to thing: the diminished apotheosis of object-oriented ontology.

One might trace the legacy of Rousseau's thinking here across a whole archive of nineteenth-century doll-focused children's books and articles that sought to socialize or domesticate the female child by way of the object lesson of the doll.[29] However, at this stage I want simply to contrast Rousseau's doll with the first doll to appear in Klein's case studies: that of two-year-old Rita.[30] According to Klein, who analyzed Rita in her own home in Berlin in the early 1920s, Rita would play mother and child with her doll. She would tuck it into bed very tightly, in one instance with a toy elephant, who was told to ensure the doll did not get up, steal into the parents' bedroom and "do some harm there or take something away." Playing mother, Rita was "excessively strict and cruel."[31] In *The Psycho-Analysis of Children* (1932) Klein describes her mode of attacking her toys:

> On another occasion, she put a triangular brick on one side and said: "That's a little woman"; she then took a "little hammer," as she called another long-shaped brick, and hit the brick-box with it exactly in a place where it was only stuck together with paper, so that she made a hole in it. She said: "When the hammer hit hard, the little woman was *so* frightened."[32]

I shall return to Rita's "little woman" and other Kleinian toys in my ensuing discussion of Edgeworth, but for now, I want to note a series of differences between Klein's and Rousseau's formulations of doll and girl. Rita's doll is a child that she punishes, not an adult to be grown into, while her version of the "little woman" is a block-like object, activated by Rita with the "movement and noise" Rousseau attributes to the male child at play. It is non-anthropomorphic, neither dressable nor imitable. In Rousseau's dream of a female created to meet Émile's needs, a doll is educative, modeling a passive and supplementary self-fashioning. In Klein's analytic session a toy is being beaten. Rather than suggesting that the two "little women" simply indicate historical changes in the conception of the female child, my argument is that, from its inception in the work of Rousseau and Edgeworth, the educative imperative of the object lesson was always shadowed by the "hostile impulses" of object relations.

"Want of Proper Objects"

Practical Education, the educational treatise coauthored by Maria Edgeworth and her father, is a text built from infant observation. Maria's step-mother Honora Sneyd Edgeworth had initiated a "'register of the remarks of the children'" in 1770 when she took over the parenting of the unruly Maria and her three surviving siblings as Richard's second wife. According to Marilyn Butler, Maria's relationship with Honora was "a classic case of daughter/(step)mother friction"; nonetheless, Butler concedes that Honora's methods "may have initiated much of the avant-garde pedagogic system that became the family's corporate trademark."[33] In her register, Honora recorded the ways in which the children responded to both object lessons and domestic things, the questions they asked and the constructions they placed upon unfamiliar terms and practices. *Practical Education; or, The History of Harry and Lucy* by Honora Sneyd and Richard Lovell Edgeworth grew from this material, and was published in 1780, the year of Honora's death from tuberculosis. It was described by Richard Lovell Edgeworth as intended "to inculcate the plain precepts of morality, not by eloquent harangues, but by such pictures of real life, as may make a Child wish to put himself in the place of the characters intended to excite his emulation" while also attempting "as much as possible to lead the understanding from known to unknown problems and propositions."[34] The book's ambition, then, recalls that of Rousseau's proposed *Crusoe* redaction, in combining principles of imitation and interrogation. Honora's register was resumed by Maria in the early 1790s as her father's family, which eventually extended to twenty-two children from four different mothers, continued to grow. Honora and Richard Lovell's *Practical Education* was revised as the first part of Maria Edgeworth's 1801 collection of juvenile tales *Early Lessons*, and continued to resurface in a number of Edgeworth's publications for children until 1825.

Maria and Richard Lovell's *Practical Education* appeared in 1798, eighteen years after Honora's death. Noting that "When a book appears under the name of two authors, it is natural to inquire what share belongs to each of them," the preface situates Edgeworth senior as the author of "all that relates to the art of teaching to read in the chapter on Tasks, the chapters on Grammar and Classical Literature, Geography, Chronology, Arithmetic, Geometry, and Mechanics," while Maria's chapters, which include "On Temper," "On Vanity, Pride, and Ambition," "On Attention" and "Books," are all animus and objects (ix–x).

Despite the acknowledgment of dual authorship the treatise was termed "Maria's great work" until late in its production, and grew organically from her revival of the registers, which were appended as "Notes containing conversations and anecdotes of children."[35] The preface makes clear not only that Maria wrote the lion's share of *Practical Education*, but that her inspiration was maternal rather than paternal: "She was encouraged and enabled to write upon this important subject, by having for many years before her eyes the conduct of a judicious mother in the education of a large family" (x). Here the stepmother Honora Sneyd, coauthor of the first *Practical Education*, is revived as the guiding spirit of the second *Practical Education*, authored by the stepdaughter Maria.[36] Maria acknowledges a further guiding influence in Rousseau, acclaimed early in the book as "able champion" (3) of educative play. These intricacies of authorial debt, both acknowledged and occluded, in a father/daughter copublication founded on infant observation, seem worth highlighting here as they anticipate the context and terms in which Anna Freud's contributions to an educatively framed child analysis were initiated and formulated. As noted in the introduction, Anna Freud's promotion of infant observation techniques, from her early teaching in Vienna to the practices of the Hampstead War Nursery, was predicated on an understanding of the child as categorically different from the adult. Developing a psychoanalytic version of the Rousseauian thesis that "childhood has its ways of seeing, thinking, and feeling which are proper to it" (90), Anna Freud argued that children's play could not be equated, as Klein had proposed, with adult free association. Instead she defended the notion of analytical transference promulgated by her father, which excluded the child because it was understood still to be operating within a dominant relationship to the parent. The degree of codependence between Maria Edgeworth and her father has been the focus of much Edgeworth criticism, well summarized by Caroline Gonda, who quotes, among others, Frank Swinnerton's comment that "when once the father is dead [the literary daughter] can be relied on as the acme of loyalty [. . .]. She will extol his scholarship [. . .]. She does this, not from a strained sense of duty, but because she really believes that the man she saw first from her cradle has god-like qualities."[37] Equivalent characterizations dogged the psychoanalytic daughter Anna Freud as she sought to perpetuate her father's scholarly and personal legacy. Edgeworth's explicit adherence to the lessons of her two pedagogic fathers, Richard Lovell and Rousseau, is rendered ambivalent, this chapter argues, by the violent toy stories that complicate *Practical Education*'s project of rational child-rearing.

Mitzi Myers notes that "until late in the game" when her father added his chapters on scientific and philosophical topics, Maria Edgeworth referred to her *Practical Education* project as "'toys and tasks.'"[38] The book's first chapter, penned by Maria, is simply entitled "Toys."[39] However Edgeworth presents us first up, not with the intact objects of the conventional object lesson, but, as noted earlier, with toys destroyed: "disjointed dolls, maimed horses, coaches and one-horse chairs without wheels, and a nameless wreck of gilded lumber" (1). "'Why don't you play with your playthings, my dear?'" the mother intones, the internal repetition nonetheless intimating the tedious redundancy of simply employing objects as they are nominated. Edgeworth moves swiftly into damage control, recuperating the child she has figured as "idle and miserable" as enlightened investigator examining the how of the toy, or productive laborer whose aggression is rightly directed toward time-wasting: "Is it not rather unjust to be angry with him for breaking [his toys] to pieces? [. . .] He breaks them, not from the love of mischief, but from the hatred of idleness; either he wishes to see what his playthings are made of, and how they are made, or whether he can put them together again if the parts be once separated" (1–2).[40] The object is held responsible for the damage it provokes: infant destructiveness is attributable to "want of proper objects to occupy the [. . .] attention" (9). Only the bad object, in other words, attracts unruly behavior; it is a cause rather than a symptom. Edgeworth's chapter goes on, again presumably with the able champion Rousseau in mind, to distinguish the useful toy from the "gilded lumber" that incites appropriate aggression. In Edgeworth's account ornate and complex toys displace the child as the ill-developed object: they are "frail and useless," and the child's will to destruction becomes indicative of a natural virtue that privileges use over consumption and exercise over passivity. Foreshadowing Baudelaire's virtuously and cerebrally violent infant, she writes: "as long as the child has sense and courage to destroy the toys, there is no great harm done" (3).[41] For Edgeworth, "proper objects" include strong wooden carts, simple wooden and ivory pegs, balls and cubes, pencils and scissors, rather than fancy coaches, fine dolls and their houses, or those philosophical toys (gilt lambs and churning milkmaids) that resist the kinds of inquiry into their makings that "snaps the wire or perforates the bellows" (5).[42]

In her "Toys" chapter, Edgeworth more than once invokes the fantasy of a "rational toy-shop" where useful educative objects might be purchased: a concept she elaborated in one of her 1801 *Moral Tales*, "The Good French Governess." In this story *Émile's* masculine preceptor has become an ideal preceptress, Madam De Rosier, an aristocratic émigré with a name that echoes Rousseau's, who, on arriving in England, becomes governess to the children of the negligent Mrs. Harcourt. The two eldest Harcourt girls, Isabella and Matilda, represent overweening intellect and sensibility: the former too confident in her mnemonic powers; the latter strongly sympathetic, but in the absence of intellectual encouragement ("she had more hopes of pleasing by the graces of her person than of her mind") beginning to mature into Rousseau's doll-woman, with "her attention gradually turned to dress and personal accomplishments."[43] The youngest daughter Favoretta "had been, from birth, the plaything of her mother and her mother's waiting maid" (412), while Herbert, a rough, clumsy boy, is growing into "a little surly rebel, who took pleasure in doing exactly the contrary to every thing he was desired to do, and who took pride in opposing his powers of endurance to the force of punishment" (413). Petted toy and hostile child, each introduces itself to the new governess via a preferred object: Herbert "Held his whip fast in his right hand"; Favoretta cried "'Will you love me? I have not my red shoes on to-day!'" (414). Although the children to some degree anticipate Austenian types—sense and sensibility, pride and persuasion—their depiction incorporates an understanding of the family psychology informing their difficulties that renders them something closer to child-psychoanalytic case studies. Madame de Rosier observes, not the normative mottling of sensibility on Matilda's cheeks, but a "timid, anxious blush" (412); Herbert is characterized as "neither caressing nor caressed" (411).

Rational toys form an early gambit in Madame de Rosier's educational reformation of her charges:

> After Mad. de Rosier had been some time at Mrs. Harcourt's, and had carefully studied the characters, or, more properly speaking, the habits of all of her pupils, she took them with her one morning to a large toy-shop, or rather warehouse for toys, which had been lately opened, under the direction of an ingenious gentleman, who had employed proper workmen to execute rational toys for the rising generation. (419)

The double qualification—habit for character, warehouse for toy-shop—signals Edgeworth's conscientious implementation of Rousseauian terminology (his "empire of habit" and workshop as play space.) The children learn from tradesmen, visiting "the coachmaker's, the cooper's, the turner's, the cabinet-maker's, even the black ironmonger's and noisy tinman's shop" (427), and a version of Rousseau's bean sermon is enacted as Herbert learns about private ownership via a packet of radish seeds. The tale thus emplots not only *Practical Education*'s version of the ideal toy but its author's stated debt to Rousseau. Yet while she follows Rousseau in advocating "great carts and wheelbarrows" over fancy phaetons, Edgeworth explicitly excludes from this rational toyshop those very toys reclaimed by Rousseau in the final book of *Émile*: "'No [. . .] dressed dolls!' said Favoretta, in a reproachful tone—[. . .] 'Nor soldiers—nor a drum!' continued Herbert" (420). The children are ultimately converted to rational play by finding their own favored objects co-opted or substituted. Herbert becomes horse to a sturdy cart, "whipping himself" as he gallops away (420); Favoretta moves from thinking of lacework as something "such as [the nursemaid] Grace laces me with" (421) to an item she can manufacture herself. Toys that have been used to express angry or shamed feeling are reclaimed as the child displaces ambivalence with what Klein would come to call "*the desire to restore*."[44] Within the tale this transformation goes hand in hand with renewed relations with the mother: Mrs. Harcourt in turn becomes distracted from a life of dissipation as her interest is kindled in her children's new modes of reparative play.[45]

There are certainly ways of reading Edgeworth's pedagogic agenda as a conservative one, and Edgeworth's figuration of the rational toy might easily be adduced to such arguments.[46] Where Rousseau railed against moribund luxury and refigured proletarian or agricultural labor as healthy play, and Pestalozzi and Montessori, as Anna Freud would later, focused their attention on the deprived children of the peasantry or the urban proletariat, in *Practical Education* the toy is an instrument of bourgeois subjectivity. Just as the sturdy artisanal toy is pitted against the "frail and useless" coach or dollhouse of aristocratic pretensions, so Edgeworth maintains a firm distinction between the potential and play of "children of the poor" who are to be beguiled by watching their older siblings labor into habits of "sympathetic industry" (14), and bourgeois children, whose induction into work-*like* play must negotiate "the hazard of their keeping company with servants" (25). As Gary Cross points out, citing both Edgeworth and Locke, the educative equation of "the plain with the creative," the injunction that "toys were not to be novelties, miniatures of aristocratic whimsy, mechanical curiosity or commercial dazzle [. . .] is firmly anchored in a middle-class culture of self-improvement with deep roots in the historical aspirations and ascent of the bourgeoisie."[47] In her discussion of nineteenth-century autobiographies of non-human characters, which "trace the education and upbringing of owner and object alike," Lynn Festa observes a related privileging of the "hand-hewn, nonindustrial" thing: "the objects are all raised and educated on an individual basis; none of them are industrially manufactured. The manner of their crafting is lovingly described."[48] Festa suggests that the process of careful manufacture mirrors the educative process to which the child must submit: objects and children are fashioned by a hand that is both nurturing and disciplining. Conflating personal and cultural nostalgia, Walter Benjamin was later to celebrate the handmade wooden toy as peasant object. "The entire process of their production and not merely its result—is alive for the child in the toy, and he naturally understands a primitively produced object much better than one deriving from a complicated industrial process," Benjamin wrote, privileging "wood [as] the most important among these materials. There is an incomparable mastery of its handling—of carving, coloring, and lacquering—."[49] And Roland Barthes would express a similar preference for carpentry over mechanics in the realm of the toy: "If it dies, it is in dwindling, not in swelling out like those mechanical toys which disappear behind the hernia of a broken spring. Wood makes essential objects, objects for all time."[50] Barthes pays tribute to the wooden toy as both first and enduring object, whose innocence of manufacture and special location between nature and culture offer a perfect analog for infancy. For Benjamin and Barthes, "primitively produced" is to "complicated industrial process" as the child is to the adult, illuminated by distance. The handcrafted toy is always the good, whole object, "alive for the child" not, as Klein argued, as partial projection, but as embodied formation.

Yet *Practical Education* is a much more ambivalent text than readings of its conservatism allow, and the figure of that ambivalence is the broken toy. In the treatise's version of the rational toy-shop, playthings are not so much crafted as effectively defanged: "wood properly prepared" (22); chemicals provided with proper directions so that "parents would not be afraid of burning or poisoning their children in the first chemical lessons" (25). If these "rational" objects are intended to anticipate and waylay childish violence, what reciprocal animosity renders parents afraid of harming their child? When Edgeworth writes "the first toys for infants should be merely such things as may be grasped without danger" (5), does she speak of danger to the infant or the toy? In her "Toys" chapter, aggression bounces, unresolved, between object and child, parent and thing. For all the effort that Edgeworth spends recuperating the destructive child as nascent thinker and worker, the exasperated antagonism manifest in the opening scene of toy carnage cannot quite be put to rest. It resurfaces across the chapter in the repeated figuration of the child as ever eager to "divert him-self with forbidden objects" (10), making ordinary domestic things casualties of brutal play. Even sensible toys such as a father's gift of a mini carpenter's tool kit risk producing "dreadful marks of the file and saw upon his mahogany tables" (21). Parents who "tremble for their furniture" (15) are encouraged to engage their children mentally with their playthings to prevent them being "so actively hostile in their attacks upon inanimate objects" (16).

As Fröbel and Montessori would later, Edgeworth advocates the use of tex-tured toy objects to enable infants to distinguish between shapes: "Round ivory or wooden sticks should be put into their little hands," she writes; "by degrees they will learn to lift them to their mouths, and they will distinguish their sizes: square and circular bits of wood, balls, cubes, and triangles, with holes of dif-ferent sizes made in them, to admit the sticks, should be their playthings" (5–6). But Klein's little patient Rita, whose "'little hammer,' as she called a [. . .] long-shaped brick, [. . .] hit the brick-box [. . .] exactly in a place where it was only stuck together with paper, so that she made a hole in it," models a different use of block-like toy objects; one that is less about protecting the little hands of infants than absorbing their unexpressed fury, envy and shame.[51] Rita's hammer and hole are comparable to Edgeworth's "square and circular bits of wood," with their equally suggestive "holes of different sizes in them to admit the sticks" (5), in their solidity and graspability, not to mention their capacity to represent Oedipal drama. In Rita's play the most basic of objects, the wooden block, stands for both human figure and tool. When she patented her play-technique via a series of bespoke toy objects, Klein continued to use the wooden and block-like. "It is important," she elaborated, to "enable the child to express a wide range of phantasies and experiences [. . .] that these toys should be non-mechanical. [. . .] Their very simplicity enables the child to use them in many different situations, according to the material coming up in his play."[52] Klein's later sets of playthings were "small and simple toys—little wooden men and women, carts, carriages, motor-cars, trains, animals, bricks, and houses as well as paper, scissors, and pencils."[53]

With the exception of the yet to be invented train and motor car, these are identical to Edgeworth's privileged toy objects: Edgeworth also mentions little human and animal figures, "a substantial cart" (2), carriages, houses, and bricks, focuses on the importance of drawing, and speaks of the advantage girls have

Figure 2. Toys used by Melanie Klein in her psychoanalytic work with children, 1920s–1930s. Reproduced by permission of the Wellcome Collection (wellcomecollection.org) [Attribution-NonCommercial 4.0 International (CC BY-NC 4.0)]

Figure 3. Wooden carts and other farm toys used by Melanie Klein in her psychoanalytic work with children. Photograph by Vanessa Smith. Objects: author's own.

over boys "in their exclusive possession of the scissars." (13) Where Edgeworth saw the child's investigation of the complex mechanical toy's interior, which inevitably "snaps the wire or perforates the bellows" (5), as spurred by the will to know, Klein, as we have seen, saw simple wooden toys as ideal for conveying psychic states. The material of the toy is understood to be integral to the material that "comes up" in play.[54] And where for Edgeworth the wooden toy is always, in the first instance, pedagogic—"they will learn to lift them to their mouths, and they will distinguish their sizes"—for Klein it is both symbolic and mediating. Klein's insistence on simple toys effectively brings out the "repressed" of Rousseau's and Edgeworth's elementary educative objects, speaking to that hostility that their pedagogy seeks to defeat or tame.

The significance of wooden objects for Klein rests on physical properties with specific psychic affordances. Unlike Edgeworth, Rousseau, and Baudelaire, she recognizes that the destruction of the toy signifies something beyond intellectual dissatisfaction or curiosity. Not only intricate but simple toys will therefore be equally subject to "actively hostile" attacks. The ideal toy should be designed, it follows, not simply to avert harm, but to absorb it. Both malleable and enduring, wood is susceptible to but able to survive assault. Barthes expands on the benign characteristics of wood, which he refers to as

> an ideal material because of its firmness and its softness, and the natural warmth of its touch. Wood removes, from all the forms which it supports, the wounding quality of angles which are too sharp, the chemical coldness of metal. When the child handles it and knocks it, it neither vibrates nor grates, it has a sound at once muffled and sharp. It is a familiar and poetic substance, which does not sever the child from close contact with the tree, the table, the floor. Wood does not wound or break down; it does not shatter, it wears out, it can last a long time, live with the child, alter little by little the relations between the object and the hand.[55]

Barthes's toys register mild, accretive handling from a developing child that has little in common with those furious infants exercising their "natural" sadism on the toys in Klein's consulting room. He can only envisage and repeatedly deny the possibility of the wooden toy "wounding" the child; not the child, who in his formulation gently wears out its objects, injuring the toy. But wood, as Klein understood, has a use value for the childish imaginary because it resists love and accommodates anger. The wooden toy, like the analyst herself, allows inarticulable hostile feelings to find expression, and sustains their onslaught.

Edgeworth's commencement of *Practical Education* with a chapter of toy stories seems to me far from coincidental. Klein's model of child's play gives us a way of understanding the scene of destruction that opens that chapter, as a toy story which the volume's educative and maturational thesis is unable to explain away. But the question of where the aggression that scene manifests goes within Edgeworth's text persists. Who is relieved by this angry play? When Edgeworth turns from the "disjointed doll" to a discussion of the generic doll as educative toy, it is as the subject of polite, qualified demurrals: "our objections to dolls are offered with great submission and due hesitation" (4). This reluctance to interrogate a toy that, like others she robustly criticizes, is characterized by fussy ornamentation and unnecessary intricacy, is attributed to the precedent of Rousseau, that "able champion" of the doll as ideal girl's object. As I noted earlier, Rousseau's doll is the toy the female child grows into rather than out of: the perfect correlative for adult femininity. Edgeworth alludes to the "sensible remark of a late female writer" who questioned Rousseau's advocacy of doll-like behavior, most likely invoking Catharine Macaulay, who critiques Rousseau in these terms in the twenty-third of her *Letters on Education*.[56] But she was in fact more immediately cognizant of the potential failures of Rousseau's educative principles. Her oldest brother, Dick, had been raised on the model of Émile by her father. In his memoirs, Richard Lovell Edgeworth records the mixed success of the experiment. His son early showed signs of "too little deference for others, and [. . .] an invincible dislike of control." Richard took him to France in the company of his close friend Thomas Day, another Rousseau enthusiast who was later to adopt two foundling girls and attempt, unsuccessfully, to educate them to be his potential wife. In passing through Paris they met with Rousseau who "took a good deal of notice of my boy." Rousseau invited Dick with him on his morning walk, but found him dogmatically chauvinistic, reporting, to his father's embarrassment, that every good object the boy observed, "even down to a pair of shoe buckles" was "pronounced by him to be English."[57] Dick continued to evince a persistently wayward character, eventually entering the navy and dying at the early age of thirty-two.

Practical Education is, then, the early coproduction of a daughter whose father attempted to literalize Rousseau's philosophy of education for his son; it is also the first notable work of a soon-to-be female novelist whose authorial career would take her very far from Rousseau's example of Sophie, the matured doll helpmeet for the ideal male subject Émile. Edgeworth's veiled reference, via the unnamed Macaulay, to a female literary, and specifically educative heritage of articulate dissent, obliquely amplifies her hesitant quibbles with Rousseau. Yet the anger that is surely tamped down in Edgeworth's very civil demurrals finds a different form of release. While carefully refusing to do so, she repeatedly frames the possibility of explicit dissension from Rousseau as an attack upon the toy. "Dolls" she writes, "can boast of such an able champion in Rousseau that it requires no common share of temerity to *attack* them." And having therefore offered her "objections to dolls" only "with great submission and due hesitation," she proposes "with more confidence we may venture to *attack* baby-houses" (3, 4: my emphases). The toy whose destruction is checked by Edgeworth's polite acknowledgment of Rousseau's authority here is surely the same "disjointed doll" that provides such an arresting opening to *Practical Education*: Rousseau's model of female education, dismembered. That toy story represents an anger that will not quite be subsumed as object lesson or example of natural curiosity or work ethic. The destructive rage that the child appears, in Kleinian terms, to be exhibiting in Edgeworth's imagined scenario may also, perhaps, represent the elsewhere-stifled protest of the author herself.

Pupil or Plaything?

Edgeworth's first full-length-novel *Belinda* (1801) can, as several critics have pointed out, be read as a continuation of *Practical Education*'s pedagogic project.[58] Lady Percival is an extension of Edgeworth's homage to Honora Sneyd Edgeworth, the emotionally measured and eminently rational maternal preceptress, while the portrait of Virginia Saint-Pierre, the child-woman Clarence Hervey has raised and educated "to be given to him," to use Rousseau's formulation, reanimates and gives more explicit expression to Edgeworth's arguments with Rousseau over female education. In the following brief reading I suggest that a subtext of projective identification again underwrites *Belinda*'s dialogue with educational method. In the Advertisement, Edgeworth casts her work as another "Moral Tale—the author not wishing to acknowledge a Novel." Given that "so much folly, errour and vice are disseminated in books classed under this denomination," she hazards that "the wish to assume another title will be attributed to feelings that are laudable, and not fastidious."[59] Edgeworth's proposition is that by changing the generic designation of her text from novel to fable she can change the sentiment with which it is charged. Formal re-attribution will reconfigure the book from vector of bad feeling to product of laudable impulses. Like the nineteenth-century children's moral tales of which Edgeworth provided early examples, *Belinda* can be read as a story in which emotional attachment renders things animate and people thing-like. Its complex marriage plot involves determining whether the beloved might prove to be a good object that would allow for the expulsion of bad feeling and the flourishing of reparative dynamics.

The novel opens with Belinda's move from country retirement to London, where she is established at the home of the witty, reprobate Lady Delacour due to the machinations of her aunt Stanhope, a notorious matchmaker who has successfully united "half a dozen nieces" with men of superior fortune (7).[60] Belinda soon attracts the interest of Clarence Hervey, a wealthy heir who has been damaged by an ill-conceived education. "Early flattered" with notions of his own genius, he has become entitled, "imprudent, wild and eccentric," while at the same time "so dreadfully afraid of passing for a pedant, that when he came into the company of the idle and the ignorant, he pretended to disdain every species of knowledge" (14). If Clarence is the spoiled child who has thrown away his education, Belinda is early figured as a toy object: a "puppet in the hands of others" (10). Moreover Mrs. Stanhope's formative influence renders her not merely a toy, but the worst kind: a potentially artificial object. Clarence is "prejudiced by the character of her aunt" into resisting his burgeoning feeling for Belinda, conceiving of her as a carefully manufactured decoy: where he "would have thought Belinda an undesigning, unaffected girl [. . .] now he suspected her of artifice in every word, look and motion" (15). Yet despite her fashioning at the hands of Mrs. Stanhope, Belinda remains "more undesigning, and more free from affectation and coquetry, than could have been expected" (10). Characterizing her heroine as a paradoxical puppet free from affectation, whose "levers," in Rousseauian terminology, "unsettle the human heart" (*Émile*, 387), Edgeworth anticipates Heinrich von Kleist's observations in "Über das Marionettentheater," published nine years after *Belinda*. In that essay, Kleist records an exchange with a principal in the local ballet, who claims that "any dancer who wished to perfect his art could learn a lot" at the puppet theater. While Kleist argues that the marionette can be operated "entirely without feeling—rather like turning the handle of a barrel organ," his interlocutor proposes that its movement is motivated by its strong center of gravity. A puppet, by this understanding, "could never be guilty of affectation[, f]or affectation is seen [. . .] when the soul, or moving force, appears at some point other than the centre of gravity of the movement." It is self-consciousness that "can disturb natural grace," and, lacking self-consciousness, the ostensibly mechanical puppet can "be more graceful than a living human body."[61] Like Kleist's marionette, Belinda has the capacity to emerge as both a more natural object and a more effective conduit of feeling than her counterparts on the London marriage market, but first she must overcome the self-consciousness with which Clarence's derogations imbue her, finding her own "centre of gravity."[62]

Belinda hears Clarence denigrate her artificiality firsthand at a masked ball she attends in the second chapter of the novel. Clarence has been informed that Lady Delacour and Belinda are to appear as Tragic and Comic Muse, respectively, but at Lady Delacour's caprice the pair have switched roles at the last minute. Thinking she is the disguised Lady Delacour, Clarence and his friends exercise their wit at Belinda's expense before the Tragic Muse, Clarence eventually declaring, after much ribbing, "'Do you think I don't see as plainly as any of you, that Belinda Portman's a composition of art and affectation?'" (26). Her immediate sense of mortification ensures that Belinda becomes the figure she imitates, her tragic mask giving true expression to her feelings as she sighs and turns pale beneath it. Clarence has described her as "an errant flirt of Mrs Stanhope's training," but nonetheless acknowledges "a kind of electricity about that girl," that leaves him with a "sort of cobweb feeling, an imaginary net coming all over me" (24). His hesitant metaphors ("a kind of"; "sort of") may incorporate a confused reference to experimental science of the kind *Practical Education* had advocated. Benjamin Franklin's *Experiments and Observations on Electricity* (1751) used what was effectively a spider puppet in order to demonstrate the animating powers of electricity:

We suspend by fine silk thread a counterfeit spider, made of a small
piece of burnt cork, with legs of linnen thread, and a grain or two of
lead stuck in him to give him more weight. Upon the table, over which
he hangs, we stick a wire upright as high as the phial and wire, two or
three inches from the spider; then we animate him by setting the elec-
trified phial at the same distance on the other side of him; he will immediately fly to the wire of the phial, bend his legs in touching it, then
spring off, and fly to the wire in the table; thence again to the wire of
the phial, playing with his legs against both in a very entertaining
manner, appearing perfectly alive to persons unacquainted.[63]

Like Franklin's "counterfeit spider"—itself a kind of automaton or toy—Clarence's
mixed metaphor ultimately blurs rather than clarifies the distinction between
the natural and artificial.

His criticisms of the artfully composed Belinda notwithstanding, Clarence
is a devotee of intricate automatons. He has himself appeared at the ball un-
disguised, due to his failure to transform himself into a highly complex marionette. He had designed a serpent costume heavy on special effects:

For this purpose he had exerted much ingenuity in the invention and
execution of a length of coiled skin, which he manoeuvered with great
dexterity, by means of internal wires; his grand difficulty had been to
manufacture the rays that were to come from his eyes. He had contrived a set of phosphoric rays, which he was certain would charm all
the fair daughters of Eve. He forgot, it seems, that phosphorous could
not well be seen by candle light. When he was just equipped as a serpent, his rays set fire to part of his *envelope*, and it was with great difficulty that he was extricated. (23)

While "he escaped unhurt, [. . .] his serpent's skin was utterly consumed; nothing remained, but the melancholy spectacle of its skeleton" (23). Already exposed
by the failure of his contrivance, his subsequent inability to distinguish between
Belinda and Lady Delacour in their muse's garb ensures that, at least as regards
his impression of herself, the scales fall from Belinda's eyes. In *Practical Education*'s terminology, he "snaps the wire [and] perforates the bellows" of his
costly mechanical toy, and in the process fails to establish Belinda's solid worth.

Practical Education features among its toys "a set [. . .] which are made to
imitate the actions of men and women, and the notes and noises of men and
beasts" (4). Like Clarence's serpent "many of these are ingenious in their construction, and happy in their effect, but that effect unfortunately is transitory."
These are among the toys whose destruction Edgeworth regards as a sign of

infant health and virtue: "When the gilt lamb has ba-ad, the obstinate pig squeaked, and the provoking cuckoo cried cuck-oo, till no one in the house can endure the noise; what remains to be done?" The child will rightly take the toy apart, "spoiling a new plaything" (4–5). In *Belinda*, such objects are poor substitutes for intimacy: gimcrack assemblages of spurious effect, they provoke false insight. Yet the alternative is not the utterly artless construct. The subplot involving Virginia St-Pierre mocks the notion of a love object brought up in untainted seclusion, showing the child of nature to be the most artificial of entities. As the dilettante "genius," the spoiled Émile, Clarence is a devotee of Rousseau, whose "declamations produced more than their just effect on an imagination naturally ardent." He therefore "formed the romantic project of educating a wife for himself" on the model of Rousseau's Sophie. Clarence struggles for a while, we are told, with "the difficulty of finding a proper object for his purpose," but he eventually stumbles upon "an object formed expressly for his purpose" (362). The repetition of the phrase "for his purpose" alerts us, in a now familiar Edgeworthian syntactic move, to the redundancy inherent in the purpose-designed object. As Belinda, over the course of the novel, comes to be perceived by Clarence as anything but artificial, Virginia is catachrestically reconfigured as toy: "the one he saw could be a companion, a friend to him for life; the other would merely be his pupil, or his plaything" (379).

In an astute essay that also links *Belinda* with Edgeworth's educational writing, Yoon Sun Lee has argued that the tests by which characters and things are co-evaluated across the novel must be viewed in the context of the later eighteenth-century development of experimental science, and the challenges that its "protocols and structures" presented for the concurrent development of the novel form. Lee observes that Edgeworth even-handedly combines "trials of fact, in addition to ethical or sentimental tests" as part of the evolution of this particular marriage plot, and suggests that, unlike the sentimental novelists that preceded her, "instead of inviting the reader to feel along with the characters, Edgeworth asks us to *watch how things happen*."[64] In my reading, there is no either/or dividing feelings from things in *Belinda*. The novel's love tests are equally examples of object relating: learning is acquired as much through damage and reparation as through controlled experimentation. Clarence's misrecognition of good object as artificial and child of nature as vector of appropriate feeling revisits the provocation of Rousseau, who has proposed a doll-woman as ideal companion. Edgeworth characterizes Clarence as a poor reader of Rousseau. Not only is he overly literalist (Rousseau's writings have "produced more than their just effect" upon him, just as they did upon Edgeworth's own father and his friend Thomas Day), he is guilty of genre confusion, doggedly following as educational instruction manual what should be understood as *Émile*'s marriage plot. In order to assess Rousseau's "romantic project" properly, Edgeworth instead reinstates the novelistic sensibility she has disowned in *Belinda*'s advertisement: revision and reeducation are managed by the workings of narrative. Fiction, it turns out, constitutes an apt hermeneutic for exposing living doll as automaton and artificial puppet as feeling subject.

Rejecting Rousseau's toy model, Edgeworth's critique instead anticipates Hoffman's tale "The Sandman" (1816), written fifteen years after *Belinda*'s publication. In that text, the protagonist Nathanael becomes enamored of the automaton Olimpia, whom he believes to be a living woman; meanwhile he rejects his fiancée Clara, castigating her as a "lifeless cursed automaton."[65] Freud meditates on Hoffman's life-like doll in his paper on "The Uncanny." Contesting the supposition that feelings of uncanniness are generated rationally, when "there is intellectual uncertainty whether an object is alive or not, and when an inanimate object becomes too much like an animate one," Freud argues that the automaton returns us to "childhood life." Freud's essay, in which he first adumbrates the insights of *Beyond the Pleasure Principle* on manifestations of repetition compulsion, offers a through-line from Edgeworth and Hoffman's early nineteenth-century meditations on artificiality to the fort/da game with which I began this chapter. In his reading of Nathanael's confusion of doll and woman, Freud reminds us "that in their early games children do not distinguish at all sharply between living and inanimate objects, and that they are especially fond of treating their dolls like live people."[66] If Clarence's quest to prove Belinda a good object is at times adduced to his sentimental practical education, it is also, by this psychoanalytic trajectory, a toy story, bearing the traces of this "infantile wish."

2

Possible Persons

Tackleton the Toy-merchant, the villain of Dickens's 1845 Christmas tale *The Cricket on the Hearth,* runs a far from rational toy shop. Serving no apparent educative purpose, his toys are vehicles for their maker's aggression and ambivalence. Tackleton has been misdirected into the business "by his Parents and Guardians," and "cramped and chafing in the peaceable pursuit of toy-making, he was a domestic Ogre, who had been living on children all his life, and was their implacable enemy."[1] He is not in the market for his own product: "he despised all toys; wouldn't have bought one for the world," and his business risks its profit margin ("he had even lost money [and he took to that toy very kindly] by getting up Goblin slides for magic lanterns," while "in intensifying the portraiture of Giants, he had sunk quite a little capital") in favor of a psychic payoff (180). His toy-making is his "relief and safety-valve," giving vent to unacceptable feelings. He "insinuate[s] grim expressions" onto little human figures, and fashions "appalling masks [. . .] to stare infants out of countenance," creating playthings that frighten rather than soothe (180). And Tackleton's insinuations as well as his objects cast him as the enemy of "the Hearth." The suspicions he raises regarding the actions of Dot Peerybingle, the tale's keeper of the home, risk the authority of the family and its hold upon domestic meaning. Tackleton, himself keen to forge a winter/spring union with Dot's friend, the aptly named May Fielding, claims to have caught Dot in the arms of a stranger. Her much older husband, the carter John Peerybingle, concludes that he must surrender his wife to the younger man. However, Dot proves true: her stolen embrace has in fact been one of friendly welcome for May's long-lost lover Edward Plummer, who has returned from abroad in disguise to claim his bride. In its defense of domesticity against the perverse

constructions of a harmful toy-work, this "Fairy Tale of Home" seems uncannily to preempt the Anna Freudian position on Melanie Klein's child therapy.
Hearth will eventually triumph over the hostile hermeneutics of the toy world
because, as Anna Freud would come to claim, "all the relations of everyday
life, and all its gratifications and disappointments" are dependent upon the
domestic template.[2]

Yet despite its overt loyalty to an ethics of domesticity, Dickens's tale is an
equivocal advertisement for family values, its fireside certitudes repeatedly
unsettled. Dot's parental authority is itself a form of child's play.[3] She readies
dinner "as briskly busy as a child at play at keeping house" (171), and produces
"a very doll of a baby" (170) at the moment of her husband's return: "Where
the baby came from, or how Mrs. Peerybingle got hold of it in that flash of
time, I don't know. But a live baby there was in Mrs. Peerybingle's arms" (169).
The narrative remains innocent of "where babies come from" for the Peerybingles are playing family. As the story proceeds, we find this real "live baby"
subjected to something closer to a toy's casual brutalization at the hands of the
child than maternal care. Tilly Slowboy, the kind-hearted but clumsy-fingered
domestic helper, is an inadvertent female Punch: a beater of Baby, who "had
several times imperilled its short life, in a quiet way peculiarly her own" (172).
The narrator repeatedly mentions the infant's endangered head, also a particular focus of Punch's violence: according to Henry Mayhew's 1861 performance
transcript, Punch "knocks [Baby's] head up against the side of the proceedings
several times."[4] Tilly brings Baby's cranium into regular "contact with deal
doors, dressers, stair-rails, bed-posts, and other foreign substances" (172); she
must be "isolated [. . .] from every article of furniture but the chair she sat on,
that she might have nothing else to knock the Baby's head against" (203). The
slapstick theatrics of the tale's concluding marriage party involve a comic cre-
scendo of harm to Baby:

> Everybody tumbled over Tilly Slowboy and the Baby, everywhere.
> Tilly never came out in such force before. Her ubiquity was the theme
> of general admiration. She was a stumbling-block in the passage at
> five-and-twenty minutes past two; a mantrap, in the kitchen at half-past
> two precisely; and a pitfall in the garret at five-and-twenty minutes to
> three. The Baby's head was, as it were, a test and touchstone for every
> description of matter,—animal, vegetable, and mineral. Nothing was
> in use that day that didn't come, at some time or other, into closer
> acquaintance with it. (237)

Tilly takes over from the Dutch clock, key object of the hearth, marking time
for this "happy ending" with a contingent sadism.

The title page of the tale, drawn by Daniel Maclise and engraved by G. Dalziel in the form of a Dutch clock's painted face, reinforces the co-presence of domestic peace with cluttered and curiously self-motivated quotidian objects.

Figure 4. Frontispiece for *The Cricket on the Hearth*, by Daniel Maclise. Reproduced by permission of victorianweb.org. Scan: Philip V. Allingham. [https://victorianweb.org/art/illustration/cricket/1.html]

Scenes of domestic life from cradle to grave revolve, not just around an image of the cricket, ridden stably by its fairy, but also the kettle, from which a more childlike cherub figure (another neglected baby?) looks set to tumble. Rather than functioning as markers of domestic verisimilitude or virtue, household objects in *The Cricket on the Hearth* are playthings. The central and centering fireplace is itself a shadow-box of toylike objects: animated articles, characters in their own right—a "little waxy-faced Dutch clock" (165) with a bony, skeletal interior, featuring a "terrified" (166) and "convulsive little Haymaker" (165); the kettle which is by turns "aggravating and obstinate," "quarrelsome," "sullen and pig-headed" (166), resonant of "invitation and welcome" (167), and humming "like a great top" (168). The tale never quite resolves its contest between hearthside comfort and eruptive play.[5] In a final tableau Anna Freud's and Klein's emblems are held in equipoise: "a Cricket sings upon the Hearth; a broken child's-toy lies upon the ground: and nothing else remains" (242).

The thing-like qualities of Dickensian characters and the reciprocal animate qualities of his objects have long been observed. G. K. Chesterton read *The Old Curiosity Shop*'s (1841) cast as one of motivated curiosities: "The comic characters in the book are all like images bought in an old curiosity shop. Quilp might be a gargoyle. He might be some sort of devilish door-knocker, dropped down and crawling on the pavement. The same applies to the sinister and really terrifying stiffness of Sally Brass. She is like some old staring figure cut out of wood."[6] Dorothy Van Ghent proposed that in Dickens's novels inanimate objects are curiously animated, while "the animate is treated as if it were a thing."[7] She characterizes Dickens's language as one in which "predications about persons or objects tend to be statements of metabolic conversion of one into the other" (426).[8] George Orwell accounted for the vividness of Dickensian character as an object effect: "Dickens's people are [. . .] always in a single unchangeable attitude, like pictures or pieces of furniture"; J. Hillis Miller noted the "metonymic reciprocity" between Dickens's characters and their contexts.[9] For Herbert Sussman and Gerhard Joseph, Dickens's shifts "between representing characters as self-acting 'things' and as 'people' [. . .] registers a Victorian discursive practice where the boundary between the machine and the human tends to dissolve", an insight crucially amplified and nuanced by Tamara Ketabgian in her examination of the intertwined "animal, mechanical and prosthetic traits" of Dickens's and other Victorian literary characters.[10] But in *The Cricket on the Hearth*, that always semi-permeable boundary between character and thing seems to have been explicitly dismissed. Moreover, with its conspicuous toy-making the tale invites us to understand Dickensian character, not just as any old thing, but as a toy. Tackleton sketches out toy designs with "a certain furtive leer for the countenances [. . .], which was safe to destroy the

peace of mind of any young gentleman between the ages of six and eleven"
(180). "What he was in toys," writes Dickens, "he was (as most men are) in other
things" (180). Tackleton's projections, as we have seen, derive their impetus
from his own worst feelings. Equally, the toys provide a template for his own
depiction, their furtive leer becoming his one-eyed peer, and his dry, twisted
face and jerky stance seemingly indicative of wooden pieces screwed in place:
"he stood in the Carrier's kitchen, with a twist in his dry face, and a screw in
his body, and his hat jerked over the bridge of his nose, and his hands tucked
down into the bottoms of his pockets, and his whole sarcastic ill-conditioned
self peering out of one little corner of one little eye" (181). Caleb Plummer, the
artisan in Tackleton's employ, reads a new character immediately as an assemblage of movable parts. When an apparently elderly stranger (the disguised
Edward, Caleb's own son) enters the Peerybingle home, he muses:

> "A beautiful figure for a nut-cracker; quite a new model. With a screw-
> jaw opening down into his waistcoat, he'd be lovely. [. . .] Or for a fire-
> box, either," observed Caleb, in deep contemplation, "what a model!
> Unscrew his head to put the matches in; turn him heels up'ards for the
> light; and what a firebox for a gentleman's mantel-shelf, just as he
> stands!" (184)

Caleb's understanding of identity as toylike and reconfigurable here confounds
his capacity to pierce disguise and recognize his flesh and blood. It also underpins his relationship with his blind daughter Bertha, for whom he willingly
assumes the role of a disarticulated body part—"'my eyes, my patient willing
eyes'" (195).[11]

Enraged, paranoid, reparative: Tackleton and his workers produce proto-
Kleinian toys with incidental therapeutic capacities. And Dickens's characterization is of the same mold. As he moves from the earliest picaresque fictions
to the psychologically rich portraiture of his "mature" novels, Dickens's increasingly interiorized protagonists are surrounded and mirrored by toylike figures
that problematize the thesis of novelistic maturation, proving as essential to
the depiction of a complex psychology as internal monologue, and reflexively
highlighting the importance of wooden character and creaky plot to the production of Dickens's sentimental effects. Moreover, in his deployment of toy
characters Dickens appropriates for the novel a prescient understanding of the
psychic work that toys can perform.[12] His virtuous protagonists are tailed by
minor characters that, while explicitly foils, give expression to the rage that lies
repressed in that other figure so central to his oeuvre, the sentimental child.
In *Little Dorrit* (1857), for example, Tattycoram doubles not only the spoiled
Pet, for whom she has been effectively purchased as a toy, but Amy Dorrit herself,

as she rails against and threatens to overwhelm her minor status. Tattycoram's role as another of Dickens's lucky foundlings is belied by her sobriquet, which combines "tatting" (rag-gathering) with discipline, identifying her as an abused rag-doll.[13] Maggy evokes an alternative version of the cherished soft toy, accompanying the heroine's maturation in benign arrested development. Bald, with "one tolerably serviceable eye" and a fixed smile, she is a broken doll destroyed by childhood beatings, which she reenacts by way of self-introduction ("Maggy [. . .] beat an imaginary child, and said, 'Broom-handles and pokers'").[14] As the outsized object of belated care, Maggy allows Amy Dorrit in turn to adopt the reparative role of "little mother," much as *Cricket*'s recovered Tilly Slowboy both reinforces and ironizes Dot Peerybingle's domesticity. Tilly is depicted as a shabbily dressed wooden doll or puppet: "She was of a spare and straight shape, this young lady, insomuch that her garments appeared to be in constant danger of sliding off those sharp pegs, her shoulders, on which they were loosely hung" (172); her legs have "a fatality about them which rendered them singularly liable to be grazed; [. . .] she never effected the smallest ascent or descent, without recording the circumstance upon them with a notch, as Robinson Crusoe marked the days upon his wooden calendar" (198). Her woodenness and impromptu brutality with Baby are of a piece, the latter attributed to the "constant astonishment" of this foundling child ("only differing from fondling by one vowel's length"), at "finding herself so kindly treated" in her domestic situation with the Peerybingles (172). Unfondled foundling found, Tilly is no soft plaything, but rather the clunky toy embodiment of her hard-knock life. Alex Woloch has observed that Dickens's characters "[f]amously tend to resemble one another, accruing features that thus seem to transcend any particular structure"; John Frow has identified family typologies that pattern Dickensian fiction, proposing that "in Dickens's novels the social order is imagined through and as a family, and family relations—seen, above all from the perspective of the child—take on a charged intensity."[15] My suggestion is that the child's perspective renders such reiterative characters, like the Kleinian object, toy-types before they are familial types, and that the work they perform in relation to the "charged intensity" of the parent-child relationship is therapeutic as well as representational. Toy characters, aggressed or repaired, cycle through Dickens's fiction in order that a later novel might reengage with and potentially resolve the childish affect of an earlier novel.[16]

There is much evidence across Dickens's fiction that he understood the more aggressive cathexes of childhood play. Take its depiction as tormenting "sick fancy" in *Great Expectations* (1861); Esther Summerson's "half ashamed" burial of her favorite doll before she leaves a substitute home in which she has been mistreated; or Sally Brass's first games: she was "remarkable, when a tender prattler, for [. . .] her exquisite manner of putting an execution into her doll's house."[17] Dickens's recognition of the ways in which aggression, rage, envy, and shame are acted out in play is matched by his insistence on its therapeutic benefits. David Copperfield must retrieve "the first objects" that surround, focus, and express childish feeling as a way of coming to terms with his past.[18] The depiction in *Hard Times* (1854) of the Gradgrind children's relentlessly rational education and its role in stunting their emotional growth indicates that Dickens believed play to be essential to maturation, and phantasy to adaptation to reality. Excluded by her father from any toy imaginary, Louisa claims, "You have trained me so well, that I never dreamed a child's dream," conflating dream and play in a perfect Kleinian equation.[19] Might we extend these insights beyond a cursory acknowledgment that Dickens, like Sleary the circus-rider, embraced the ludic principle, to think more concertedly about why characters that verge on caricature—that are toylike—carry such affective weight and generate such, often counterintuitive, narrative sympathy?[20]

Whether as social issue, pedagogic problem, or symbol, the child has been a significant focus of Dickens criticism.[21] His fiction, it has often been observed, features a series of characters that seem suspended between childhood and adulthood. Rosemary Bodenheimer puts it that "the Dickensian child does not grow up in the ordinary sense. Instead of developing, it changes places; it moves on."[22] Noting the difficulty of determining the age of Dickens's younger characters she in particular references "Dickens's 'little women,' Nell Trent, Amy Dorrit and Fanny Cleaver, a.k.a. Jenny Wren": figures that occupy an "amorphous borderland between childhood and adulthood," and whose exhibited smallness "presents them to the world as children" even once they are grown in years.[23] John Kucich lists Nell, Paul Dombey, Oliver Twist, and Smike, among others, as a set of "child-like, prepassional" death-driven characters.[24] Laurie Langbauer notices that such miniatures establish an uncanny seriality across Dickens's oeuvre: "all the Little Nells and Tiny Tims, in their seemingly redundant appellations—'Little,' 'Tiny'—insist on a kind of uncanny reiteration that we regard them as small children, hence as different, diminutive, in need of our care."[25] Lauren Byler, on the other hand, refers to the "self-miniaturizing rhetoric" of the Dickensian little woman, arguing that insistent minimization is a key weapon in the arsenal of the sentimental Dickensian heroine.[26]

While Dickens's child-women were beloved by his wider readership, *fin de siècle* aesthetes advertised their imperviousness to their appeal, withholding the emotion that mass audiences notoriously displayed. Oscar Wilde laughed at the death of Little Nell. Swinburne was unsettled by "the child [that] has never a touch of childhood about her," claiming that Nell's invariable evenness of temper makes her "a monster as inhuman as a baby with two heads."[27] Henry

James dwelled at length on what he regarded as the disturbing abnormality of Jenny Wren:

> Miss Jenny Wren is a poor little dwarf, afflicted, as she constantly reiterates, with a "bad back" and "queer legs," who makes dolls' dresses, and is for ever pricking at those with whom she converses, in the air, with her needle, and assuring them that she knows their "tricks and their manners." Like all Mr. Dickens's pathetic characters, she is a little monster; she is deformed, unhealthy, unnatural; she belongs to the troop of hunchbacks, imbeciles, and precocious children who have carried on the sentimental business in all Mr. Dickens's novels; the little Nells, the Smikes, the Paul Dombeys.[28]

James's characterization of Dickens's sentimental monsters is formulated as a response to a wager: "What do we get in return for accepting Miss Jenny Wren as a possible person?"[29] He invokes the fictional compact that bridges the sentimentalism to which Dickens remains, in his opinion, too wedded, and the realism which was to be his own preferred genre: that we acknowledge character as human substitute. James's and Swinburne's brutal displacement of character with caricature, purported humanity with Gothic monstrosity, attempts to disrupt the flow of sympathy toward Dickens's "eccentric children" by asserting that there is no possibility of readerly identification with these fictional subjects.[30]

The wager of possible personhood, as both a mode of characterization and the potentiality of Bildung, is something Dickens had preemptively queried through the two types of undeveloped figures that populate his novels: the children who fail to reach maturity ("the little Nells, the Smikes, the Paul Dombeys"), and the wooden characters that never take on flesh. This chapter argues that these two types of incomplete subject are brought into conscious, indeed self-reflexive contact within the play space of his novels, in order to manifest the kind of psychological dynamic that would soon be acted out and articulated within the Kleinian play-therapy session. James's invocation of the "possible person" anticipates the terms of recent debate about the relationship between character and personhood. In *The Economy of Character* (1998), Deidre Shauna Lynch posed the radical question: "What happens if we do not assume that the history of character and the history of the individual are the same thing?"[31] Contesting developmental histories of the novel that assume an evolution of character from the flat to the rounded or fleshed out, Lynch drew attention to "characters' quality of eerie thing-hood—their quality of being at once 'out there' and 'other-than-us,' the way that, like the commodities in *Capital*, they seem more autonomous, memorable, and real than their makers."[32] Lynch recognized the coexistence of exteriorized and vivid characterization, and questioned the imbrication of the notion of characterological interiority with claims for critical distinction: the deep character ratifying the deep reading. In his influential *The One vs. the Many* (2003), Alex Woloch identified Dickens's "radically distinct formulation of the minor character," which he argued "catalyzes new kinds of affective presence."[33] He observed that Dickens's minor characters have a capacity, despite their instrumentalized roles, to somehow exceed the framework of their "narrative duties," compelling "intense attention, in-and-of themselves."[34] John Frow subsequently contested Woloch's reliance, in such formulations, on a notion of "implied being," and sought to bear in mind the ontological hybridity of character: the fact that its identificatory appeal is always dependent on its constitution as a set of textual signs.[35] Frow proposed that characters be strictly understood as "quasi-persons" or "person-like entities": part modeled on living human subjects, and part purely "pieces of writing."[36] Toril Moi has in turn recently questioned the formalist "taboo on taking characters to be real" that she sees as exemplified by Frow's approach, arguing that the split between sign and signified to which he draws attention is something unproblematically solved in the everyday experience of ordinary readers.[37] Where Lynch sees psychological depth as the critical hallmark of achieved post-Romantic character, Moi notes the formalist critical pressure to reject notions of characterological interiority in favor of rigorous attention to characters' textual and semiotic constructedness, linking this to the modernist moment in which literary scholarship consolidated its relatively recent status within the academy.[38]

Each of these arguments might, in fact, engage the toy as well as it does literary character. We understand anthropomorphic toys as "person-like entities," that are "able to do emotional as well as representational work."[39] Their "eerie-thinghood" renders them the archetypal uncanny object. They serve as both model and metaphor for minor character, catalyzing "new kinds of affective presence." And they embody and enact both the tendency toward and the taboo against treating character as real (indeed they provide the primal scene for this approach to literary character). So why insert the toy, surely a superfluous mediating term, into the well-nuanced evolving account of character's relationship to selfhood? My suggestion, via *The Cricket on the Hearth*, has been that Dickens uses toy-making as an explicit analogy for his mode of creating character: character that is situated between personhood and thinghood. Toy character makes manifest the slippage between a dream of the lifelike and rough-hewn construction. Furthermore, this book's broader hypothesis, derived from Klein's practice of child analysis, is that toy-work bears a particular relationship to the formation of selfhood, that extends beyond anthropomorphism.

Klein, we recall, chose "a number of small and simple toys" to use in her child analysis, including "little wooden men and women, carts, carriages, motor-cars, trains, animals, bricks and houses."[40] In this context too, toys were both models and metaphors. As she was to show, their woodenness as much as their verisimilitude allows toys to perform significant affective labor. "Little [. . .] men and women" are not simply mini-persons, approximating being, but also unequivocal things, which can be treated with expedient sadism.

Dickensian characters perform the intricate dance between charged interiority and recalcitrant exteriority of Kleinian projective identification, interacting through intense repudiation and equally intense recognition, and demonstrating their author's prescient understanding of the ways in which attachment is object oriented. By formulating character as toylike, Dickens offers a self-reflexive alternative to implied personhood. Dickens's oeuvre arguably fits with the broader developmental account of the nineteenth-century novel, demonstrating a shift from the picturesque and crudely sentimental to the richly interiorized portraiture of an ascendant realism. Alternatively, according to criteria not dissimilar from those we have seen deployed in later nineteenth-century criticism of *Robinson Crusoe*, he can be represented as having failed quite to achieve psychological credibility because of his tendency to create character objects rather than quasi-human subjects.[41] But if, as Lynch has noted, the evolution of the novel toward the representation of "psychological depth" as a corollary of Romantic individualism has become an "article of our literary faith," how might that assumed teleology look different if the psychological paradigm is not one geared toward depth and sophistication but rather toward regression and the expressivity of clumsy objects?[42] This chapter develops its arguments from child analysis in the arena of literary character to propose that we might reconceive the way in which thing-like qualities and psychological interiority work together. Being toylike does not preclude psychological depth: rather, toy-object relations divulge a vexed interiority—an ambivalence that complicates the surface didacticism and apparently simple characterological oppositions of Dickens's representations of persons.

Ugly Playthings

In the preface to the 1848 edition of *The Old Curiosity Shop*, Dickens casts the novel's eponymous setting as a space of object relating: "In writing the book, I had always in my fancy to surround the lonely figure of the child with grotesque and wild, but not impossible companions, and to gather about her innocent face and pure intentions, associates as strange and uncongenial as the grim objects that are about her bed when her history is first foreshadowed" (8).

The opening chapters elaborate this relationship between Little Nell and the things that surround her. Master Humphrey, the soon-to-be-discarded narrator, who has encountered Nell lost among the London backstreets and escorted her home, finds he cannot dismiss the thought of the "child in her bed: alone, unwatched, uncared for" (20), among an array of objects "that might have been designed in dreams" (13). Curiosity might itself be defined as object-oriented affect: in the curiosity shop where Nell resides with her infirm grandfather, affect is both amplified and contagious. Master Humphrey conjectures, "I am not sure I should have been so thoroughly possessed by this one subject, but for the heaps of fantastic things I had seen huddled together in the curiosity-dealer's warehouse. These, crowding upon my mind, in connexion with the child, and gathering round her, as it were, brought her condition palpably before me" (20–22). The loneliness of the child is here made palpable by "external objects," which in turn figure as self-motivated: huddling, crowding, gathering. Where Master Humphrey understands her curious companions, both material and characterological, as contextual background, situating Nell within "a kind of allegory" (22), they function in a more immediate sense metonymically, within a chain of grotesque and sinister objects charged with negative feeling that can only be expelled by violent destruction. As the novel progresses Nell will find herself one of a cast of characters that further constitutes an object world. When she and her grandfather leave their curio business, ruined by his debt to the villainous Quilp, and are pursued from London through England's industrial midlands, they encounter explicitly toylike troupes of fairground performers, are befriended by dubious Punch showmen, and sojourn in a waxwork museum. Such picaresque encounters throw up ludic models for Dickens's practice of characterization. But more significant actors in Nell's story—her soft-hearted champion Kit, the harsh Brass siblings, and the gradually reclaimed antihero Dick Swiveller—are equally toylike: semi-anthropomorphic, strangely jointed, poorly stuffed, or impervious.

The most overtly thing-like character of *The Old Curiosity Shop*, and also its most articulate enactor of negative feeling, is Nell's nemesis Quilp, whose description, as other critics have noticed, links him with the puppet Punch.[43] George Speaight, in his comprehensive *History of the English Puppet Theatre* (1955), provides an evolving portrait of Punch commencing with his first appearance in England as Pollichinella or Punchinello during the Restoration.[44] Initially a large marionette, Punch was traditionally rendered as a stout, stooped figure with a wooden baton, conical hat, and huge and bent phallic nose. Grotesque as he was, and certainly not to be termed "more graceful than a living human body," Punch nonetheless partook of that absence of affectation that Kleist attributed to the gravity-impelled movement of the marionette.[45] In the nineteenth century, with the introduction of the traveling puppet theater, carried on the back of itinerant puppeteers, Punch evolved into a smaller glove puppet. The wooden body of the marionette was replaced by a cloth torso that allowed it to be motivated by the motions of the human hand; however, the puppet retained its wooden head, and little wooden bowlegs would hang over the rim of its traveling theater box. Lack of affectation evolved, with this change of form, into an increasingly brutal shamelessness. Punch's domestic violence was also introduced in the nineteenth century, coincident with the elaboration of a domestic context as Judy, or Mrs. Punch, and Baby entered the show.

Like the nineteenth-century Punch, Quilp is "low in stature" with a dispro-portionately large head with "remarkable hard features" topped by a "high-crowned hat"; his expression is at once exaggerated and static, emphasized by "a ghastly smile, which, appear[s] to be the mere result of habit and to have no connexion with any mirthful or complacent feeling" (29). When he is presumed dead, Brass and Mrs. Jiniwin memorialize him in Punch-like terms: "'Large head, short body, legs crooked'" (372), while drinking glass after glass of punch ("Nothing but punch!" observes Quilp, in a surely not accidental pun). His reappearance is announced first by his protruding nose: "'Aquiline!' cried Quilp, thrusting in his head, and striking the feature with his fist" (373). Quilp's voice is characterized as high pitched: he vents delight "in a shrill scream" (368). He is described baiting his nemesis Kit and Mrs. Nubbles with the un-canny combination of squeaky voice and hard features:

> Making his voice ascend in the scale with every succeeding question,
> Mr Quilp finished in a shrill squeak, and subsided into the panting
> look which was customary with him, and which, whether it were
> assumed or natural, had equally the effect of banishing all expression
> from his face, and rendering it, as far as it afforded any index to his
> mood or meaning, a perfect blank. (362–63)

His timbre recalls the sound produced by the swazzle, the instrument devised to render Punch's distinctive shrill and rasping voice; his features, at once fro-zen and exaggeratedly expressive, recall those of the puppet. He is repeatedly described "hanging [. . .] out" of beds or window frames (103), from the edge of a carriage roof or over the back of chairs, like Punch either at rest or at the edge of the stage, and has a jack-in-the-box tendency to pop up unexpectedly from cupboards or behind doors ("'Such an amazing power of taking people by surprise'" [373]). He has a disconcerting habit of "screwing his head very much on one side" (42) as though unjointed. He flourishes a wooden stick or cudgel, and displays a sadism characterized by its randomness and nonsensi-cality: "'I'll pinch your eyes'" he threatens Tom Scott (48); "I'm in the humour now. I shall be cruel when I like" he tells his wife (375). He is most at home when he confines himself to his wooden countinghouse full of wooden furniture, a habitat that matches his astoundingly hard interior: a singular manifestation of his idiosyncratic violence is his ability to smoke and drink burning hot rum to the great discomfort of not only his tender wife, but the otherwise harsh and inhuman Samuel Brass, and Richard Swiveller (himself a well smoked and soaked individual).[46] Indeed, he twice sneaks up unexpectedly on his wife and mother-in-law as they are apparently reveling in his absence, in scenes so similar as to have the feel of the repeat performances of favorite requisite scenes in a puppet show or pantomime.[47]

The representation of Quilp as something between glove puppet and marionette, combining the flexible and unpredictable movement of the former with the impenetrable interiority and absence of affectation of the wooden marionette, is reflected in the mixed iconography of both Punch and Quilp in Phiz's illustrations to *The Old Curiosity Shop*. Nell and her grandfather come upon the "exhibitors of the freaks of Punch," Codlin and Short, behind the scenes. They have retired to "make some needful repairs" to the puppets (129), a task which must be undertaken out of the public eye, in order not to "destroy the delusion" (130) of the Punch and Judy show: "one of them was engaged with binding a small gallows with a thread, while the other was intent upon fixing a new black wig, with the aid of a small hammer and tacks, upon the head of the radical neighbor, who had been beaten bald" (129). Over their preparations presides Punch, Quilp-like with his frozen smile, hooked nose, and tiny legs "dangling in a most uncomfortable position, all loose and limp and shapeless" (129). These are clearly depicted not as the vestigial legs of the Punch glove puppet, but those of a marionette, while at least one of the puppets in Short's box is attached to string from a wooden cross bar (Figure 5).[48] Nonetheless, as both Figure 6 and Codlin's constant complaints testify, this puppet theater is a manually transportable stage of the kind that could only be used for glove performances operated from below. In a subsequent illustration (Figure 7a), Quilp drops in over the Brasses' doorframe in his conical hat, looking, as David Amigoni has pointed out, like Punch peeping over his theater frame.[49] He is consistently figured with long coattails behind and little legs akimbo, as though he might well be subtly manipulated by an inserted hand.

Kenneth Gross, in his extended meditation on the poetics of puppetry, focuses on Punch's "wit, violence, shamelessness, and unkillableness," which he relates to the puppet's constitution as "a thing with a head of wood, without human feelings of pain and shame."[50] Gross argues that Punch's peculiar strength is that of "a puppet who knows himself to be a puppet."[51] This "knowledge" of his materiality, rather than his tenuous anthropomorphism, is

Figure 5. *Punch in the Churchyard.* Wood engraving by Hablot Knight Browne (Phiz) for *The Old Curiosity Shop.* Reproduced by permission of victorianweb .org [https://victorianweb.org/art/illustration/phiz/263.html]

Figure 6. *The Grinder's Lot.* Wood engraving by Hablot Knight Browne (Phiz) for *The Old Curiosity Shop.* Reproduced by permission of victorianweb.org [https://victorianweb.org/art/illustration/phiz/264.html]

Figure 7. *Quilp Leering at the Brasses* (7a); *Little Nell Is Anxious* (7b); *Uproarious Hospitality* (7c). Wood engravings by Hablot Knight Browne (Phiz) for *The Old Curiosity Shop*. Reproduced by permission of victorianweb.org [https://victorian web.org/art/illustration/phiz/80 .html; https://victorianweb.org/art /illustration/phiz/254.html; https://victorianweb.org/art /illustration/phiz/298.html]

key to his effectiveness. His murderous violence "tries to teach the other puppets he beats and kills with his stick [. . . —] puppets who want Punch to obey human rules, to stop being a puppet, or at least to be a puppet that, like human beings, is obedient to law and custom [— . . .] to know what they themselves are."[52] Punch embraces the subversive possibilities of pure puppetry. While Gross's emphasis is on stage dynamics, the wooden violence he identifies is also integral to Punch's appeal to audiences, which delight in the emotional release provided by enacted beatings. Focusing on audience dynamics, Rosalind Crone has related the effectiveness of this catharsis to the puppet's failure convincingly to approximate personhood: to its lack of realism. "In performance," she writes "the comical and exaggerated features of Punch and Judy, as well as the inability of their wooden faces to express emotion or pain, are crucial as the audience is distanced from the violence and the characters become difficult to identify with."[53] For both Gross and Crone, wooden manufacture is essential to the channeling of negative affect that the Punch show enables. Again, we might think forward here to Klein's therapeutic objects. When she came to patent her play-technique using a series of bespoke toys, Klein, as we have seen, also favored the wooden and sturdy, affordances she felt best enabled "the child to express a wide range of phantasies and experiences," for "their very simplicity enables the child to use them in many different situations, according to the material coming up in his play."[54] "Touching wood" channeled the violence and sadism of child's play, which Klein's analysis then rendered explicit in its aggression and anxiety.

Dickens drew attention to the carnivalesque status of the Punch show's violence in a letter of November 6, 1849:

> In my opinion the street Punch is one of those extravagant reliefs
> from the realities of life which would lose its hold upon the people if
> it were made moral and instructive. I regard it as quite harmless in its
> influence, and as an outrageous joke which no one in existence would
> think of regarding as an incentive to any kind of action or as a model
> for any kind of conduct. It is possible, I think, that one secret source
> of pleasure very generally derived from this performance . . . is the
> satisfaction the spectator feels in the circumstance that likenesses of
> men and women can be so knocked about, without any pain or
> suffering.[55]

For Dickens the puppet show's harmlessness inheres in the "relief" Punch affords from literal thinking—an insight that comes close to Klein's understanding of play as enabling a non-literal representation of real feeling.[56] Klein would argue that the toy "bridges the gulf to reality."[57] The child uses the play space to articulate what it finds unspeakable: it deploys "dolls and other play-things" turned up in the "box of toys" in her rooms to depict internal associations, with the analyst "follow[ing] up the child's symbolic mode of representation."[58] Klein recorded the progress the child makes "in adaptation to reality" through a combination of play-object relating and the enabling interpretation of the analyst. To recall the sequence outlined in the Introduction, "children begin to distinguish between the 'pretence' mother and the real mother and between the wooden baby-doll and the live baby brother. They then firmly insist that they wanted to do this or that injury to the toy-baby only—the real baby, they say, of course they love."[59] In the next stage of the analysis, and "only when very powerful resistances have been overcome," children come to "realize that their aggressive acts were directed against the *real* objects."[60] The shift witnessed here is one in the perception of object substitution, which might equally translate to an understanding of character. The child claims that its relationship to its toy is determined by the object's material status, only to reach an awareness that the feeling the toy generates has a real-world referent.

The toy can function in the way Klein theorizes because, like Gross's Punch, more than a crude analog for the human, it is a "violen[t], shameless [. . .] and unkillable" thing.[61] The affect it channels can therefore wreak mediated havoc that exacts no consequences. The Punchmen in *The Old Curiosity Shop*, who perform Punch's brutal story and then discreetly repair their toy objects in order that they may undergo further battering to the delight of audiences, elaborate Dickens's proto-Kleinian recognition that the pleasurable secret of Punch is the expression of aggression devolved onto objects. During the nineteenth century, and concurrent with its increased emphasis on domestic violence (the most deliciously scandalous scene of which was the destruction of Baby, the representative infant), the Punch and Judy show nonetheless moved from being primarily adult to child entertainment. Children watching a child being beaten thus came to form an aspect of the puppet show's "secret source of pleasure." In his letter Dickens is explicit about the therapeutic effect of the performance, one dependent on the audience's understanding that its character world comprises insensate "likenesses of men and women." Like toy therapy, the theater of Punch works, not, as Crone says, because "characters become difficult to identify with," but because they render identification without real-world harm or punishment possible.

Dickens's recognition of the "secret . . . pleasure" of the Punch show—that "*likenesses* of men and women" can be subjected to violence without pain, anticipates the insights Klein gained into the sadism of the child through her play-technique. In Mayhew's transcript of the Punch and Judy play we witness erratic shifts between love and aggression:

> Punch. Bless your sweet lips! *(Hugging her.)* This is melting moments.
>   I'm very fond of my wife; we must have a dance.
> Judy. Agreed. [*They both dance.*]
> Punch. Get out of the way! you don't dance well enough for me. *(He
>   hits her on the nose.)* Go and fetch the baby, and mind and take care
>   of it, and not hurt it. [. . .]
> Judy. *(Returning back with baby.)* Take care of the baby, while I go and
>   cook the dumplings.
> Punch. *(Striking Judy with his right hand.)* Get out of the way! I'll take
>   care of the baby. [. . .] *(Punch continues rocking the child. It still
>   cries, and he takes it up in his arms, saying,* What a cross child! I
>   can't a-bear cross children. *Then he vehemently shakes it, and
>   knocks its head up against the side of the proceedings several times,
>   representing to kill it, and he then throws it out of the winder.)*
> Enter JUDY
> Judy. Where's the baby?
> Punch. *(In a lemoncholy tone.)* I have had a misfortune; the child was
>   so terrible cross, I throwed it out of the winder. *(Lemontation of Judy
>   for the loss of her dear child. She goes into asterisks, and then excites
>   and fetches a cudgel, and commences beating Punch over the head.)*
> Punch. Don't be cross, my dear: I didn't go to do it.
> Judy. I'll pay yer for throwing the child out of the winder. *(She keeps on
>   giving him knocks of the head, but Punch snatches the stick away
>   and commences an attack upon his wife, and beats her severely.)*[62]

The symptomatic play of Klein's six-year-old patient Erna manifested the same abrupt and violent transitions evident here. In one game, she placed a toy woman and man in a wooden carriage:

> The two loved and kissed one another and drove up and down all the
> time. Next a toy man in another carriage collided with them, ran over
> them and killed them, and then roasted and ate them up. Another
> time the fight had a different ending, and the attacking toy man was
> thrown down; but the woman helped him and comforted him. She got
> a divorce from her first husband and married the new one. This third
> person was given the most varied parts to play in Erna's games. For
> instance, the original man and his wife were in a house which they
> were defending against a burglar; the third person was the burglar, and

slipped in. The house burnt down, the man and woman burst and the third person was the only one left. Then again the third person was a brother who came on a visit; but while embracing the woman he bit her nose off. This little man, the third person, was Erna herself.[63]

Erna's play in Klein's analytic space displays the wooden brutality, shamelessness and anarchic identificatory freedom that Gross regards as essential to the effectiveness of the Punch theater. Klein remarks that her room "used to look like a battlefield after Erna left it," for "she used to break her toys or cut them up, knock down the little chairs, fling the cushions about, stamp her feet on the sofa, upset water, smudge paper, dirty the toys or the washbasin, break out into abuse, and so on, without the slightest hindrance on my part."[64] As in Punch, such "domestic violence" is the corollary of a domestic narrative, in terms of which objects provide a way for the child (audience member or analysand) to "abreact her affects."[65]

Quilp's brutality is echoed and enabled by a cast of equally toy-resembling minor characters. Sally Brass, whose name possibly alludes to an "Aunt Sally," the figure of an old woman with a clay pipe in her mouth used as a cockshy in a fairground game, and occasionally represented by a puppet, is a "brazen" Judy to his Punch, the narrative hinting that the Marchioness is their much-abused Baby. This Dickensian ludic speculation, like Erna's, reimagines the primal scene as an unceremonious and violent union of toy figures, producing an infant whose resilience is necessarily sadistic. (Quilp's other abused "child," Tom Scott, tumbles while Quilp waits, Punch like, to beat him with a piece of wood. His nurture by "blows and threats on one side, and retorts and threats on the other" has nonetheless produced "a strange kind of mutual liking" that bespeaks a Kleinian child's fractious relationship with the symbolic family of its wooden toys (49). Swiveller is subject to "strange influences" in relation to Sally Brass, "mysterious promptings" to treat her as a fairground Aunt Sally and "knock her head-dress off and try how she looked without it" (258). He wishes she might, like a hard toy, survive assault ("If you could manage to be run over, ma'am, but not seriously") and flourishes a ruler near her head as play-therapy, to calm "the agitation of his feelings" (269, 258). The Marchioness is, in turn, beaten by Sally, who is "impelled" by "some extraordinary grudge [. . .] to rap the child with the blade of the knife, now on her hand, now on her head," and to deal her "some hard blows with her clenched hand" (279). Sampson Brass asserts that, like a toy, she can deflect such violence without experiencing pain: "she's a light weight, and it don't hurt her much" (268). The Marchioness only properly emerges as a character (eventually graduating from a self-nominated "nothing" to the aristocratic-sounding Sophronia Sphynx) once Nell has started to show symptoms of her demise, and this negative correlation heralds a number of significant substitutions between these two "little" characters. Like Little Nell, she is repeatedly referred to as "the child." Frances Armstrong describes the Marchioness and Nell, along with Barbara, as a trio of "housekeepers" who exercise a "diminutive competence" within the novel's "doll's house" or "toy-shop world."[66] She comes to occupy the place imagined for Nell as Dick Swiveller's girl, his own Sophie in the Rousseauian narrative, "growing into a woman expressly on my account, and [. . .] saving up for me" (75, 552).[67] Educated, matured, and partnered, she eventually reclaims those possibilities lost to the other child-woman: Bildung and marriage plot.

Toy characters reconfigure narrative as abrupt, unhinged, and apparently unmotivated. And as a supporting cast, they provide expression for the anger and sadism of the ostensibly angelic "little" heroine: a toy box of unbreakable avatars. The term sadism is often applied to Dickens's fiction, but it is typically considered as something done to the child rather than by the child. Robert Newsome, for example, writes that "it is a striking characteristic of the children in the early novels especially that, far from being revered, they are often objects not just of neglect, but of an abuse that is active and sadistic."[68] Adult characters repeatedly brutalize children; by extension, Dickens is figured as an author who cruelly tortures his readers with depictions of tortured children.[69] Little Nell is often understood as one such abused child, sacrificed to Dickens's sentimental effects. Indeed, she seems more immediately of a type with Anna Freud's case studies of "altruistic surrender" than a character akin to the Ernas and other children who engaged in violent play in Klein's therapy room. She is figured as "unassuming" and characterized by "the modesty of demands which she made on life," while her experience of gratification is solely as projected onto others.[70] Her identity is constituted through displacement, and "instead of exerting herself to achieve any aims of her own, she expend[s] all her energy in sympathizing with the experiences of people she care[s] for."[71] Yet my suggestion is that the childlike protagonist's retaliation is mediated through interactions with characters rendered toylike and unharmable, in a dynamic that preempts that of Klein's therapy session. Although others have also noticed the anger that underwrites the modesty and humility of Dickens's most explicitly "little" heroines, Amy Dorrit and Nell, they have tended to frame this insight as ethical judgment. Lauren Byler, for example, has argued for the "passive aggression" of these little women, whom she regards as enacting a covert sadism through the limited but potent medium of self-control. This diagnosis posits a problematic composite of the "knowing" child and the cunning woman ("Nell . . . is adept at using her own vulnerability to influence the behavior of certain adult characters"; Little Dorrit's "hard work at being invisible draws all kinds of attention").[72] Where Byler asserts that for Dickens's child-women "selfhood can only be discerned through the violence done to a person (or to one's person) and can only be asserted through aggressive acts towards others," Klein would allow the child's relationship to persons to be mediated through violence done to objects. One of the most demonstrably therapeutic aspects of Kleinian toy-work and the analyses it motivated was a complete absence of judgment regarding the psychic rewards of childish bad feeling. Though they acted as stand-ins for human objects, things were precisely not persons; harm was enabled but also contained by the toy world. Placing his childish protagonists in toy landscapes allows Dickens, too, to give nonjudgmental rein to the monstrousness of the minor; to act out the violence that lies dormant in the disciplined and virtuous Victorian child.

As little Quilp shadows Little Nell, he articulates the violence that attends her story, manifesting an aggression whose absence in Nell herself has struck many critics as an inadequate registration of that abuse apparent in her narrative.[73] He enters the narrative in Nell's wake ("the child was closely followed"), the hard-surfaced puppet to her "wax-work child" (29, 240).[74] We understand that she has visited Quilp regularly on her grandfather's behalf, and she initially indicates more amusement than fear in his presence: "plainly showing by her looks that while she entertained some fear and distrust of the little man, she was much inclined to laugh at his uncouth appearance and grotesque attitude" (51). Like the tantalized child-audience at the puppet show, she witnesses Kit and Tom Scott tussle violently and Quilp intervene:

> "I'll stop 'em," cried Quilp, diving into his little counting-house and
> returning with a thick stick, "I'll stop 'em. Now, my boys, fight away.
> I'll fight you both. I'll take both of you, both together, both together!"
>   With which defiances the dwarf flourished his cudgel, and dancing
> around the combatants and skipping over them, in a kind of frenzy
> laid about him. (54)

The scene, which reads particularly like a Punch script, discloses an impetus for Quilp's rage. Kit has reportedly commented that Quilp is "an uglier dwarf than can be seen anywheres for a penny" (55). Quilp adverts to this insult with growing fury as the novel progresses, seeking first to contain and expel Kit with threats of imprisonment and transportation, and then acting out his thwarted aggression on a giant toy, "a great, goggle-eyed, blunt-nosed figure-head of some old ship," made to stand for Kit and be punished as such:

> "Is it like Kit—is it his picture, his image, his very self?" cried the
> dwarf, aiming a shower of blows at the insensible countenance, and
> covering it with deep dimples. "Is it the exact model and counterpart

of the dog—is it—is it—is it?" And with every repetition of the question, he battered the great image until the perspiration streamed down his face with the violence of the exercise. (463)

As with Klein's child patients, Quilp's exaggerated toy "bring[s] out his aggressiveness," the figurehead's combined resemblance and insensibility providing palpable relief. [75]

Yet the taunt with which Kit has irreparably offended Quilp is hinged to an identical insult, directed at Nell. Kit's remark has been provoked, he explains, by Tom's Scott's denigration of Nell: "'Then why did he say,' bawled Kit, 'that Miss Nelly was ugly?'" (55). Quilp's brutal intercession here, we might notice, comes at Nell's request ("'Oh pray stop them, Mr Quilp!'" [54]). The insult recalls the taunt of later nineteenth-century critics that Nell is monstrous. It links Quilp and Nell as shamed and denigrated small creatures, his violence enacting an enraged protest that the sentimental child heroine cannot voice. Where Quilp as small person insistently asserts heft and resistance, Nell is reflexively slight. She walks "printing her tiny footsteps in the moss, which rose elastic from so light a pressure and gave it back as mirrors throw off breath" (187); after her death her grandfather, unable to tell the difference between her living and dead form, tells "'I often tried to track the way she had gone, but her small fairy footsteps left no print upon the dewy ground to guide me'" (536). That Nell fails to make an impression is reiterated by every critic that cyclically declares a failure to attach to her character, and instead confesses their "secret pleasure" in the more obviously monstrous Quilp, who demonstratively resists any imputations of flatness ("'Aquiline, you hag. Do you see it? Do you call this flat?'" [373]). Just as The Old Curiosity Shop anticipates and thematizes reader responses to its little characters, however, so it makes explicit their codependence. Quilp's perfect, Baby Bear fit in Nell's little bed as he occupies her house of curiosities marks their characterological symmetry. And his unintentional drowning occurs two days before Kit, Garland, and the Single Gentleman reach Nell, only to find her two days' dead. As Quilp's small corpse is battered and cast up, a shift is registered in the third-person pronoun: converted from a "him" to an "it," Quilp's status as brutalized object rather than person is underlined, even as Nell's body resists decomposition. Yet the sentimental child and the "ugly plaything," "toyed" with by the tide, expire, necessarily, together (512).

Miniature Work

Almost a decade later, Dickens would construct another "ugly plaything" in David Copperfield's (1850) Miss Mowcher. A dwarf hairdresser and manicurist,

Miss Mowcher purports to find her "tiny way" through the Bildungsroman
Dickens called his "favourite child" as "a plaything for you giants."[76] Yet, unlike
the unwoundable Kleinian toy or the hard-interiored Quilp, Miss Mowcher
lays claim to injured feeling. She rails against the "inconsiderate young people,
fairly and full grown" that "make a plaything of me, use me for their amusement, throw me away when they are tired, and wonder that I feel more than a
toy horse or wooden soldier!"[77] Miss Mowcher's assertion, as maltreated plaything, of affective interiority speaks to the second phase in Kleinian toy-work.
As well as observing the abreactive aggression of children's play, Klein, as we
have seen, noticed the move toward reparation that succeeded injury of the
toy. She observed that "Feelings of guilt may very soon follow after the child
has broken, for instance, a little figure."[78] The child's guilt in turn generates a
"variety of processes by which the ego feels it undoes harm done in phantasy,
restores, preserves and revives objects."[79] This sequence might apply to the
evolving narrative of *The Old Curiosity Shop*'s second, shabbier "little" female,
the Marchioness, whose happy ending offers compensation for Nell's tragic
destruction. In the case of Miss Mowcher, however, the minor character is
ventriloquizing the complaint of an injured person. Jane Seymour Hill, a chi-
ropodist and neighbor of Dickens's, recognized herself at Miss Mowcher's first
appearance in the serial of *David Copperfield* and wrote to him, pleading for
the rehabilitation of her character: "I have suffered long and much from my
personal deformities but never before at the hands of a Man so highly gifted
as Charles Dickens."[80] As Julia Rodas speculates, Hill's appeal to Dickens's
sentimental ethics may have been unsuccessful, had it not been backed up by
a legal letter that made clear that the character had recourse to real-world
modes of advocacy.[81]

Rodas sees the eventual repair that Dickens offered Miss Mowcher, which
restored her character from procuress to avenger of "Lil Emly," as a form of
chary restitution to disabled subjectivity. In my reading, its only partially resolved aggression encapsulates the precarious resolution offered by Kleinian
reparation. As I noted in the Introduction, the relatively limited literary critical
uptake of Kleinian theory, most of it in the wake of Eve Kosofsky Sedgwick's
turn to Klein, has shown a tendency to regard reparation as an affirmative and
ameliorative process: the goal of, rather than a stage in, analysis. This has
morphed the Kleinian model into something closer to her rival Anna Freud's
"altruistic surrender": a form of restorative action, purportedly in favor of the
object, that is essential to the ego constitution of the subject. Yet the effort to
repair damaged objects does not, as Elizabeth Wilson discerns, "abolish sadism
itself."[82] Rather, she cautions, "reparative gestures require [. . .] the recognition
that sadistic attacks are inevitable."[83] Quoting Klein, Wilson reminds us that

"the best we can hope for is that 'a relative balance between love and hate is attained.'"[84] In proposing that this less consoling version of reparation, as counterweight rather than synthesis, best describes the psychic work performed by Dickensian character, I want to turn to a character-type that "grows up" between a "minor" and a "mature" Dickens text: that of the doll's dressmaker. My suggestion is that such explicitly restorative figures can only function in robust play worlds populated by breakable and mendable toy characters.

Tracing Dickens's evolution of the doll's dressmaker will involve first returning to *The Cricket on the Hearth* and the character of Bertha Plummer. "Blind Bertha" and her father Caleb form a toy-making team: Caleb constructing, painting, and glazing toys and Bertha dressing dolls and inserting their equally unseeing eyes. They dwell in "a little cracked nutshell of a wooden house" where toys have long been fashioned for "boys and girls, who had played with them, and found them out, and broken them" (188). The house itself is a toy object waiting to be destroyed by similarly investigative Edgeworthian children or angry little Ritas: "you might have knocked down Caleb Plummer's dwelling with a hammer or two, and carried off the pieces in a cart" (188). Within it Caleb labors to construct "dolls of all stations of life" (189) and their houses, and a supply of proto-Kleinian "melancholy little carts" (190) and roughly carved men and women that Dickens again defends as "harmless" (191) analogs for human behavior.

Bertha, as I mentioned earlier, relies on her father's eyes as visual prostheses. Motivated by a misguided sympathy, Caleb has designed for his daughter a further imaginary dollhouse within the frame of their impoverished home: one in which the broken walls and ceiling are repaired, his own aged figure appears rejuvenated, and Tackleton features as benign benefactor rather than cruel master:

> The Blind Girl never knew that ceilings were discoloured, walls
> blotched and bare of plaster here and there, high crevices unstopped
> and widened every day, beams mouldering and tending downward.
> The Blind Girl never knew that iron was rusting, wood rotting, paper
> peeling off; the size, and shape, and true proportion of the dwelling,
> withering away. The Blind Girl never knew that ugly shapes of delft
> and earthenware were on the board; that sorrow and faintheartedness
> were in the house; that Caleb's scanty hairs were turning greyer and
> more grey, before her sightless face. (188–89)

If Caleb's overcompensation here is a form of overt amelioration, this reparative gesture is laced with hostility. The benign father, motivated by a sentimentalizing care, effectively pimps his daughter to the old man he hates, while setting her up for a cruel but in some ways accurate diagnosis by her beloved as "'poor Idiot'," with "'no gleam of reason,'" her fantasies "'Bedlam broke loose'" (193). Elisabeth Gitter, who also notices that "the story's sentimental veneer barely conceals a punishing aggression," sees Bertha as the target of Dickensian callousness: through her Dickens "invites his sighted readers [. . .] to participate in the sadistic pleasures of teasing the blind."[85] The Blind Girl, for Gitter, is the preeminent object of narrative cruelty: a character who "surrounded by eyes and games of seeing, is herself stranded in sightlessness," and who, "irredeemably ineligible for marriage" is set up for a "punishing exclusion from the fairy-tale ending."[86] Gitter understands Bertha simply as victim of a broadly defined sadism. Focusing on her work in the toy world, on the other hand, allows us to note her own repressed animus. She elicits a visually exclusive fantasy from her father, ignoring the evidence of her other senses as, like the Kleinian child patient, she compels him to repeat a specifically worded object narrative.[87] When his doll's story strays from her preferred script, she applies a strangling grip:

> "tell me something about May. She is very fair? [. . .] Her shape—"
>   "There's not a Doll's in all the room to equal it," said Caleb. "And her eyes!—"
>   He stopped; for Bertha had drawn closer round his neck, and, from the arm that clung about him, came a warning pressure which he understood too well. (196)

Her work fitting equally unseeing eyes into the faces of dolls she nonetheless deftly manufactures and clothes betrays an unsighted intimacy with how things look in the outside world akin to the percipience of the Kleinian child, whose play discloses its unarticulable awareness of the primal scene.

Our Mutual Friend's (1865) Jenny Wren, a doll's dressmaker fashioned almost ten years after Bertha Plummer, belongs to what is generally understood to be Dickens's "mature" late fiction. Another reflexively underdeveloped minor, she proves crucial to one of the novel's paired Bildungsromane, mediating the relationship between the beleaguered heroine Lizzie Hexam and her delinquent suitor Eugene Wrayburn. Jenny makes her living from doll-work, supporting her shabby, infantile, alcoholic father. A designer and restorer, she nonetheless remains both object and agent of violence and destruction, exemplifying the complexities of a reparation that fluctuates rather than synthesizes.[88] Although, as we saw, Henry James regarded her failure to grow as commensurate with an inability on Dickens's part to give up childish things and develop from caricature to rounded character, most recent critics have built a notion of complex characterization into their analysis of Jenny's role. Katherine Inglis refers to her as "Nell, reinterpreted for the less sentimental 1860s as [a] glorious, contrary visionary"; Helena Michie argues that she represents an advancement upon *Bleak House*'s (1853) first-person conception of female selfhood by underscoring, through her doll-work, "the self's necessary fragmentation."[89] Hilary Schor reads her as a self-reflexive character, "a sign for Dickens's fiction"; Ben Moore credits her with "continually pull[ing] apart identity, the basic category of realism."[90]

Jenny is introduced in terms that evoke a composite of Nell and Quilp: "a child—a dwarf—a girl—a something"; Charley Hexam calls her "a little crooked antic" but puzzles as to whether "a child, or old person, or whatever."[91] Yet she explicitly avoids that charged descriptor "ugly" that enrages Quilp, showing a "queer but not ugly little face," and a mesmerizing head of golden hair (222).[92] She is nonetheless susceptible to a similar sense of insult, indulging fantasies of harm toward the children who have mocked her twisted back and legs with a comparable, if primarily verbal, aggression to that of Quilp assaulting the figurehead:

> "Ever so often calling names in through a person's keyhole, and imitating a person's back and legs. Oh! *I* know their tricks and their manners. And I'll tell you what I'd do, to punish 'em. There's doors under the church in the Square—black doors, leading into black vaults. Well! I'd open one of those doors, and I'd cram 'em all in, and then I'd lock the door and through the keyhole I'd blow in pepper. [. . .] And when they were all sneezing and inflamed, I'd mock 'em through the keyhole. Just as they, with their tricks and manners, mock a person through a person's keyhole!" (224)

Words, it appears, *can* harm Jenny, requiring brutal but also childish "redress," to choose an apt term for Jenny's version of retaliation. Her repeated location of aggressive impulses "through the keyhole" looks forward to the locked drawers of the Kleinian therapy room, from which child analysands would each draw their own toy box, and begin to enact their sadistic fantasies in a curtailed world of play. The scissors she flourishes, which fashion and threaten at once, also reappear among the toy objects of the child analytic session, where "cutting out [came to] play a large part."[93]

If Jenny indeed represents a more developed exploration of the psychology of play than Quilp or Bertha: the former pure enraged projection; the latter whose doll-work masks the complicity of reparation with aggression, this is not because she serves as a figure of restorative resolution, equatable with the maturation of either character or author. Rather Jenny models a therapeutic play figured as continued oscillation between sadism and reparation. Her interactions with her toys, both inanimate and human, express rage and shame in dialogue with a skilled practice of material and metaphoric amelioration. Jenny occupies a world of projective identification, where dolls are fine ladies and fine ladies are mannequins. As she observes high society women on the streets of London, she quips, "'I dare say they think I am wondering and admiring with all my eyes and heart, but they little think they're only working for my dolls!'" (431). Reciprocally, her impoverished family life finds expression in perverse games of parenting. Her father is an errant child, conflated in Jenny's angry response to his "tricks and manners" with those who mock her through her keyhole. Before meeting "Mr. Dolls," Eugene Wrayburn assumes that when the childlike Jenny speaks of her "troublesome bad child" who "costs me a world of scolding," she refers to a toy: "'A doll?' said Eugene, not understanding and looking for an explanation" (239). Jenny berates her father as "'a pretty object for a parent's eyes'" (523), and wishes that his chattering teeth would "all drop down your throat and play at dice in your stomach" (522). Her fantasized disarticulation of her wayward "child" is matched by castigation of herself as failed parent. The *"desire to restore,"* Klein was to observe, "springs" from the unconscious wish for the death of the father or mother: reparation in the play world makes amends to those injured in phantasy.[94] Jenny's needle and scissors stab at her imagined victims, even as they clothe and repair.

Jenny has one recurrent dream in the earlier part of the novel, of children that arrive "all in white dresses, and with something shining on the borders, and on their heads" when she is in pain. If this comes perilously close to the death-driven angel visions of those other Dickensian suspended children—Smike, Little Nell, Paul Dombey—Jenny's supernatural visitants have a different mission. They call: "'Come and play with us!' When I said 'I never play! I can't play!' they swept about me and took me up, and made me light" (238). Jenny's relief, unlike Nell's, is survival rather than eternal rest, a survival mediated by what Mark Hennelly calls her "play stance."[95] Her domestic life and her work in the toy world involve a quotidian conflation of character and person: the same substitutive logic allows her to refigure disappointing parent as failing child, or reposition fine lady as servant of her vision. In the resolution of the novel's marriage plot, this flexibility proves crucially therapeutic. Jenny's ability to locate that critical word, "wife," that will reclaim both Eugene Wrayburn and Lizzie Hexam is attributed to her dexterity in the microcosmic realm of dolls: "the natural lightness and delicacy of touch which had become very refined by practice in her miniature work, no doubt was involved in this" (720). Her doll's-dressmaking-as-therapy is not a version of Anna Freud's analytic seduction, "zealously crochet[ing] and knit[ing] during her [child patient's] appointments, and gradually cloth[ing] all her dolls and teddy bears"; nor is it solely informed by a hindsighted "ethics" of repair.[96] It is an act of explicit sublimation. Dickens suggests that manual and material skills morph seamlessly into the linguistic: Jenny's capacity rightly to understand human subjects is mediated and refined through her toy-work.[97] In this sense she is, as other critics have noted, a substitute for the author and his work in the world of character. But she is also the proto-child-analyst, moving life plots forward through the astute and enabling decipherment of object-mediated human relations.

3

Our Plays

The Brontës' literary careers commenced with a toy story. Charlotte drafted it first, in March 1829, when she was twelve years old:

> Papa bought Branwell some soldiers from Leeds. When Papa came home it was night and we were in bed, so next morning Branwell came to our door with a box of soldiers. Emily and I jumped out of bed and I snatched up one and exclaimed, "This is the Duke of Wellington! It shall be mine" When I said this, Emily likewise took one and said it should be hers. When Anne came down she took one also. Mine was the prettiest of the whole and perfect in every part. Emily's was a grave-looking fellow. We called him "Gravey." Anne's was a queer little thing, very much like herself. He was called "Waiting Boy." Branwell chose "Bonaparte."[1]

Charlotte refers to events in June, 1826, when her father Patrick Brontë returned from Leeds bearing a number of toy gifts: "a set of ninepins, a toy village, and a dancing doll" for the girls, and the box of wooden soldiers, which her brother Branwell had requested "to supplement older sets now battered and broken."[2] It is the latter toys, wooden and anthropomorphic, christened alternately "The Twelve" or "The Young Men," that, as is evident here, captured all the children's imaginations.[3] Each adopted and named one, which became their lieutenant in an unfolding series of games that they would refer to as "our plays." A year later Branwell felt compelled to correct Charlotte's record, writing in his "Introduction to the History of the Young Men,"

It was sometime in the summer of the year AD 1824 when I being de-
sirous to possess a box of soldiers asked papa to buy me one which
shortly afterwards he procured me from Bradford They were 12 in
number price 1s 6d and were the best I ever had Soon after this I got
from Keighly another set of the same number These soldiers I kept for
about a year untill either maimed lost burnt or destroyed by various casualties they "departed and left not a wreck behind!"

Now therefore not satisfied with what I had formerly got I purchased at Keighly a band of Turkish musicians which I continued to
keep till the summer of AD 1825 when Charlotte and Emily returned
from school where they had been during the days of my former sets I
remained for 10 months after they had returned without any soldiers
when on June the 5th AD 1826 papa procured me from Leeds another
set (those were the 12s) which I kept for 2 years though 2 or 3 of them
are in being at the time of my writing this (Dec 15 1830) Sometime
in 1827 I bought another set of Turkish Musicians at Halifax and in
1828 I purchased the Last Box a band of Indians at Haworth Both
these I still keep. here now ends the catalogue of soldiers bought by
or for me[.][4]

Between three and four years after the receipt of the soldiers, the children
began to record the stories and describe the worlds—Glass Town, then Angria
and Gondal—that they had elaborated around the wooden figures, in tiny
books "made quite literally" Carol Bock explains, "from what lay close at hand
in their home. A scrap of wallpaper, lined music sheets, fragments of book
advertisements, a used Epsom salts bag," a blue sugar bag, and other "household leftovers."[5] The early Glass Town books, in which the two quoted accounts
take their place, are calibrated to the realm of child's play: filled to their margins
with minuscule script, most likely intended to be proportionate to the toy soldiers that were imagined as their first readers. As projected audience, demanding
a miniaturized archive, the toy soldiers shielded the plays from prying adult
eyes, but the books' tiny format may also have contributed to the later short-
sightedness of their authors. The ways in which the Brontë children themselves
figured as characters within their scripts further attests to a series of primary
encounters with material objects. They were represented by the Genii: giants
who might enter the frame at any point and pick up and shift around other
characters with their huge hands, when necessary bringing those damaged or
destroyed back to life.[6] These avatars make sense first and foremost as a reflection of the real-world proportional relationship between human body and toy

soldier, and secondarily offer a commentary on the relationship between author and literary character.

Critical discussion of the juvenilia moves, without exception, immediately from toy to book, object to text. This is evident in even the most object-oriented Brontë criticism. Deborah Lutz, whose *The Brontë Cabinet* (2016) excavates nine significant Brontë "objects" from the written archive, imaginatively revivifying quotidian material as perishable as potato peelings, focuses on the "tiny books" in her discussion of the siblings childhood play, rather than the toys or wooden furniture that she briefly acknowledges prompted them.[7] And Kate E. Brown, in an exquisite examination of the plays as acts of mourning, focuses on the production of the little books, rather than the "physical plays" which she concedes they only "partly consolidated," as performing complex reparative work: "in their objectness [. . .], the miniature books of the Angrian legend function to restore the body imaginary, even as they also perpetuate its loss."[8] The elision of a primal scene of play is more noteworthy when we consider that there was a period of three to four years between the commencement of "our plays" and the generation of the first scripts that detailed them; a space of unscripted play that becomes lost in archival hindsight. In his essay on "Creative Writers and Daydreaming" (1908), Freud elaborated the traces of complicity between child's play and theater found in a number of European languages, and observed that "language has preserved [the] relationship between children's play and poetic creation."[9] Freud sees both child's play and poetry as versions of object-relating, sharing a requirement "to be linked to tangible objects and [. . .] capable of representation."[10] This chapter seeks to keep both the creative and ludic resonances of play in mind, by holding on a little longer to the toy objects that prompted the Brontës' childhood inventions: hard objects that served, like actors in a play, to ventriloquize phantasy. Returning to Klein's insights about the role that the toy, and in particular the wooden toy, plays in the child's representation of unconscious processes, it proposes that thinking of the juvenilia as toy stories rather than little books can offer new understandings of the Brontës' expansive fantastic worlds, and the ways these parlayed with the restricted domestic scenes in which they were seeded.[11]

Charlotte's and Branwell's versions of the original toy-soldier story instance a sibling rivalry that plays out across the Glass Town/Angria corpus.[12] The particularly piquant competitiveness of a young sister and brother who might both consider themselves entitled to be put first, Charlotte by virtue of age, Branwell by virtue of gender, is negotiated as a rhythm of acquisition, donation, and nomination, all held within the framework of play that is predicated on collaboration. The two passages I have quoted advance a series of claims about primacy, and only belatedly about authorial primacy: more immediately they concern who was gifted, owned, and took the object, and what it was made to stand for. While Charlotte's account acknowledges Branwell's position as original recipient of the gift of the soldiers, she emphasizes her role as the first to "snatch up" and to "exclaim": to take possession and to name. Emily and then Anne follow her example, "when I said this, Emily likewise took one and said it should be hers. When Anne came down she took one also." Branwell, the owner of the toys, is repositioned as the belated claimant. In each instance, recalling Rousseau's imperious infant, clutching precedes naming; touch precedes speech. The rivalrous "snatching" creates a retrospective hierarchy: Charlotte seizing upon the "prettiest" and "perfect" Wellington figure, Emily and Anne, the minors, taking up minor characters (Gravey and Waiting Boy would, however, soon be renamed Parry and Ross, after the then-topical Arctic explorers) and Branwell grasping the archetypal strong opponent. The toys, which were not carefully viewed and assessed but instantaneously grasped, serve nonetheless, in Charlotte's telling, as touchstones of each child owner's character, as well as their personae within their imagined worlds. Branwell's counter-version reasserts his precedence by commencing with request rather than gift. His father's present is figured as a response to Branwell's primary demand, not for original but for replicant objects, which form part of a series of wooden figures to which he has omnipotently laid waste.

In his analysis of Branwell's "Introduction," Michael Moon emphasizes this destructive element, which he opposes to the logic of preservation that motivates Charlotte's account. Moon argues that "[p]erhaps the most striking feature of Branwell's retelling of the story is the high casualty rate among the successive waves of his toy soldiers," focusing on the "extravagance and instability" registered in Branwell's inventorying of toys "maimed lost burnt or destroyed."[13] Yet the two versions of the story have more in common than this reading allows. There is something closer to fort/da game than ritual sacrifice going on in Branwell's "desire to possess" and then casting away of his toys. Moon's privileging of the four verbs at the center of the passage, "maimed lost burnt or destroyed" is at the expense of the hum of acquisitive activity that runs through this passage. Magisterially demanding that his "desire to possess" be satisfied, Branwell takes turn about with his father in this passage in buying, procuring, getting, keeping, purchasing, and again, procuring, buying, purchasing, and keeping. And his list of losses is counterpointed by his reiterated collective nouns, "set" and "band," which testify to an interest in completion, and an equal imperative to hold on to rather than sacrifice the toy. It is, in fact, only the first box of soldiers that is "maimed lost burnt or destroyed"; Branwell concludes with a healthy total of "these I keep." His account is ultimately, as he sums up, a "catalogue of soldiers bought by or for me," not a memorial to dead toys. The emphasis on preservation is even more apparent in a note to a later chapter of "The History of the Young Men," where Branwell writes:

> The truth of this respecting the Monsters is when I first saw them in the morning after they were bought I carried them to Emily Charlotte and Anne They each took up a soldier gave them names which I consented to and I gave Charlotte Twemy (ie Wellington) and to Emily (Parry) to Anne Trott (Ross) to take care of them though they were to be mine and I to have the disposal of them as I would—shortly after this I gave them to them as their own—PB Bronte.[14]

Branwell's insistent self-authorization (I saw, I carried, I consented, I gave) is ratified by an investment in capacities for caretaking: the necessary condition and probation for devolved ownership of the soldier. The text to which the note refers similarly stresses guardianship, alluding repeatedly to the Genii's protective role: "I am the cheif Genius Brannii with me there are 3 others she Wellesly who protects you is named Tallii she who protects Parry is named Emmii she who protects Ross is called Annii."[15] Even if we acknowledge the violence of Branwell's "Introduction," the distinction between "the actual damage done [and] what the toy stands for," to invoke Klein, is not carefully maintained.[16] He speaks of a couple of soldiers as "still *in being*," and goes on "to conclude this Introduction already to [*sic*] long with saying, that what is contained in this History is a statement of what Myself Charlotte Emily and Anne *realy pretended did happen*."[17] The real and the imaginary, being and object, are inextricable in his formulation. Writing a year after Charlotte has snatched the toys into text, Branwell's version asserts paternal favor and his own entry into the world of consumer spending. But his references to purchasing power, whether his own or through the father, also place his acts of destruction within a dialectic in which aggressive omnipotence alternates with replication, restitution, and revivification.

If play with toy objects is widely understood as a negligible stage in the Brontë children's production of a miniaturized textual archive, there is a further consensus among critics that the little books grow up. As Moon observes, foundational criticism of Charlotte's juvenilia (he cites the work of Winifred Gérin, Helen Moglen, Christine Alexander) tended to offer "a highly teleological developmental narrative about her alleged repudiation of her 'narcissistic,' excessively romantic juvenilia in favor, ultimately, of the disciplined and sober ('mature') realism of *Jane Eyre* and *Villette*."[18] Meg Harris Williams regards the juvenilia as evincing increasing stagnation until Charlotte begins to allow "the external world to enrich the dynamism of her fantasy life"; Conover argues that by leaving the collaborative partnership with Branwell in 1836 "Charlotte opens the way to an even greater growth for herself as a writer of adult fiction." Bock, even as she pieces together a materialist account of the little books' construction, situates this within an authorial developmental trajectory: "these were the homely materials from which the future authors fashioned their first literary productions."[19] Her diction reminds us that Charlotte Brontë herself set the standard for this teleological approach, writing in the belated preface to her first written, last published novel *The Professor* (1857), of "many a crude effort, destroyed almost as soon as composed" in which she had purportedly "got over any such taste as I might once have had for ornamented and redundant composition, and come to prefer what was plain and homely."[20] Yet the distinction between the "homely" and the elaborate cannot be straightforwardly mapped onto "adult" reclaimed text and disowned childish object. Williams observes that the tale in which Charlotte records the arrival of the toy soldiers already situates its anecdotes within a "homely realistic setting."[21] As Kate E. Brown notices, the claim in Charlotte's preface to *The Professor* that her early writings were destroyed is "not quite true": the little books survive in archives today because they were "carefully preserved until her death."[22] And the youthful "scriblomania"[23] that disconcerted Elizabeth Gaskell when she first came upon the juvenile archive ("they are the wildest & most incoherent things. [. . .] They give one the idea of creative power carried to the verge of insanity"), emerged from between deceptively plain, home-fashioned covers.[24] The attempts to police a boundary between homeliness and hyperlogia recall the terms of contention between Anna Freud and Melanie Klein: both Anna Freud's insistence that the domestic "real" takes precedence over phantasy in infant ideation, and her assertion that ordinary and everyday explanations might offer more direct insight into children's symbolizing than Melanie Klein's, in her view over-inflated, interpretations. In those arguments too, as we have seen, distinctions collapsed as both Klein's and (despite her intentions) Anna Freud's toy stories disclosed everyday objects symbolically co-opted to the schizoid or reparative excesses of childhood phantasying.

The juvenilia's play-driven approach to story-telling was not a "childish thing that, while perhaps leading to the adult novels, was none too soon put aside",[25] whose spatial and temporal boundlessness would be constrained in grounded domestic fiction; whose narratives of hasty material and sexual gratification would be supplanted by the extended and complex plots of Bildung. But in making this case, this chapter does not argue, as other critics have, for either the aesthetic complexity of the juvenile works, or the sustained Gothic or Byronic legacies of the "homely" adult novels.[26] Nor does it speculate about traumas of which the "plays" might be the symptom.[27] Rather it reconceives

Charlotte Brontë's oeuvre, from juvenilia to realist novel, as an evolving series of toy stories in which phantasy life is worked through with a particular violence, meted out to declaratively "little" characters.[28] In *The Professor* and *Villette* (1853) this mode of creating worlds and characters subsists in tension with the imperatives of a more traditional version of Bildung, centered around the figure of the developing pedagogue.[29] The novels reprise an ambivalence reiteratively invoked in the Brontës' journal jottings and letters, which testify to the siblings' repeated attempts to make beginnings as teachers, only to have their pedagogical intentions disrupted by outbreaks of aversion or desire and by the pull of their "plays." The conflict between the imperatives of a novel of education and the eruptions of toy story that I trace in this chapter, focusing first on the juvenilia and then on Charlotte's "homely" first novel, *The Professor*, rehearse the lineaments of Anna Freud and Melanie Klein's dispute about the relevance of pedagogy or play for understanding the childhood psyche and its fluctuating investments in the real and phantasy.

Real Worlds

The characters of the early, "Glass Town" juvenilia recurrently face moments in which they are forced to understand themselves to be toys. In Charlotte's affectively motivated, multi-chaptered tale "The Search After Happiness" (July 28, 1829), an old man tells of having lain down for the night outdoors only to find himself "raised in the air by invisible hands. In a short time I lost sight of the earth and continued on my course through the clouds till I became insensible. [. . .] What may be my future destiny I know not" (51). Morphing from character back to insensible object, he reverses the process by which the Brontë children snatched the toy soldiers into play, reminding the Genii that their precocious psychological projects ("The Search After Happiness") are constrained by toy parameters. In "Strange Events by Lord Charles Wellesley," dated September 1, 1830, the first-person narrator seeks to conquer a state of suicidal ennui by visiting a Public Library. Taking down a "ponderous volume" and turning its "huge leaves," he suddenly has the strong impression that he is "the mere idea of some other creature's brain" (257). He perceives, in turn "dimly and indistinctly, beings that really lived in a tangible shape, that were called by our names and were US from whom WE had been copied by something—I could not tell what" (257). As he tries to fathom this confounding intuition,

> I was roused by a loud noise above my head. I looked up and thick
> obscurity was before my eyes. Voices, one like my own but larger and

dimmer (if sound may be characterized by such epithets) and another
which sounded familiar, yet I had never, that I could remember, heard
it before, murmuring unceasingly in my ears.

I saw books removing from the top shelves and returning, apparently of their own accord. By degrees the mistiness cleared off. I felt
myself raised suddenly to the ceiling, and ere I was aware, behold two
immense, sparkling, bright blue globes within a few yards of me. I was
in [a] hand wide enough almost to grasp the Tower of All Nations, and
when it lowered me to the floor I saw a huge personification of myself—hundreds of feet high—standing against the great Oriel.

This filled me with a weight of astonishment greater than the mind
of man had ever before to endure, and I was now perfectly convinced
of my non-existence except in another corporeal frame which dwelt in
the real world, for ours, I thought, was nothing but an idea. (258)

Giant figures interrupt Wellesley's browsing, taking up the wooden soldier narrator, despite the "weight" of his astonishment, with infinitely greater ease than
he does the book, and offering, in their corporeality, a significantly more tangible
projection of his subjectivity than that buried within its pages. Character is
forced to know itself not just as invention, but as ventriloquial object, and to
internalize a commensurate understanding of "the real": a space that the toy
world analogizes, but in which its violent abreactions do not manifest.

Michael Moon links the tendency to pathologize Branwell Brontë's writings,
less evident in critical discussion of the sisters' juvenilia, to their depiction of
"grotesque extremes of behavior, including violent behavior."[30] Yet Charlotte's
early writings reveal comparable brutality, with a particular focus on dismemberment (many of her Glass Town Tales, for example, show an obsession with
grave robbing). Whereas in Branwell's tales bloodshed takes place in the context
of battle, however, Charlotte brings it into domestic and pedagogic settings.[31]
In the first volume of the "Tales of the Islanders" she records: "In June 1828,
we erected a school on a fictitious island, which was to contain a thousand
children" (22). The Duke of Wellington's sons, Wellesley and the Marquis of
Douro, guard the students with the nonchalant sadism of children playing
with toy soldiers: "finally coming home with about a dozen wanting, who are
found a few days after in hedges or ditches with legs or head broken" (25). (In
another elision of story and play worlds mediated by violence, Charlotte adds
"I forgot to mention that Branwell has a large black club, with which he thumps
the children upon occasion and that most unmercifully.") The second volume
of the "Tales" narrates the further history of "[The School Rebellion]" (October
6, 1829). The school is now running smoothly: "all the rules were observed with

scrupulous exactness, the governors attended admirably to their duty"; children whose natural behaviors are understood to be violent and wild "were absolutely becoming something like civilized beings, to all outward appearance at least: gambling was less frequent among them; their quarrels with each other were less savage; and some little attention was paid by themselves to order and cleanliness" (100). Pacing her story against recent historical events, Charlotte then mentions Wellington and Peel's passing of the Roman Catholic relief act, recalling the arrival of the newspaper, and "with what eagerness Papa tore off the cover, and how we all gathered around him, and with what breathless eagerness we listened" (100). While the swerve of topic makes for bumpy reading, the conflation of narrative and story-time is seamless. A real-world domestic scene in which Patrick Brontë finds himself surrounded by his politically invested children, all eager to hear the news, flickers briefly into focus within an imagined scenario in which the toy-soldier "Papa" of the island tales, the Duke of Wellington, is a chief actor.[32] The school, meanwhile, is neglected by both narrator and governors, and a rebellion ensues. The "little queens" (minor Genii) take an air-balloon to the island where they meet Wellington's sons, one of whom is injured and near death. In one of those displays of omnipotent reparation that underwrite the "plays," they "in the plenitude of our goodness and kindness of heart, cured him instantaneously" (104). Although the school then prospers, "we, becoming tired of it, sent the children off to their own homes" (104). Again, content and scene of play are melded: we understand that, just as the queens are bored with school governorship, so are the Brontë children with this game.

Such magisterial and insouciant shifts of object identification—their kinship, that is, with the world of child's play—make the juvenilia juvenile. But the obvious domestic correlatives for the tales' roughly handled character-objects also allow them to be read as therapeutic narratives. Charlotte's "The Silver Cup: A Tale" opens with Lady Dunally "reading aloud a most beautiful and affecting novel," which lulls her unsentimental husband to sleep, "for he had no feeling" (70). When a man comes to the door with an object for sale, Captain Henry Dunally purchases the "beautiful silver cup," and is berated by his wife for acquiring such a "great ugly thing" (70). Lady Dunally values a different object, "a miniature ship composed of glass and made with the utmost skill and ingenuity," which is kept locked in a rosewood box in the library. The next morning she comes upon her youngest child, Cina,

> busily engaged with an elegant parasol, now all torn and broken, in
> smashing the beautiful ship to pieces and about to crack the delicate
> masts and cordage. [Cina] gave a laugh like an idiot. For a moment the

lady stood transfixed with horror at the heart-rending scene, then rush-
ing in she snatched up the child and shaking her furiously threw her
down on the floor. (71)

Captain Dunally shouts "'I've a great mind to knock your brains out against
the wall (giving her a great slap),'" but settles with telling Cina "'get along about
your business, you nasty little thing'" (72). His son, Henry Fearnothing, "a very
wicked, wild boy" secretly attends the public execution of the maternal uncle
after whom he is named (70). Captain Dunally then has a dream linking the
family's misfortune with the purchase of the silver cup. "Odours," a substance
regularly employed in Glass Town to undo the work of the Genii, split the cup
to pieces; meanwhile the glass ship is "mended by invisible hands" (73). In
Kleinian "projective identification," the child projects repudiated aggression
outward, before learning, through the object world, to tolerate its own ambivalence and reassimilate bad feeling. Here Charlotte and Branwell's competing
aesthetics and narrative rivalry are projected into objects (the cup of the martial
Captain Dunally; the ship of his readerly lady) that are aggressed verbally and
physically until interpretation, mediated by dream-work, produces a
resolution.

"The Silver Cup" appeared in the October 1829 issue of "Blackwoods Young
Men's Magazine," a Glass Town journal edited by Charlotte's avatars, based
on *Blackwood's Edinburgh Magazine* (1817–1980), to which her father subscribed
(her brother's competing version was "Branwell's Blackwoods Magazine"). In
the tale's manuscript copy the "Cup" of the title replaces a scratched-out word
"JAR."[33] If Charlotte's intended title was "The Silver Jar," it is possible she sought
to echo or rewrite one of the most famous of Maria Edgeworth's children's
tales, "The Purple Jar" first published in *The Parent's Assistant* in 1796, and a
staple of early reading throughout the nineteenth century. In that tale, which
is reminiscent of "The Good French Governess" in its emphasis on training a
child to make useful purchases, but which has also been read as a female pu-
berty allegory, young Rosamund chooses to spend her money on a beguiling
purple jar rather than a much-needed pair of shoes.[34] However, practical experimentation soon exposes the jar's striking color as an illusion created by an
odorous black liquid filling its plain glass form. When her father notices that
her old shoes are down at heel, he refuses to take her on a visit to a glass-house,
vowing "no one must walk slipshod with me" and "looking at her shoes with
disgust."[35] "The Silver Cup" is similarly a tale of mis-purchasing and brutal
parental rejection, though use-value and rational acquisition have no place in
Charlotte's version. Rather, her tale exposes and amplifies the injured family
feeling that underpins Edgeworth's object lesson.

   The easy slippage in these four typical early tales, between phantasy and scenes of reading or writing, between objects as heavily laden symbols and as material things, taken up and put down in gestures of alternate violence and reparation, cannot but seem to preempt the work of the Kleinian playroom, where the aggressed and petted wooden toys of a Rita or an Erna would come to be deployed in brutal and logically random yet psychically resonant imaginary narratives. Charlotte shows the same disconcerting capacity for "moving with untroubled literalness between phantasy and its objects" that Mary Jacobus identified in Klein's analyses.[36] The exemplary "soldier" play of the Kleinian corpus is her longest and last published case study, that of Richard, a ten-year-old boy she analyzed when she relocated to Pitlochry in Scotland in 1941 to escape the London blitz. Richard's war games, acted out with toy and furniture objects and through a series of drawings, and which mapped onto vengeful phantasies about a neighborhood child, Oliver, were interpreted by Klein as family stories. Richard spent much of his time anxiously following the progress of World War II via news reels and maps, and his games were filled with naval battles between accurately named destroyers and U-boats. Klein diagnosed a conflation of Hitler with his father in Richard's phantasy life, suggesting that Richard was directing his Oedipal anger outward onto current events. She also analyzed his ambivalent feelings toward his mother and his older brother, Paul, who was serving as a soldier, and was an object of both envy and admiration. Klein quite quickly observed the lessening of Richard's anxiety as she delivered her explicit oral, anal, and genital focused interpretations.

   When Richard began the analysis Klein laid out drawing materials and some little toys: "little wooden figures, some of them dressed as men, others as women, some small, some larger," swings, trains, "little animals, houses," a coal and a timber truck, and some wooden fences and trees.[37] Richard ignored the toys and instead "seemed extremely keen to tell all about himself, as if he had been waiting for this chance for a long time. [. . .] He said he had noticed the toys, the pad, and pencils on the table, but he did not like toys, he liked talking and thinking" (22). By the thirteenth session, however, he asked Klein to bring "the toys which he had seen in the first hour; he might now like to play with them" (63). When play commenced it was evident that he had internalized the key symbols of Klein's analysis to the extent that he was almost able to self-soothe:

> Mrs K. had brought the toys and put them on the table. Richard was very interested and at once began to play. He first picked up the two little swings, put them side by side, made them swing, and then laid them down beside each other, saying: "They are having fun." He

Figure 8. Toys used by Melanie Klein in her psychoanalytic work with children, 1920s–1930s. Reproduced by permission of the Wellcome Collection (wellcomecollection.org) [Attribution-NonCommercial 4.0 International (CC BY-NC 4.0)]

filled one truck of the train which he called the "goods train" with small figures, and said "the children" were off on a pleasure trip to Dover. He added a slightly larger toy woman in a pink dress, whom he at once called "Mummy." (In all his subsequent play she figured as Mummy.) He said that Mummy, too, was going on the pleasure trip with the children. He added one of the bigger men, whom he called "the minister" because he was wearing a hat, but soon took him out of the truck, sat him on the roof of a house, added the pink woman, and they both tumbled down. He put them by themselves in a truck facing one another and said: "Mummy and Daddy are making love." He had taken out the small figures from the first truck and put one of them in the second truck, turned towards the couple in the first one. (64)

Richard's game recalls Erna's perverse and enraged carriage scenarios, which I compared in Chapter 2 to a Punch script. In Richard's case, family figures are explicitly consigned to the "*goods* train" (my emphasis), indicating his understanding of their object status and its therapeutic rewards. The wooden figures can enact both Oedipal "pleasure trip" and rough tumbles without accruing harm, either to themselves as objects, or commensurately to Richard by generating unmanageable envy or rage. After this first play Richard was at times able, as Klein acknowledged, to take the reins of the analysis himself. When she interpreted a plant in one of his drawings as representing his mother, "Richard pointed out to Mrs K. that Mummy was also there in another form because she was the ship *Nelson* and Daddy the submarine *Salmon*" (69). In this and numerous subsequent examples Richard demonstrated not just his ability to understand the symbolism of his play, but the lessening of anxiety and indeed active enjoyment that came with his flexing of that capacity.

Richard's games were at times attended by a similar sense of cathartic apathy to that evinced by the Brontës, as at the end of the "The School Rebellion." Taking up the toys and setting aside "a few figures that had some small defects [. . .] suddenly Richard bit the tower of a house (which he called a 'church'). Then the dog bit somebody and disaster followed. Everything collapsed and the dog was the only survivor" (72). At this point "Richard again put the toys aside, as he had done after the previous disasters, and said that he was 'tired' of them" (72). Such moments were counterbalanced by others in which he phantasized not just destruction but revivification, or introduced color panels into drawings that were formerly simply pencil outlines, demonstrating reparative and creative skills that recall the omnipotence of the Genii. Richard's analysis was Anna Freud's notion of harm writ long: a ninety-three-session series of graphic exegeses whose key symbols were transferred to and internalized by the receptive child. Klein alludes to Anna Freud's concerns in a note to the twenty-first session, where she remarks the "fact that, by making unconscious material conscious through interpretation, anxiety is somewhat diminished (which does not prevent its return)," and notes that this is "in keeping with a well-established principle of technique. Nevertheless, I have often heard doubt expressed whether it is advisable to interpret and make manifest to children (and for that matter to adults) anxieties of such a deep and particularly painful nature" (99–100). Anna Freud's objections to what she regarded as Klein's dubious interpretative ethics have been amplified by recent revisionist psychoanalysis. Carolyn Laubender, for example, notes that Klein "routes the grammar of war that animated Richard's manipulation of [toy figures] from his external world to his internal one."[38] Observing that Richard at times disputes Klein's interpretations or drives the analysis, but without registering the manifest relief he obtains from both the content of such interpretation and his increasing facility in self-soothing, Laubender insists that "for Klein the realist purchase of [Richard's] concerns has little appeal."[39] Her focus on what she refers to as Klein's "ahistorical" disregard of "Richard's political anxieties," like

Anna Freud's insistence that a handbag may simply be a handbag, literalizes and delimits the therapeutic scope of the "real."[40]

There is, however, also common ground between a number of Anna Freud's child therapy case studies and the Brontë "plays." She too encountered Genii-like fantasies of omnipotence: children's dreams of the violent destruction, sometimes followed by reanimation, of a family member. In one instance, the family friend of a patient (a boy of a similar age to Richard's) fell ill. At his therapy session he described a scenario in which his mother visited the invalid and found that he was dead:

> At that moment the dead man's little son came in. She called him and said, "Come here, look, your father is dead." The boy came up to the bed and spoke to his father. The father was alive and answered him. He turned to my patient's mother and said, "What is the matter? He is alive." Then she spoke again to the father, but again he made no reply and was dead. But when the boy came up again and spoke, the father was alive again.

As was her wont, Anna Freud underplayed the work of analysis in this case, remarking that "the fantasy is [. . .] transparent," and that "further interpretation is superfluous."[41] She remained adamant that the toy space that Klein created and the interpretations she concocted from omnipotent play with objects were redundant and top-heavy. For understanding both the strangeness and ameliorative capacity of play such as Richard's and the Brontë siblings', however, Klein's toy-work remains compelling. In Richard's wooden pleasure trip, "having fun" can incorporate the primal scene. In "The Silver Cup," we witness the transformation of domestic life and its envy-inducing favoritisms and hierarchies through object-work. And in "Strange Events" the toy itself comes slowly to understand that its world is not "the real," yet that it nonetheless carries the burden of reality-directed feeling, manifest in the interaction between its materiality, living and larger bodies, and the perversely therapeutic work of story.

Klein's notion of play as a "bridge" (more often than not made of wooden blocks) between the unconscious and the real is preempted, in a highly reflexive way, by the entire corpus of the Brontë juvenilia. Claire Harman encapsulates this bridging capacity neatly, writing: "the booklets connected with the 'Twelves' soon evolved from props to something much more central, very consciously a way of bolstering the reality of the games they played, and making their everyday world a little less real, creating a zone where the two would coexist."[42] The role of the object world in mediating between figure and ground is apparent from the earliest plays. In her second surviving manuscript, "The History of the Year," the arrival of the soldiers is framed by a scene of writing. Charlotte references "an hundred and twenty years old" geography book "at this moment lying before me while I write this," (4) and goes on to establish further coordinates, arranging her family in their domestic setting like figurines in a doll's house, performing the hierarchized tasks of a song of sixpence:

> I am in the kitchen of the parsonage house, Haworth. Tabby the servant is washing up after breakfast and Anne, my youngest sister (Maria was the eldest) is kneeling on a chair looking at some cakes which Tabby has been baking for us. Emily is in the parlour brushing it. Papa and Branwell are gone to Keighly. Aunt is upstairs in her room and I am sitting at the table writing this in the kitchen. (4)

Only the mention of the deceased sister, Maria, briefly shifts tense into the past: emphasis is otherwise on "this moment" and the objects and actions that bear witness to it. Emily and Anne Brontës' "diary papers," begun in November 1834 when Emily was sixteen and Anne thirteen, some years after they had commenced their Gondal saga, are equally resolutely presentist: "Taby said just now Come Anne pilloputate (ie pill a potato [)] Aunt has come into the kitchen just now. [. . .] It is past Twelve o'clock Anne and I have not tided [sic] ourselvs, done our bed work or done our lessons and we want to go out to play."[43] These dispatches from the scene of (again, minute) writing are interwoven with others in the same present tense from the Gondal kingdom: "The Gondals are discovering the interior of Gaaldine Sally Mosley is washing in the back kitchin."[44] But Emily and Anne also use immediate objects and spaces to project imagined futures. The first paper ends: "Anne and I say I wonder what we shall be like and what we shall be and where we shall be if all goes well in the year 1874."[45]

The early diary papers are soon incorporated into a series, reviewed and renewed every four years on Emily's birthday. Each opens with a recitation of present coordinates that touches base with familiar objects; most report of the progress of the Gondal narratives; all conclude with a reiteration of wishes that all will be well at the next four-year ceremony, often framed as a hope of finding themselves in the same setting among the same things. "I guess that this day 4 years we shall all be in this drawing room comfortable I hope it may be so," writes Emily in 1837.[46] While imagination is expansive within their imaginary worlds, its play in relation to their own real-world, real-time futures is highly restricted. Sandra M. Gilbert and Susan Gubar understand this fundamental recourse to the domestic space as indicative that "psychodynamic 'play,' [. . .] is an activity at once as necessary and as ordinary as housework: ironing and the exploration of alternative lives are the same kind of 'business'."[47] Yet it is

difficult to read these texts either in Anna Freudian terms, as indicative of a
primary domestic allegiance that resists incorporation into phantasy, or as early
gestures toward a homely realist aesthetic. Present, phantasy and future are
blended in an object-focused, incantatory ritual whose numerous errors of
spelling contribute to its regressed feel.[48] In the final paper Anne again situates
the other family members in relation to her writing self in the present moment:
"Charlotte [. . .] is now sitting sewing in the Dining-Room Emily is ironing
upstairs I am sitting in the Dining Room in the Rocking chair before the fire
with my feet on the fender Papa is in the parlour."[49] Her report of Gondal, "The
Gondals in general are not in first rate playing condition—will they improve?"
indicates a sustained conception of character as inherently play-object, battered
by wear.[50] She concludes, again, with anxious projection:

> I wonder how we shall all be and where and how situated on the
> thirtyeth of July 1848 when if we are all alive Emily will be just 30
> I shall be in my 29th year Charlotte in her 33rd and Branwell in his
> 32nd and what changes shall we have seen and known and shall we be
> much chan[g]ed ourselves? I hope not—for the worse [a]t least—[. . .]
> Hoping for the best I conclude.[51]

The desire for change that will revivify play is canceled by an apprehension
that superstitiously confines hope to the framework of an enduring present. The
sisters would both have died by the time the next four-year reckoning came
around. While the brevity of the series as a whole—its fall into silence—is poignant, the intense anxiety about the possibility of futurity, which renders these
tiny texts superstitious articles, is there from the earliest entries.[52] The objects
on and around the Brontë writing table become opportunities for touching
wood, and warding off the force of an equally manifest death-drive.

Charlotte's equivalent of Emily and Anne's later diary papers, her Roe Head
journal of 1836, reveals a similar structure, moving from spatial and object-
oriented self-location to the world of imaginative reverie. Charlotte was a young
teacher at the school at which she had spent time as a student when she kept
the journal, ostensibly now under the aegis of "educative agencies."[53] Nonetheless it is in this context that violent and erotically charged phantasy shifts
from what she terms "the infernal world" (162) of Angria to the school domicile,
and from character to person, in a mode that anticipates the regressive acting
out of Kleinian play-therapy. The first of the journal entries reestablishes a by-
now-familiar structure, commencing by taking spatial and temporal coordinates:
"Well, here I am at Roe-Head. It is seven o'clock at night. The young ladies
are all at their lessons, the school-room is quiet, the fire is low. A stormy day
is at this moment passing off . . . ," before slipping into an "ecstasy" of reverie

(158). The return to the domestic space is initially simply bathetic: "in the bower of Zamorna's lady!—while this apparition was before me, the dining-room door opened and Miss W[ooler] came in with a plate of butter in her hand" (160). By the third entry, however, her surrounds are no longer stabilizing but disruptive, inducing a rage that cannot fully shift the focus of its violence from real objects to phantasy narrative. As she completes a lesson, Charlotte finds herself "sinking from irritation & weariness into a kind of lethargy" (162). She envisions, with fury, a future strained by constant repression of her own, internal, "School Rebellion": "forcibly suppressing my rage at the idleness, the apathy and the hyperbolical & most asinine stupidity of those fat-headed oafs, and on compulsion assuming an air of kindness, patience & assiduity" (162). Her violent anger gives way, promisingly, to "vague sensations" that might "have settled down into some narrative better at least than any thing I ever produced before" (163). However once again her context obtrudes itself, producing visceral rage: "just then a dolt came up with a lesson. I thought I should have vomited" (163). She returns to her teaching in a state of barely contained aggression, recording "the violence of the irritation [one student's] horrid wilfulness [sic] excited and the labour it took to subdue it to a moderate appearance of calmness" and intimating unspecified threat: "if those girls knew how I loathe their company, they would not seek mine so much as they do" (163). Finally free to slip into reverie in her own room, her thoughts turn naturally to soldier play: "statesmen & kings, a revolution, thrones & princedoms subverted & reinstated" act out the "violence" that just recently "nearly killed me," and the mental cleansing this affords is figured as a "washing [of] bloody hands" (165). The threat to real-world relationships is averted in play phantasy.

Klein's *Narrative of a Child Analysis* (1961) demonstrates the complexity of psychic shifts between phantasy and "real" scenes of battle. Richard's war games and drawings and Klein's explications of the desire and envy underwriting them lead, by the thirty-third session, to a moment of recognized ease and happiness. Richard tells Klein, "this morning, feeling bolder, he made up his mind that when the war was over and they moved back to their home (in 'Z'), he would not be afraid to fight his enemy Oliver" (157). His plans to punish his "real-life" enemy (an ambivalent figure, who is sometimes a friend), recall, in their childish remit, Jenny Wren's fantasy of blowing pepper through a keyhole: "He said that after the war he was planning to take Oliver prisoner. There was an untidy corner in the garden with bushes and lots of bees and wasps. It was not actually filthy but was certainly not a clean place. There Oliver would be kept. He would be guarded so that he could not escape, and the bees and wasps would sting him" (158). Richard describes previous battles with Oliver in which "he nearly broke Oliver's bones; they also threw stones at each other"

(158). Richard first claims he "would have liked to kill him," but quickly modifies this: "he added, no, not really, but he hated him very much" (158). Klein notes that "meanwhile Richard had been making another empire drawing" (158). Richard's play moves back and forth between phantasy focused around contemporaneous real-world war coordinates and events and a planned, future-dated acting out in the realm of childhood play's enmities and allegiances, all advancing in a context of gradually understood and soothed feeling and greater freedom of play. Charlotte on the other hand, attempting to maintain a phantasy life scripted in childhood in a context of adult pedagogy, finds that acting out is curtailed, and the aggression that play might alleviate must be repressed. Her rage derives in part, then, from the fact that the shift from real-world writing space to fantasy realm can no longer, as in her childhood "plays," be seamlessly, indeed self-reflexively, enacted.

Homely Materials

The Roe Head journal depicts Charlotte angrier than Angria can relieve. Some years later, probably at the end of 1840, she penned her "Farewell to Angria." A brief prose piece, ostensibly marking a departure from the world of romance and heralding her realist turn, the "Farewell" is in fact conspicuous for its conflation of the two genres. Charlotte confesses her previous tendency toward natural supernaturalism and the delineation of emotional extremity: "I have shewn my landscapes in every variety of shade &light"; "So it is with persons— my readers have been habituated to one set of features [. . .] varied but by the change of feeling or temper or age—lit with love, flushed with passion, shaded with grief, kindled with ecstasy, in meditation & mirth, in sorrow &scorn &rapture."[54] The regretful mood she records has its foundations, however, not in excess, but in a version of the quotidian repetition that anchors many of the juvenile writings. Extreme "characters & scenes & subjects" have become over-familiar, declining into an "empire of habit." While sketching the therapeutic promise of a reprieve from wild imaginings ("the mind would cease from excitement"), she renders the phantasy world domestic, a realm of "friends" and "intimate acquaintances," to surrender which feels "almost as if I stood on the threshold of a home & were bidding farewell to its inmates."[55] In the Farewell's configuration, Charlotte seems to anticipate Anna Freud's assertion that childish phantasy and its symbols remain fundamentally confined to a domestic ambit of feeling. It would be another six years before the Brontë sisters invented their next "play," establishing three new alter-egos, Currer, Ellis, and Acton Bell, in order first to self-publish a collectively authored volume of poems, and then to send their "big books" (one- and two-volume novels) out into the "real" world of British publishing. *Wuthering Heights* (1847), *Agnes Grey* (1847), and *The Professor* were sent out together. The former two were accepted for publication as a three-volume set by Thomas Newby. *The Professor* was roundly rejected, but a response from Smith, Elder and Co. encouraged "Currer" to try her hand at another novel. She finished *Jane Eyre* promptly, and it was published earlier in 1847 than Emily and Anne's joint volume. Emily would die of tuberculosis only a year after *Wuthering Heights* was published; Anne half a year later, having completed her second novel, *The Tenant of Wildfell Hall* (1848).

Those first three forays into the novel genre, *Wuthering Heights*, *Agnes Grey*, and *The Professor*, works that Charlotte and her critics consider the maturational telos and generic obverse of the infantile, miniature "plays," are nonetheless riddled with and discomposed by toy stories. I shall conclude this chapter with a reading of *The Professor*'s toy animus, but Emily and Anne's initially more successful works also hearken back in fundamental and reflexive ways to play legacies. Heathcliff turns up at Wuthering Heights in circumstances that echo the nocturnal arrival of Branwell's toy soldiers. Like Patrick Brontë, Mr. Earnshaw has promised his children gifts to be purchased on a trip to town: "What shall I bring you? You may choose what you like; only let it be little."[56] Hindley chooses a fiddle and Cathy, then "hardly six years old," chooses a whip. Instead, they are presented with a child termed an "it," that has "crushed to morsels" Hindley's toy fiddle while being transported in his father's arms.[57] Hindley "blubbered aloud, and Cathy, when she learned the master had lost her whip in attending on the stranger, showed her humour by grinning and spitting at the stupid little thing, earning for her pains a sound blow from her father."[58] Earnshaw proposes to "let it sleep with the children," but they "entirely refused to have it in bed with them, or even in their room."[59] The substitute toy eventually becomes the object of Cathy's sadistic love and Hindley's steadfast hate, showing a wooden soldier's aptitude for violent play, and imperviousness to abuse: "hardened, perhaps, to ill-treatment: he would stand Hindley's blows without winking or shedding a tear."[60] In *Agnes Grey*, spitting, uncontrollable children use whip and spurs to goad a toy rocking horse, and co-opt Agnes's objects in their wild play:

> Meantime, Fanny had possessed herself of my work-bag, and was rifling its contents—and spitting into it besides. [. . .]
>   "Burn it, Fanny!" cried Tom [. . .]. I ran to snatch it from the fire, and Tom darted to the door.
>   "Mary Ann, throw her desk out of the window!" cried he.[61]

The governess struggles but fails to convert toy to object lesson, and finds her-self lapsing into a reciprocal aggression ("I would shake her violently by the shoulders or pull her long hair").[62] In this slender novel Anne resolutely depicts the family feelings that stymie the developmental narratives of youngest daugh-ters, preemptively addressing Charlotte's belittlement of her mature literary productions. Agnes, consigned to perpetual childhood by her parents and sibling, proposes to become a governess. Yet as she outlines her hopes for Bil-dung, her determined infinitives subside into infantilism: "to go out into the world; to enter upon a new life; to act for myself; to exercise my unused facul-ties; to try my unknown powers [. . .] to show papa what his little Agnes could do; to convince mama and Mary that I was not quite the helpless, thoughtless being they supposed."[63] The developmental plot is here a series of baby steps, the Bildungsheldin's projected advancement teetering as she glances backward for parental approval.[64]

In 1850 Charlotte set herself to write prefatory material for the posthumous republication of her sisters' novels. In the "Biographical Notice of Ellis and Acton Bell" and the editor's preface to the 1850 edition of *Wuthering Heights*, she charged herself with a double task of revivification: not only ensuring that her sisters' works and literary reputations remained alive, but also resuscitating their moral reputations in the face of hostile reviews that had repeatedly reg-istered the enraged vehemence and sadism of their novels. Yet her gestures of reparation have almost universally been read as damaging. J. Hillis Miller has demonstrated how Charlotte's recasting of *Wuthering Heights* attempts to neu-tralize the ferocity of the novel by representing Emily via contradictory and effectively self-canceling models of authorship; Katherine Hallemeier observes that Charlotte's depiction of Anne's "honest" writing has led subsequent critics "to characterize Anne Brontë's style in similar terms, describing it as straight-forward, moral, and instructive"; and Catherine Han suggests that "as well as limiting the dissemination of *Wildfell Hall*, Charlotte Brontë laid the founda-tions for her younger sister's reputation as the least talented, blandest Brontë."[65] Marianne Thormählen and Beth Newman both recognize that the prefaces' effect of making "the younger Brontë sisters look less complex and serious in their artistry than present-day scholars can see they were" has morphed into a myth of Charlotte's deliberate and self-aggrandizing deflation of her sisters' literary legacies.[66] Newman cites recent biographical novels that have repre-sented the executor role as one of literal domestic violence, such as James Tully's *The Crimes of Charlotte Brontë* (1999), which "implicates the eldest sister in sibling murder."[67] However Charlotte's interventions are not, as such reassess-ments suggest, manifestations of a passive aggression fermented in the strong brew of incomplete mourning and unfinished rivalry: her "cuts" and recharacterizations are best understood in terms of an ongoing lexicon of play, whose earliest activities put toy soldiers into the brutalizing and reparative hands of child-giant editors with sweeping powers.

Charlotte was in part prompted to republish *Wuthering Heights* by the appearance of a review by Sydney Dobell in the *Palladium* of September of 1850, which she believed finally did some justice to Emily's writing. Dobell mistakenly identified *Wuthering Heights* as the first literary effort of Currer Bell, author of *Jane Eyre*. For Charlotte, Dobell's misattributed critical recognition was, notwithstanding, an act of resuscitation, capable of breathing new life simultaneously into Emily's dearest objects, book and sister: "it revived me for many a day to find that [. . .] dead as she was—the work of her genius had at last met with worthy appreciation."[68] Bearing her reference to revivification in mind, it is worth attending to the terms in which Dobell evoked the "genius" of this presumed first, rather than sole, novel: "It is the unformed writing of a giant's hand: the 'large utterance' of a baby god. [. . .] The child's hand wanders over the strings."[69] In conjuring a sense of immature and disproportionate power, as capable of destroying as creating, Dobell stumbles on the language of the "plays": the "giant's hand" of the Genii merging with the "child's hand," tentatively "playing" a too large instrument. When Charlotte frames her "Biographical Notice of Ellis and Acton Bell," written in direct response to Dobell's error of identity, she takes her cue from his image of the presiding Genius with the clumsy hand of a child, highlighting the "immature but very real powers revealed in *Wuthering Heights*."[70] But it is her declared project of extricating person from character—delineating the real-world identities behind the assumed names Ellis and Acton—that in fact resonates most strongly with the language of the early toy-soldier stories. Each sister, she relates, chose an "ambiguous" name from a combination of "conscientious scruple at assuming Christian names, positively masculine" and reluctance to declare themselves female to a prejudiced publishing world.[71] This name-game itself revives that which accompanied the arrival of the toy soldiers ("it shall be mine"): Emily and Anne's early avatars, "Gravey" and "Waiting Boy," preempt their ambiguous *noms de plume*. Reciprocally, in 1850 the sisters and their writings are sketched by Charlotte in toy-soldier-like terms: Emily an "unbending" "hero"; Anne the author of tales she will neither "varnish" nor "soften."[72]

Giving up the "play" of false identity and reviving the sisters' real-world characters, Genius-like, is a task that, as in the "Farewell to Angria," or the conclusion to "The School Rebellion," is attended by a withdrawal of libido: "the little mystery, which formerly yielded some harmless pleasure, has lost its interest."[73] Sounding like Anna Freud, Charlotte declares, in effect, that the

alias "may [. . .] admit of a harmless explanation."[74] Indeed, Charlotte's domes-
tication of the violent subtexts of her sisters' fictions employs a similar lexicon
to that later deployed by Anna Freud, when she turned her skeptical attention
to the sadistic extremes of Kleinian analysis. Anne's *The Tenant of Wildfell
Hall*, a novel Charlotte admits is underwritten by hatred ("she hated her work"),
purportedly "did her harm."[75] In the further "Editor's Preface to the New
Edition of *Wuthering Heights*" that novel's "rude" and "wild" prose is subtly
converted to the "homely," as Charlotte advises readers to weigh the "homely
fidelity" of Nelly Dean against Heathcliff's sadism and Cathy's "perverted
passion and passionate perversity."[76] And if the novel is "moorish and wild,
and knotty as a root of heath," "hewn in a wild workshop,"[77] we are asked to
recall that it was fashioned by an author who felt "no inducement to seek social
intercourse beyond our own domestic circle,"[78] with "simple tools out of homely
materials."[79]

This disavowal of the crude in favor of the homely is reiterated in the preface
to *The Professor*, drafted in 1851, at one of a number of points at which Charlotte
sought to publish her first, hitherto rejected, novel. She here refers obliquely
to the juvenilia, confessing that she had honed her authorship on "many a
crude effort, destroyed almost as soon as composed," and that in so doing, she
"got over any such taste as I might once have had for ornamented and redundant composition, and [came] to prefer what was plain and homely" (37). Yet
even as she retrospectively repudiates her juvenile writings, Charlotte revives
the language of Branwell's "Introduction to the History of the Young Men,"
with its logic of cyclical creation and annihilation. Resonant within her claim
to have made an aesthetic shift to "plain" style is a phantasy of the destruction
of playthings: rudimentary little objects, "destroyed almost as soon as composed," are again thrown aside. The preface further hints that sober realism
retains an undisciplined underside, which manifests transferentially in the
reading subject. Having written a Bildungsroman whose protagonist works "his
way through life as I had seen real living men work theirs," Charlotte encountered unforeseen proclivities among the "real living men" of the publishing
industry, who rejected the reflection offered by her uncompelling aspirational
protagonist: "men in business are usually thought to prefer the real; on trial
the idea will often be found fallacious: a passionate preference for the wild,
wonderful, and thrilling—the strange, startling, and harrowing—agitates diverse
souls that show a calm and sober surface" (38). Where she had farewelled Angria by avowing that "the mind would cease from excitement & turn now to a
cooler region, where the dawn breaks grey and sober,"[80] she found, when first
attempting to publish her "homely" text, that "something more consonant with
highly wrought fancy" was in fact sought by the ostensibly sedate reader (37).

This instinctive rejection of the novel's reality-effects has persisted in *The Professor*'s critical reception. The perception that *The Professor* (eventually published posthumously in 1857) is a formally "immature" work tends to be linked to the observation that it remains a more Angrian text than Charlotte admits. Robert Keefe reads the novel as "an unconscious and unsuccessful attempt to escape [. . .] the garish sunsets of Angria"; Stevie Davies recognizes that "the adult antagonists of *The Professor* bawl puerile abuse like characters from Branwell's and Charlotte's juvenilia."[81] More generally, as William Cohen notes, "readers have always considered it minor, ill-conceived, and uncompelling."[82] *The Professor* has registered as repellent in mood and effect: an "unpleasant and oddly disquieting book," as Heather Glen puts it.[83] The biographically inclined have interpreted it as the unsuccessfully processed residue of Charlotte's depression and repressed anger in the wake of her own Belgian story of failed intimacy with her "professor," Constantin Heger, an episode that is understood to have required expulsion before she could begin to resolve feeling more effectively into art in the canonical novels *Jane Eyre* and *Villette*.[84] Cataloging the book's aesthetic failures, others conflate *The Professor*'s tendency to leave a bad taste with bad taste; its capacity to convey bad feeling with being a bad object. Terry Eagleton calls it "a more dishonest and idealized version of *Jane Eyre* and *Villette*"; Robert Keefe sees it as harboring "a disturbing undertone of melancholy"; Juliet Barker claims that the dissonances of the novel can be attributed to Charlotte's speaking through a male first-person narrator.[85] In the brief reading that follows, I bring these two sets of critical intuitions (affective and aesthetic unease) together, suggesting that the play legacies of the novel are the vehicle for its unsettling yoking of repressed aggression and sadistic envy with the "sober" everyday.

In her first full-length fiction, Charlotte manifested her turn from the juvenile and impassioned to the grey and sober in both setting and character, establishing a self-referential preference for the "poor, obscure, plain, and little" that would persist through her published oeuvre.[86] William Crimsworth, a narrator, "not handsome, and no dressing can make me so, [. . .] no object to win a lady's love, no butt for the shafts of Cupid" (106), having passed up both a conditional inheritance and employment at his wealthy brother's mill, finds himself in the suitably "flat," "dull," "unromantic and unpoetic" landscape of Belgium, embarking on a humble pedagogic career (86). He commences teaching in a boys' school, and then extends his ambit to the neighboring girls' academy, where the *directrice* briefly toys with his affections. Crimsworth quickly disciplines his feelings as he does his pupils, eventually ending up in an explicitly doubled position of mastery as head of his own school and of a domestic household (his wife, Frances Henri, both former student and fellow teacher, insists, even in intimate exchange, upon designating him "master").[87] The novel concludes with a "brief" word regarding their son: an unsmiling boy, who, like his parents, is cast in the anti-heroic mold, and is "as little of a pretty child as I am of a handsome man, or his mother of a fine woman" (286). Much of the resistance readers experience in relation to this text derives from the particular way in which Charlotte has chosen to fashion a "hero" modeled on "real living men" (38). In Crimsworth the switch from romance to realism manifests as bathos, with conspicuous ordinariness evinced as a querulous acting out of injured narcissism and envious spoiling. The juvenilia's language of battle has not quite been abandoned, but it is transmuted to tropes of self-mastery: as William Cohen puts it, Brontë "enclose[es] the protagonist within metaphorical armor."[88] The "real living" hero maintains the toy soldier's hard surface as psychic defense.

If the emotionally impervious Crimsworth has the carapace of a petit bourgeois toy soldier, defeating emotional attack in domestic battles ("erelong he tired of wasting his ammunition on a statue—but he did not throw away the shafts—he only kept them quiet in his quiver" [56]), a broader toy language underwrites his Bildungsroman. Aware of his own unattractiveness, he measures the women he encounters via the figure of the doll. Crimsworth deploys phrenological terminology to master the female students who seek to mock or flirt with him.[89] Yet this overtly scientistic focus on physical surface is perversely underwritten by a more insistent tendency to describe them as made objects: dolls of different classes of material, to recall the workshops of Caleb Plummer and Jenny Wren. "Female character" as a whole is something imagined as "vague, slight, gauzy, glittering," but which proves "palpable substance enough; very hard, too, sometimes, and often heavy," like a fancily-dressed doll (126). Crimsworth describes Aurelia, "of middle size, stiffly made, body long, legs short, bust much developed but not compactly moulded, waist disproportionately compressed" (127), hair "glossy with gum and grease" (128); Adèle, "features well-chiselled and regular, well-cut eyes" (129); Sylvie "with a pale, passive, automaton air" (131); and Eulalie, whose "eyes moved a little—by these evidences of life alone could I have distinguished her from some large handsome figure moulded in wax" (114). While references to molded forms and chiseled features belong to the lexicon of nineteenth-century feminine description, Charlotte seems to intensify the allusions to doll-like manufacture, against which Crimsworth again musters toy-soldier defenses: "in less than five minutes I had buckled on a breastplate of steely indifference, and let down a visor of impassable austerity" (115).

Although, like his author, he asserts that his portraits are "from the life"—direct, embodied realist descriptions—toy terminology plays an important psychic role for Crimsworth (130). His resistance to the doll-like is his chief sexual disavowal, informing his initial attraction to Zoraïde Reuter, the directrice of the ladies' seminary: "the idea of marrying a doll or a fool was always abhorrent to me: I know that a pretty doll, a fair fool, might do well enough for the honeymoon; but when passion cooled, how dreadful to find a lump of wax and wood laid in my bosom" (137). While the horror of this phantasy is the idea of flesh revealing itself to be insensate, we might recall here Klein's insight that the toy medium, in its callous woodenness, enables the child to express aggression that it cannot in the realm of animate, woundable subjectivity.[90] Crimsworth's claim that he does not desire the doll is belied by the hyper-materialism of his doll metaphors, which render explicit what Klein perceived in her therapy room: that the wish only to harm the toy, not the real-world counterpart, masks a domestic sadism that can only be contemplated through the lens of play.[91]

Crimsworth seeks to distinguish his relationship with Frances Henri by exempting her from the toy terminology he ascribes to other women. While his account of her attractions is as repellently objectifying as his portrayal of the female students, it is embodied rather than material: "in her there was no deformity to get over; none of those prominent defects of eyes, teeth, complexion, shape [. . .] had she been either 'édenté, myope, rugueuse, ou bossue,' my feelings towards her might still have been kindly, but they could never have been impassioned" (252). Yet description falters when deprived of the doll lexicon: resorting to litotes, he sketches his future wife via a series of lacks, that in turn thinly disguise a fantasy of dismemberment: of woman as a simple assemblage of body parts. The animated human frame is effectively broken down into a Frankensteinesque toy construct, or a Kleinian series of aggressed part objects. Consonant with Crimsworth's declarative repudiation of the doll, the child the couple produces (named, with a further Shelleyan resonance, Victor) is deprived of toys: "His toys have been few, and he has never wanted more" (286). Nonetheless, "for those he possesses, he seems to have contracted a partiality amounting to affection" (286): they are the focus of a surplus of feeling that at times threatens to render him a "milksop" (285) and at others manifests as "revolt [. . .] against disappointment, mischance, sudden sorrow, or supposed injustice" (289). They possess, in his infancy, a capacity to "meet his violence" (289).

If the figuration of family relations via play (or its explicit lack) takes us to Klein, Crimsworth's repudiation of the toy and commitment to a blended pedagogy and domesticity resonate even more strongly with Anna Freud's response to play therapy. Similarly, his aggressed doll depictions of his students return us not only to the overlapping realist and phantastical sadism barely contained within the Roe Head journal, but to Anna Freud's early writing. William Cohen's discussion of *The Professor* adduces Sigmund Freud's "A Child Is Being Beaten" (among other sources on masochism), arguing that Freud's model of a subject shifting between masochistic and sadistic phases cannot fully account for the novel's depiction of "erotic Pain."[92] It is perhaps more fruitful in this context to consult his daughter's elaboration of masochism theory in her first psychoanalytic paper, "Beating Fantasies and Daydreams." In her preface to *The Professor*, Charlotte repeats the gesture inaugurated by the "Farewell to Angria," of setting aside the heated fantasy of the juvenilia, in favor of sober realism. Where fantasy life had threatened to disrupt her pedagogy at Roe Head, leading her compensatorily to characterize her affectionate pupils as "dolts," objects of rage and "loathing," in *The Professor*, I have conjectured, an ostensibly realist pedagogical Bildungsroman nonetheless allows for the symbolic beating of students figured as toy objects, by a toy-soldier-like self-made man.[93] In "Beating Fantasies and Daydreams," Anna Freud similarly negotiates a relationship between real-world context, fantasy, and writing. She purports imaginatively to reconstruct, rather than to recollect, the history of one female child patient in her father's earlier case study (a child that is in reality herself). But what she provides, as I suggested in the Introduction, is also a portrait of the development of a writer. The girl is prone to sadistic fantasies of the kind Freud had outlined, but Anna discloses that alongside these, "between her eighth and tenth year" (at approximately the age when Charlotte commenced her toy-soldier "play"), "the girl initiated a new kind of fantasy activity which she herself called 'nice stories' in contrast to the ugly beating fantasy."[94] These stories persist into adolescence in a kind of serial form:

> the girl had formed not one but a whole series of stories which deserve to be called "continued stories" in view of the constancy of the acting figures and the entire general setting. Among these continued stories one stood out as the most important: it contained the largest number of figures, persisted through the longest period of years, and underwent various transformations. Moreover, from it other stories branched off, which—as in legends and mythology—were elaborated into innumerable almost independent tales. Alongside the main story there existed various minor, more or less important stories which were used in turn but all of which were fashioned according to the same pattern. (144)

Anna Freud's essay aims to show that these "nice stories" and the beating fantasies are two sides of the same coin: where the former demonstrate sublimation, the latter give evidence of "repressed sensual strivings" (153).

Like Charlotte foreswearing the increasingly ill-repressed "sensual strivings" of the juvenilia in her preface to *The Professor*, Anna Freud's avatar, "the girl" equates earnest virtue with domestic realism: "All the figures in these nice stories had names, individual faces, external appearances that were detailed with great exactness [. . .]. The family circumstances of these figures, their friendships and acquaintances, and their relationship to each other were precisely specified and all incidents in their daily life were fashioned as true to reality as possible" (142). At approximately age fifteen she comes across a "boy's storybook" and takes the plot of one story, with a male protagonist, as a frame within which to elaborate a longer daydream narrative, "formed exactly like a real novel, containing an introduction, the development of a plot which leads to heightened tension and ultimately to a climax" (144, 145). Although she in this sense achieves the fantasy equivalent of an extended piece of prose fiction, Anna Freud finds that when its scenes are viewed "as a continuous and connected series, we are surprised by their monotony, though the daydreamer herself never noticed it either in the course of fantasying or in talking about them" (148). The attachment to intricately elaborated fantasy combined with a recognition of repetition and tedium echo the terms of Charlotte's renunciation of her fantasy world. Several years after first forming this interconnected daydream (so presumably at the end of her adolescence) "the girl put it in writing" (154). The result was that the textual object ceased to be masturbatory: "the finished story itself does not elicit any such excitement. A reading of it does not lend itself to obtaining dreamlike pleasures. In this respect it had no more effect on its author than the reading of any other comparable story written by another person would have had" (155). Anna Freud concludes that writing, as opposed to narrativized daydreaming, allows for an indirect, socially oriented pleasure gain by producing an effect upon an imagined reader, and that this supplants the direct pleasure gain of fantasizing. As she sums up, "she has found the road that leads from her fantasy life back to reality" (157).

Charlotte Brontë espouses a similar philosophy in the preface to *The Professor*, when she abjures the quick climaxes and "ornamented and redundant" style of her early works to frame a continuous Bildungsroman in which "hero" is also "real living m[a]n," enjoying a "mixed and moderate cup of enjoyment" (37). But as we have seen, her realist tale is nonetheless replete with fantasies of sadism played out upon characters depicted as objects. The purported social orientation of long-form writing is, in her case, directed toward the creation of possibly the Victorian period's most unlikable "hero," and the royal road to realism is reached, not through the construction of a "nice story," but via characters, structure, and imagery that anticipate those of Anna Freud's original, repudiated beating fantasy. For in that,

The child invented complicated organisations and complete institutions, schools, and reformatories in which the beating scenes were to take place, and established definite rules and regulations which determined the conditions of gaining pleasure. At that time the persons administering the beatings were invariably teachers. (141)[95]

With Crimsworth's narrative, her first, maligned attempt at the evolved genre of novelistic realism, Charlotte Brontë attempts to pass off sustained, pleasurable regression as mature work-ethic. Her sleight of hand sets the scene for my discussion of Victorian female Bildungsromane in this book's final chapter.

4

Bildung Blocks

Wilhelm Meister's Apprenticeship (1795–96), widely credited as the first Bildungsroman, is also a toy story. It commences with child's play in the Rousseauian mode: with a boy seeking enlightenment by exploring the interiors of objects. Wilhelm, first in conversation with his mother and later in recount to his actress lover, Mariana, recalls in loving detail the toy puppets that inspired his love of the theater. When a marionette show of David and Goliath debuted in his family home, the infant Wilhelm begged a repeat performance, determined to understand the inner workings of the life-like "dolls":

> "I had made up my mind the first time that the dolls did not really speak, and I suspected that they did not move of themselves; but, then, how was it that it all looked so pretty, and seemed as if they really spoke and moved? where could the people and the lights be? These questions disturbed me all the more, because, much as I enjoyed the enchantment of the scene, I longed to be one of the enchanters: to have a hidden hand in the game, and yet to be a spectator and enjoy the illusion."[1]

"Trying to find out *how* everything was done" leads Wilhelm to steal and damage the puppets; actions forgivable in the light of this quest for understanding (13), for, as Maria Edgeworth would soon enjoin, "Is it not rather unjust to be angry with him for breaking them to pieces? [. . .] He breaks them, not from the love of mischief, but from the hatred of idleness; either he wishes to see what his playthings are made of, and how they are made, or whether he can put them together again if the parts be once separated."[2] Yet, as in Edgeworth's well-managed play tableaux, there is domestic aggression nested in the narrative of accrued understanding. When eventually Wilhelm succeeds in putting on a performance of his own, his "hidden hand" fumbles, and "I let my Jonathan [puppet] drop" (17). The humiliating blunder, he claims, "seemed welcome to my father" (19). Years later when he brings the toy puppets to his first lover, she instinctively rejects all but "the beardless Jonathan, [which] quite took her fancy" (9). Her quick skill in manipulating this object of Wilhelm's earlier disgrace, fondling it as she strokes him, repairs the wound left by his father's mockery, while also analogizing her skill in manipulating Wilhelm: "she managed him so prettily and understood so well how to transfer her caresses from the doll to our friend, that this trifling play was the introduction to some happy hours" (9–10).[3] A transferential object relating is managed here in the interests of a narrative of sexual development.

The story of the child acrobat Mignon offers a violent counterpoint to this account of juvenile investigation maturing into consensual adult play. From her first appearance until her early death, Mignon figures as another marionette: her performances both disjointed and light; her body contorted yet curiously impervious; her appearance androgynous, and in doll-like suspension between childish and womanly form. When she performs her egg-dance, Stefanie Bach notices, "Kleist's marionette seems to have come alive. [. . .] Mignon seems to touch the ground only occasionally: she is part of the 'springende Gesellschaft.'"[4] The resemblance becomes explicit when Mignon and Felix mimic puppet-play:

> The children, as they sat in the great armchair opposite with their heads only just above the table, looked like puppets in a Punch and Judy show and began to act a little piece in that style. Mignon imitated the squeaking tone famously, and at last they knocked their heads together and against the edge of the table in a fashion which only wooden dolls could have endured. Mignon grew so madly excited, that heartily as the company had been amused at first by the fun, they were at last obliged to interfere. (51)[5]

Mignon resists, and is pictured "with her head thrown back and her limbs as it were flung into the air" (53). Her violent play crescendos across the novel. Her first spasms of psychosomatic pain register as puppet movements: "her body became convulsed, she started up, and fell on the ground as if every joint were dislocated. [. . .] The spasms continued, they spread from the heart to the poor dislocated limbs; she only hung in his arms" (54). Her death is that of a "naughty child" who has treated too wildly a toy that is also a self (351). In the later recovered history of her mother, Sperata, Mignon's body is substituted by a marionette-like assemblage. Believing Mignon drowned in a lake, Sperata wandered the shore collecting animal bones, which were supplemented by sympathizing locals with those of a recently deceased child. "She had carefully fastened every bone in its right place with threads and pieces of ribbon," strung along by the hope that the rearticulated skeleton would revive and take on flesh (368).[6]

That the story of the puppet-like child Mignon replicates and ironizes the Bildungsroman of Wilhelm's maturation from *Kinderspiel* to *Schauspiel* is a critical commonplace; however, scholars are divided as to whether toy or child is tenor of the Mignon metaphor. Stefanie Bach describes Mignon as "androgynous and childlike, resembling a puppet on a string"; Terence Cave includes "puppet-like movements" in conjunction with "outbursts of wild behavior" as characteristics traceable across the Mignon archive, "as if Goethe had discovered some economy of human comportment, irreducible to a schema or to a pallid archetype, that was both highly unusual and immediately *recognizable*"; while Marc Redfield proposes that "Mignon's crampings of the heart and epileptic seizures return us repeatedly to the puppet theater."[7] In arguing that "the story of the puppets [of Wilhelm's childhood] becomes the story of Mignon," Redfield also gives particular attention to the scene in which the children act out puppet theater from the stage of the "great armchair." He suggests that both Mignon and Felix's "condition of possibility" depends

> on an act of identification with a puppet—an impossible act that the text registers in one of its most astonishing turns of phrase ("banged their heads together . . . in such a manner as actually only wooden puppets can withstand"). The children are not puppets, but they do that which only puppets can do. It is impossible to identify with puppets, but this impossibility "occurs."[8]

Redfield deduces that "the children, the actor, and the aesthetic text 'are' puppets in the sense that they have, impossibly, been made possible by them."[9] Carolyn Steedman acknowledges analogies to the marionette figure, referencing both Freud and Kleist, as part of her investigation of Mignon's redactions in a range of post eighteenth-century texts that understand childhood as a psychically buried "component of the adult self," yet she is equally interested in those "real children (children observed, children described, children remembered by the adults they became)" that she understands to be Mignon's counterparts.[10] Michael Bell, on the other hand, in an analysis that considers *Wilhelm Meister* and the Bildungsroman genre in "fertile analogy with the pedagogical relation," regards Mignon simply as a "pre-pubescent girl."[11]

When Redfield parses "'banged their heads together . . . in such a manner as actually only wooden puppets can withstand'" (in Eleanor Grove's translation, "in a fashion which only wooden dolls could have endured" [51]) as "they do that which only puppets can do," he subtly shifts passivity to action, with-standing or endurance to doing, rendering object as subject (rather like a pup-peteer) by sleight of hand.[12] Yet as Klein understood, toys "do," psychically, by remaining objects. Klein anchored the therapeutic value of the toy on its ca-pacity to suffer damage without pain, and thus to allow the child both to act out and repair feeling in a delimited and interpretable space. The question "child or toy?" does not equate with a reality check in the Kleinian analytic schema. Her play therapy offers a way of retrospectively understanding Mignon as simultaneously representative child and the toy through which it manages feeling in the world, while her analytic praxis, through which children come to "realize that their aggressive acts were directed against the *real* objects," offers a belated template for Wilhelm's apprenticeship.[13] Whereas the telos of Wilhelm's Bildungsroman is generally understood as his renunciation of the theater and acceptance of the role of father, Mignon's parallel, non-developmental story approximates the more brutal Kleinian narrative, as aggression is expelled through the abuse and destruction of a contorted, unstably gendered, toy-like child who dies of a literally broken heart. Wilhelm's archetypal and Mignon's failed developmental narrative are two parts of the same toy story: one in which the realist and the performative intermediate first and foremost in the affective rather than educative sphere.

Mignon's subplot, hinged to the growth and self-education of the Bildung-sheld, marks, like the spasms and crampings of her puppet body, the awkward fit of the girl child to a boy's-own tale. Her toy story narrates naughtiness and (self-)destruction more memorably than maturation, reframing Wilhelm's memories of his puppet theater as a perverse nostalgia that registers develop-ment as loss rather than gain. She embodies a counternarrative of regression that continues to tug at the nineteenth-century Bildungsroman's developmental momentum, even as the form follows Goethe's ostensible lead in deploying childhood toys as metonyms of creative intelligence, which "grow up" into the book in our hands, or the works of the artist whose portrait we trace as a young man. The remainder of this chapter turns to the female Bildungsromane of Charlotte Brontë and George Eliot, focusing on the figure of the abused doll that animates their deformations of Goethe's template.[14] If, as I argue, envy is the primary affect impelling these texts, that pervasive feeling is surely seasoned by their authors' struggles to work with the intractable building blocks of a masculine maturational form.

Extemporized Playthings

Like *The Professor* (1857), Charlotte Brontë's *Villette* (1853) is a Bildungsroman in a doubled or hyper-literalist sense: a novel of education of an educator. It is often hailed as the apex of her "mature," "achieved" fictional work. Yet, as Charlotte's prefaces demonstrated, demarcations between immature and mature productions are difficult to maintain. To read this late novel in tandem with *The Professor*, as first and last versions of Charlotte's Belgian "play," is to disclose a psychic architecture only visible between the spines of the two books. From opposite attic windows, folded symmetrically across the *allée défendue*, Lucy Snowe and William Crimsworth, angry orphans foisted into pedagogic maturity, look into the same novelistic space: Genii weaving stories around their toy objects; troubled children peering down at the miniature figures of a doll's house. Christopher Lane is acutely sensitive to the "interest in hostility," indeed the "unfettered hatred," that he argues "circulates in Charlotte Brontë's novels as resentment and passionate antipathy."[15] In my reading this latent aggression manifests primarily in the violence meted out to persons understood as things. Toys taught Charlotte the power of authorial omnipotence, and the psychic rewards of punishing character-objects. The repudiation of fantasy worlds in her mature prefaces belies the fact that, rather than growing into realism, Charlotte continued to find, in her adult novels as in her childhood "plays," that resolution is reached by wreaking havoc on characters and offering them at best a tenuous repair; that maturation (both narratological and authorial) is predicated on regression.[16]

Figure 9. Wooden block houses. Toys used by Melanie Klein in her psychoanalytic work with children. One of a set of cards produced by the Child Psychotherapy Trust. Reproduced by permission of the Wellcome Collection (wellcomecollection.org.) Scan: Nicholas Keyzer. [Attribution-NonCommercial 4.0 International (CC BY-NC 4.0)]

Villette is a deeply ambivalent story of home-finding: not only, as critics have argued, because its concluding domesticity is open-ended, bringing closure to its pedagogic rather than its marriage plot,[17] but because its status as one of the "homely" adult Brontë fictions is travestied by a sequence of unsettled settings, comprised of transposable furniture, dollhouses of miniature objects, and cupboard spaces that suddenly disclose hidden spies like a jack-in-the-box. Its early scenes jointly introduce the first-person narrator, Lucy Snowe, and a minute and toy-like "personage" named "Home."[18] The novel opens on Lucy's annual visit to her godmother, an idyllic recess during which as "one child in a household of grown people" she is used to receiving all the attention generally accorded an only child. This privileged position is disrupted by the arrival of the "little visitor," Polly Home, for whose presence Lucy is prepared by the "signs and tokens" of miniature objects—"a small crib," "a tiny rosewood chest" (8). Lucy views the intruder as a doll object, noting "its minute hand" and the way it "turned and fixed its eyes" and how, "relieved of her wrapping" like a gift, "she appeared exceedingly tiny; but was a neat, completely fashioned little figure, light, slight, and straight. Seated on my godmother's ample lap, she looked a mere doll; her neck, delicate as wax, her head of silky curls, increased, I thought, the resemblance" (10). A "minute thing"; a "little figure" (19), Polly is plaything but "unchildlike" (12):

> When I say *child* I use an inappropriate and undescriptive term—a term suggesting any picture rather than that of the demure little person in a mourning frock and white chemisette, that might just have fitted a good-sized doll—perched now on a high chair beside a stand, whereon was her toy work-box of white varnished wood, and holding in her hands a shred of handkerchief, which she was professing to hem, and at which she bored perseveringly with a needle, that in her fingers seemed almost a skewer, pricking herself ever and anon, marking the cambric with a track of minute red dots; occasionally starting when the perverse weapon—swerving from her control—inflicted a deeper stab than usual; but still silent, diligent, absorbed, womanly. (19)

Polly's dutiful perseverance with her miniature weapon anagrammatically discloses an intrinsic perversity, and her wooden "toy work-box" might, with the shift of a punctuational hinge, become the "toy-work box" of the Kleinian playroom: its therapeutic function, clearly, to channel Lucy's displaced aggression as much as to help master Polly's grief.

"Unchildlike" was a word Klein often used to describe depressed children: in the case of her troubled patient Erna, "obsessive brooding and a curiously unchildlike nature" are attributed to "the suffering look upon the little girl's face."[19] Her play-therapy was in turn a reversed and perverse Bildungsroman, which helped children to mature by showing "a more childlike nature."[20] Polly, in mourning for her mother and separated from her father, also wears a "suffering look": Lucy punningly records "the signs of home sickness" legible on "her infant visage" (15). Lucy is fascinated by the manifestations of this sorrow. Where "other children in grief or pain cry aloud, without shame or restraint," Polly simply draws "a square-inch or two of pocket handkerchief from the doll-pocket of her doll-skirt" to discreetly dab at her tears (11). Typical childish behavior seems mitigated in the unchildlike plaything. But the offer of a play-therapy that will reanimate "childlike nature" in Polly will not come from Lucy. Instead Graham Bretton, her godmother's son, instigates a series of games with the doll-child by testing whether she is little woman or thing. He at first pretends to believe Polly a "gentlewoman" only to make her status as object rather than "personage" overt: "he caught her up with one hand, and with that one hand poised her aloft above his head. She saw herself thus lifted up on high, in the glass over the fireplace" (20, 21).[21] As toy, Polly makes Graham toy-like: her "officious, fidgety little body" is able to "galvanize him to new and spasmodic life" (28). She appears in turn to be animated solely by his interest in her: "one would have thought the child had no mind or life of her own, but must necessarily live, move, and have her being in another," Lucy sourly observes (29). Enlivened only when she is taken up or put down by another, she serves as a channel for affect: "she nestled to Graham, and seemed to feel by his feelings: to exist in his existence" (29).

Lucy subsequently tests Polly's apparent toy-like capacity to endure "suffering" in a series of attacks that seem provoked by her own abrupt displacement in the Bretton home, as made manifest in her exclusion from the world of "the playmates," Polly and Graham. She encourages Polly to intrude on an evening Graham is spending with his schoolfellows: "I thought perhaps they might not object to have her as playmate," provoking Graham to repudiate their play-fostered bond (30). Polly responds by lying "on the mat with her face against the flags," a discarded toy (30). When Polly's father eventually sends for her, and Mrs. Bretton empathetically speculates as to how she will "take this news," Lucy once more inserts herself into the communication: "*I* wondered, too, and took upon myself to communicate it" (33). As the italicized "*I*" signals, the desire to witness intense feeling channeled by the doll-child is in some way self-constituting for Lucy. She insistently probes what Nicholas Dames beautifully terms Polly's "backward turning reverence": her capacity to transfer her affections "from father to paternalized mate."[22] "Polly, are you not glad?," she interrogates: "Shall you not like to go to papa?" Yet Polly's "unexpected turn[]" of temper" when grilled by Lucy, and her question "What is papa to you?," hit "Home" (35). When they go to bed, Lucy finds herself "wishing, yet scarcely hoping" that she might be offered the chance to "soothe" and repair the toy-child she has aggressed (38).

Lucy's "fail[ure] to yield" what Graham calls "that precious commodity called amusement" so winningly provided by a doll-like girl named Home, and her sadistic processing of the envy that their preferential play generates, seem fundamental to her subsequent narrative of explicitly unspecified loss and vaguely motivated but piercing homelessness (20). As Klein would come to understand, envy differs from its associate terms jealousy and greed in its desire to vitiate the envied object: "Envy is the angry feeling that another person possesses and enjoys something desirable—the envious impulse being to take it away or to spoil it."[23] Relating envy's innate conflict between love and hate to the infant's alternating identifications of a good and bad feeding breast, Klein argues that "early emotional life is characterized by a sense of losing and regaining the good object."[24] She further proposes that the reactivation of such primary envy in the analytic situation leads to a desire to devalue the work of the analyst, and to spoil or circumvent the value of their interpretation.[25] A consonant rhythm underpins Lucy's blocked Bildung, whose sweeping losses and painfully achieved gains are desperately contained by a withholding first-person narrative voice that thwarts and impairs decipherment.[26]

Critics have tended to understand the overtly unnamed traumas of *Villette* as gesturing to events outside the novel's frame. Gretchen Braun, for example, argues that *Villette*'s "plot, along with Lucy's emotions and fortunes, oscillates and repeats, always circling back to the earlier tragedy whose details the narrator will not share."[27] She sees this as a way in which the novel "disappoints the reader who expects the steady and satisfying progression" offered by "the established narrative forms of the marriage plot [. . .] and the male ambition plot."[28] Rachel Ablow reads the carefully elided personal crises of the novel as "grotesquely violent allegories of emotional experience," diagnosing Lucy's embrace of the hypochondriac's isolation as a model for testing her own personhood and that of others.[29] Like Braun, Ablow proposes that "the novel calls attention to the fact we do *not* have full access to the character's interiority," interpreting Lucy's oblique yet extreme metaphorics of suffering as ultimately lodged "in and of the body."[30] Kate E. Brown fills in the blanks of Lucy's history by suggesting that "*Villette* is fundamentally about the experience of catastrophe and the impediments to mourning," again registering the ways in which the Bildungsroman's telos is thus withheld, as the novel translates "every point of culmination into the catastrophic origin of a new, radically underdetermined narrative."[31] While such analyses understand the novel as a mode of working through, in place of the Bildungsroman's more typical work toward, they struggle to understand this psychic work as process. *Villette*'s early Bretton scenes stage a disqualification for play that the novel repeats and works through in each of its settings and scenarios, in the reparative yet infinitely regressive cycle of Kleinian toy-work.

Klein's 1930 essay "The Importance of Symbol-Formation in the Development of the Ego" details the case study of Dick, a little English boy who evinces an inability to play. "Indifferent to most of the objects and playthings around him," Dick presented a particular problem for Klein's method.[32] He did not have feelings for things—"had practically no special relations with particular objects"—and so "any chance actions of his in relation to them were not co-loured by phantasy" (224, 225). He seemed, for analysis, unreadable: his affectless uptake of a toy object could not be regarded as symbolic. Klein could only proceed, in the face of this *"fundamental* obstacle" to interpretation, by praxis: by encouraging his interactions with her therapeutic toy objects, including large and small wooden trains, a wooden coal cart, a pair of scissors which Dick used to scratch and try to cut the pieces of wooden coal, and little human figures (225). Dick first unleashed a destructiveness that she understood as defensive: "he threw the damaged cart and its contents into the drawer and said, 'Gone'" (226). "On one occasion Dick lifted a little toy man to his mouth, gnashed his teeth and said 'Tea Daddy,' by which he meant 'Eat daddy'" (227). Klein observed that while the sadism vented on the toy "offer[ed] an occasion for the liberation of anxiety," it also multiplied anxiety "because the weapons employed to destroy the object are felt by the subject to be levelled at his own self as well" (220). With encouragement to further play, Dick showed an "obviously dawning curiosity," a lessening of anxiety and an impulse toward restitution (226). "Thus he would proceed to place the little toy men on my lap or in my hand, put everything back in the drawer, and so on" (227). This in turn gave way to "a far greater activity and curiosity and a stronger tendency to aggression of all kinds" (228). Dick's now active play coincided with a new interest in and capacity for communication: "the desire to make himself intelligible" was "in full force" for, as Klein says, "the hitherto-lacking object-relation has made its appearance" (228). Klein reads Dick's "lack of any affective relation to the things around him" (224) as obliquely sketching a childhood "environment rather poor in love" (223). Similarly, Lucy's early play scenes suffice to disclose a nebulous formative lack, which requires neither narratorial nor diagnostic ratification. Rather, I understand her Bildungsroman as a sequence of episodes in which Lucy too learns, therapeutically, to play. As in Dick's case, this involves not a simple evolution from sadism to reparation, but a cycling back and forth between envy and gratitude.

The novel's pedagogic situations, urban excursions, and country retreats configure the gradual emergence of a painstakingly acquired playfulness that confers transitory elasticity to Lucy's recursively impeded narrative. The most reflexive instance is the annual performance for Madame Beck's fête which, as M. Paul's triple injunction "play you must" underlines, unites the analytically paired signification of play as theater and toy-work.[33] Costumed, exquisite corpse style, half in masculine disguise, half in her signature "gown of shadow" (145), Lucy is able to rewrite the foppish male "part" she has unwillingly assumed, parodying the love triangle being enacted before her own eyes between Ginevra Fanshawe, her fellow performer on the stage, and Ginevra's competing suitors in the audience, Dr. John and "the doll—the puppet—the manikin," Colonel Alfred de Hamal (163). Joseph Litvak is deft in charting the "relational possi-bilities of Brontë's polymorphous scenario, [. . .] in which the inextricably in-terwoven strands of rivalry and desire running through the 'real-life' drama are further knotted by its 'recklessly' innovative reworking on stage."[34] Acting (out) intercedes between the felt and the real, managing, as Sharon Marcus observes, "negative aggressive affects like jealousy, humiliation, and punishment."[35] Later Lucy will confess that she had long recognized in Dr. John the same Graham Bretton she had in childhood failed to amuse: "Dr John Graham Bretton re-tained still an affinity to the youth of sixteen" (195). She will figure the privi-leged perspective this identification enabled as that of an audience member viewing an illuminated actor: "I liked entering his presence covered with a cloud he had not seen through, while he stood before me under a ray of spe-cial illumination" (196). As she manipulates the minor part of the fop, chan-neling the envy in the room to upstage the main players in the little drama in her similarly occluding "shadow" garb, Lucy acts out not only the sexual tension that pervades the immediate context of her performance, but her early exclusion from the world of the "playmates," Dr. John and Polly, and the sadistic envy it generated.

When Lucy awakens at La Terasse, following her collapse outside the Cath-olic church where she has sought relief in a (part therapeutic, part performative) act of confession, she finds herself in the regressed space of a toy-therapy drawer, confronted with a reassemblage of the same objects and attendant affects that motivate the opening Bretton chapters. She is twice "struck" by the things around her: first as they assume solidity within her gradually sharpening field of vision, and then again as they are rendered *unheimlich* by their very homely familiarity: "all these objects were of past days" (187). In a subtle analysis of this episode, Eva Badowska has shown how the furniture of the room becomes "vital to the recovery of Lucy's identity."[36] Arguing that the "material object enables her to recall herself," Badowska focuses on those recollected items that bear the signature of Lucy's own domestic labor: a pincushion embroidered with Mrs. Bretton's initials, and a pair of screens, engraved "stroke by stroke and touch by touch [by] a tedious, feeble, finical, school-girl pencil held in these fingers" (187).[37] Badowska's recognition of the aggression woven into Lucy's reencountered handicraft distinguishes her reading from a widespread critical tendency to view Lucy's childhood memories as nostalgic.[38] She traces the "minute red dots" of blood left by Polly's earlier hemming of the "shred of a handkerchief" as she played at domesticity from her "toy work-box" to the color Lucy had chosen for her satin pincushion, identifying "the sadistic violence whose source must be Lucy" to which the related objects speak.[39] This slippage between fancywork and phantasy-work is reiterated in the description of other objects that swim into Lucy's focus. On her first awakening, her eye fixes on "two little footstools," "a small ebony-framed chair," "two oval miniatures," "relics of a diminutive tea service," "little pictures," all of which are observed to the "minutest detail" (186, 187). The insistent miniaturism persists as, having swallowed her medicinal draught she awakes again, this time in a bed "in a little alcove" (190), next to a "little chintz chair" in "a small cabinet," a "tiny chamber" (189). The toy-scale of these reencountered mementos may speak to Lucy's achieved adult perspective on childish things, but their particularized tininess also invokes the doll-child Polly Home's accoutrements, conjuring Lucy's initial rejection by the "playmates" Polly and Graham at the very moment she appears to have relocated a foundational domestic security. La Terasse's defamiliarized familiar things foreshadow a repetition of Lucy's neglect by Graham in favor of Paulina, and intimate the supplanting of her renewed semi-familial relationships by their developing marriage plot.

At this juncture, Lucy's and the novel's "first objects" become subtly elided with Charlotte Brontë's own (188). Discombobulated by the sight of these artifacts, Lucy wonders "had a Genius stooped his dark wing down the storm to whose stress I had succumbed [. . .], had he borne me over land and ocean, and laid me quietly down beside a hearth of Old England" (188). She questions "what Genii-elixir or Magi-distillation" the nursemaid might be using to revive her (188). Badowska dismisses such allusions as "a predictable part of the ideology of global capitalist and colonial expansion," missing their surreptitious invocation of the reanimating powers of the Genii, whose feats within Brontë's early "plays" included the repurposing of objects and the revival of damaged protagonists.[40] Genii continue to show their "hands in the game" at other moments in *Villette*. The chandelier at the concert hall seems to Lucy "the work of eastern genii: I almost looked to see if a huge, dark, cloudy hand—that of the Slave of the Lamp—were not hovering in the lustrous and perfumed atmosphere of the cupola, guarding its wondrous treasure" (234); when she returns to the Pensionnat from her opiate-fueled visit to the park, the front door reopens to her "[a]s soundless, as unresisting, as if some propitious genius had waited

on a sesame-charm" (518). But their attendance on Lucy is fickle. One character, however, is briefly awarded a presiding Genius. Picturing Ginevra Fanshawe
as sustained by Dr. John's love, Lucy (admittedly with "overstretched nerves")
comes to believe that "Ginevra had a kind of spirit with her, empowered to
give constant strength and comfort, to gladden daylight and embalm darkness;
the best of the good genii that guard humanity curtained her with his wings,
and canopied her head with his bending form" (175). The "geniality" of Dr.
John, who figures as a Branwellesque composite—reviving presence and care-
less penfriend—in Lucy's story, is referenced fourteen times across the novel.
As object of his affections, Ginevra here becomes "a sort of heroine" for the
semi-delusional Lucy. And although much of the first part of the novel is devoted to Lucy's, initially clumsy but increasingly playful, efforts to disillusion
Dr. John of his preference for the unworthy schoolgirl, Ginevra arguably remains that heroine: vector of Lucy's bad feeling, disavowed emotional ally, and
therapeutic playmate.

In her first encounter with Ginevra, on the boat crossing the English Channel, Lucy records a striking quirk of her conversation:

"And where are you now?" I inquired.

"Oh! at—*chose*," said she.

Now Miss Ginevra Fanshawe (such was the young person's name) only
substituted the word "*chose*" in temporary oblivion of the real name. It
was a habit she had: "*chose*" came in at every turn in her conversation—
the convenient substitute for any missing word in any language she
might chance at the time to be speaking. French girls often do the
like; from them she had caught the custom. "*Chose*," however, I found,
in this instance, stood for Villette. (60–61)

Lucy's parsing here moves through five distinct stages. First, "'*chose*'" signals
"temporary oblivion": it marks a form of forgetting. Yet, secondly, this is understood as "habit": a recursive form that embeds this forgetting in a mode of
reflexive, embodied memory. Thirdly, we understand that "'*chose*'" in fact
indicates a kind of ethnographic learning, troped as infection: Ginevra has
"caught the custom." Fourthly, however, it resists translation: it can act as a
"filler" or place holder in sentences in any language. Finally, it is acknowledged
as sign: "'*chose*'" does always "stand for" something, it being the work of the
reader to identify the particular instance. In this case, it signifies the city of
Villette. But "*chose*" also references "*Villette*" as authorial name-choice. "Choseville," or "thing city," appears to have been Charlotte's first choice of designation
for Brussels, and possibly of title for the novel (556n19).[41] Ginevra's "'*chose*'" is

the trace, the scissored-off form, of the substituted title "Choseville," which is further inverted and echoed in the final title of the novel.[42] Moreover "'*chose*'," as it embeds in the English text of *Villette*, also reads as an expression of choice. Although Lucy will consistently figure her resistance to "catching [French] custom" throughout the novel, she does find here that she too has "caught" the word and transformed it to an "inward voice" directing her destination (66). In this sense Ginevra begins to teach Lucy to choose: a word for object inaugurates a capacity for self-direction and language—an "inward voice"— perhaps because, as with Klein's unplayful child Dick, "the hitherto-lacking object-relation has made its appearance" (228).[43]

Despite her ambivalence, Lucy comes to distinguish the impregnably com- placent Ginevra as preferred playmate, confessing that "if two had to share the convenience of one drinking-vessel, as sometimes happened—for instance, when we took a long walk into the country, and halted for refreshment at a farm—I always contrived that she should be my convive, and rather liked to let her take the lion's share, whether of the white beer, the sweet wine, or the new milk" (260–61). The unlikely friendship is consolidated when, after the performance for Madame Beck's fête, Ginevra forces Lucy to look at their two bodies side by side in a mirror. As she touts her obvious advantages, Lucy again figures their relationship as feeding: "I stood and let her self-love have its feast and triumph: curious to see how much it could swallow—whether it was pos- sible it could feed to satiety" (159). Always fearful of being overlooked, she is oddly satisfied by Ginevra's self-engrossed reading of their images, acknowl- edging "[a] good deal of it is true as gospel, and shrewd besides. There must be good in you, Ginevra, to speak so honestly" (161). Preferential play, fraught for Lucy, is licensed here not merely by Ginevra's robust contours, which match her laughing capacity to endure the prospect of Lucy's envy, but by her choice of a setting—the mirror's frame—which not only caters to her own narcissism but allows Lucy, relationally, to be seen. Ginevra creates a tableau of envy, only to effectively render such a response mockable. The interaction is self- constituting for Lucy in a way that chimes with Klein's accounts of analyses of envy. According to Klein, a key provocation for envy is the absence of it in the other, most often embodied in the figure of the analyst, who generates her interpretations from a position of enviable repletion and sanity. Once the patient comes to recognize their own envy analytically, that feeling gives way to a gratitude that strengthens over the course of the analysis. One of Klein's patients termed this a capacity to "experience the analytic session as a happy feed."[44]

Yet Ginevra ultimately serves Lucy best in her capacity to voice rage at the injury of displacement. Lucy's ostentatious plainness, which she claims, via Ginevra's mirror analysis, as a "chose-n" costume, betrays an antagonism that "shadows" her recurrent references to her invisibility in relationships where she is not the preferred "playmate." As she notes, the first, lost playmate Graham Bretton "knows you only as 'quiet Lucy'—'a creature inoffensive as a shadow'; he has said, and you have heard him say it: 'Lucy's disadvantages spring from over-gravity in tastes and manner—want of colour in character and costume'" (370–71). The novel avenges this slight—first ludic, then libidinal—by in turn discarding Dr. John. As in her childhood plays, Charlotte loses interest in this "genial" favorite of fortune, and takes up in his place another toy, the "little man" M. Paul (360). Her publisher, George Smith, the model for Dr. John, felt the slight, as Juliet Barker records: "What he objected to was the fact that his own character, Dr John, had almost completely dropped out of sight and that the story now pursued the growing relationship between Lucy Snowe and Monsieur Paul Emmanuel."[45] Dr. John is instead married to his preferred playmate Paulina, an outcome that George Smith found equally unsatisfying: "'She is an odd, fascinating little puss,' he had told Charlotte [. . .], but added 'crabbedly' that he was not in love with her."[46] Within the novel, however, it is Ginevra who acts out the aggression implicit in the author's shift of characterological allegiance. Forced to confront her analogous supersession in Dr. John's affections, Ginevra expresses her affront in toy terms. Applying the same imagery that Lucy had deployed to figure her childhood exclusion by Polly and Graham, she denounces rival and former suitor as an infantile couple: "'a conceited doll it is!'"; "to see [. . .] 'my son John' prohibiting excitement, etcetera—faugh! The scene was quite sickening" (299). Where Ginevra's displacement is in this instance relayed retrospectively, Lucy orchestrates a further encounter, purportedly aimed at soothing Paulina's incipient envy, at which she is present to observe Ginevra resentfully concede her relegation. Lucy has already acknowledged the power of a female staging of enraged grievance: in the actress she terms Vashti she has witnessed "what hurts become . . . immediately embodied: [. . .] a thing that can be attacked, worried down, torn in shreds. [. . .] Before calamity she is a tigress; she rends her woes, shivers them in convulsed abhorrence. [. . .] [W]icked, perhaps, she is, but also she is strong" (287). Ginevra's turn of temper in this repeat performance echoes Vashti's: "her invectives [. . .] had something venomous in them. Having found herself impotent to either charm or sting [. . .], hatred was her only resource; and this hatred she expressed in terms so unmeasured and proportion so monstrous" (356). Between Ginevra's enactments of envious rage, she confronts Lucy with the question "'Who *are* you, Miss Snowe?'" inviting Lucy in her turn to claim the mantle of Bildungsheldin: "'I am a rising character'" (342). Lucy toys with the robust and vocal Ginevra in a reiterative "play" that is revitalizing and self-constitutive.

If Dr. John's character is aggressed and abandoned in recompense for a neglect of Lucy that began in play, M. Paul's jealous recognition, like Ginevra's vocalized rage, serves to unblock her stymied Bildungsroman. M. Paul is repeatedly referred to as a "little man," the "little" functioning to encode his toy-like status. His attendant descriptors—"harsh" (371), "restive" (360), "wicked venomous" (378)—position him as another conduit for ugly feeling. In a sole instance where "little" is used adjectivally it is to highlight his negative affect. Lucy calls him "naturally a little man, of unreasonable moods," citing irritability, lack of magnanimity, and above all, an "essence of jealousy. I do not mean merely the tender jealousy of the heart, but that sterner, narrower sentiment, whose seat is in the head" (386). M. Paul's jealousy, however, is a form of notice that, like Ginevra's mirror inquisition, allows Lucy to see herself. It ensures that the apparent absence of a birthday gift from her acquires greater significance than all the feminine tokens he receives; it transforms her limited wardrobe and poor trinkets into potent articles of mysterious seduction: "This harsh little man—this pitiless censor—gathers up all your poor scattered sins of vanity, your luckless chiffon of rose-colour, your small fringe of a wreath, your small scrap of ribbon, your silly bit of lace, and calls you to account for the lot, and for each item" (371). His sustained attention converts Lucy's nebulous, play-engendered envy into an object-specific and reciprocal jealousy.

In Kleinian terms, jealousy, which seeks to snatch but not spoil, is therapeutic: "the working through of envy by means of jealousy is [. . .] an important defence against envy."[47] One afternoon, slipping into a Roe-Head reverie "gladdened, I think, by a sudden return of the golden glimmer of childhood," Lucy takes a handkerchief she has been lent by M. Paul, and "fell to playing with [it] as if it were a ball, casting it into the air and catching it as it fell" (269). The somnolent aptness of play to object—its dreamwork—is emphasized in the repetition of the word "fell." If Graham would come to diagnose, with some lexical contradiction, that Lucy's "disadvantages spring from over-gravity," her gentle casting and catching of M. Paul's toy-object, combining spring with gravitational play, epitomizes the mitigating work of their relationship. In Klein's analysis of a woman slow to admit her own envy, the patient dreamed of throwing a woolen ball up to "a young couple with whom something was very wrong."[48] Klein interprets, "the fact that this light ball never reached the couple implied that her reparation did not succeed."[49] In Lucy's case the "light ball" is intercepted: "The game was stopped by another hand than mine—a hand emerging from a paletôt-sleeve and stretched over my shoulder; it caught the extemporised plaything and bore it away with these sullen words: 'Je vois bien que vous vous moquez de moi et de mes effets'" (270). M. Paul jealously obtrudes himself into the self-enclosed field of play to insist that the "extemporised plaything" become an object of communication. Before departing for the West Indies, he installs Lucy in a "very small" house (534), replete, like the illusory home she thought she had found at La Terasse, with scaled down furnishings that are, in this case, not overdetermined objects but reparative tokens of "strong, effective goodness, that overpowered me by their proved reality" (536). Like the Kleinian toy, miniature things here lead the numbed Lucy back to the real and to feeling.[50] At their final "happy feed" together, Lucy, in turn admits her own jealousy: "Warm, jealous, and haughty, I knew not til now that my nature had such a mood" (541). Lucy's confessional impulse is this time properly addressed by therapeutic expression and recognition: "the whole history, in brief, summoned, to his confidence, rushed thither truthful, literal, ardent, bitter" (541). In terms that encapsulate the resolution of her first unsatisfactory play with Polly Home, she continues, "I was full of faults; he took them and me all home" (541).[51]

Startling Objects

Early in George Eliot's *The Mill on the Floss* (1860), the more conventional acts of childish rebellion of its Bildungsheldin Maggie Tulliver are arrestingly reconfigured in a scene of perverse play. Maggie vents rage and shame in a way with which we have become familiar across the course of this book: punishing a wooden toy.

> Th[e] attic was Maggie's favourite retreat on a wet day, when the weather was not too cold: here she fretted out all her ill-humours, and talked aloud to the worm-eaten floors and the worm-eaten shelves and the dark rafters festooned with cobwebs, and here she kept a Fetish which she punished for all her misfortunes. This was the trunk of a large wooden doll, which once stared with the roundest of eyes above the reddest of cheeks, but was now entirely defaced by a long career of vicarious suffering. Three nails driven into the head commemorated as many crises in Maggie's nine years of earthly struggle; that luxury of vengeance having been suggested to her by the picture of Jael destroying Sisera in the old Bible. The last nail had been driven in with a fiercer stroke than usual, for the Fetish on that occasion represented aunt Glegg. But immediately afterwards Maggie had reflected that if she drove many nails in, she would not be so well able to fancy that the head was hurt when she knocked it against the wall, nor to comfort it, and make believe to poultice it when her fury had abated; for even aunt Glegg would be pitiable when she had been hurt very much, and

thoroughly humiliated, so as to beg her niece's pardon. Since then, she had driven no more nails in, but had soothed herself by alternately grinding and beating the wooden head against the rough brick of the great chimneys that made two square pillars supporting the roof. That was what she did this morning on reaching the attic, sobbing all the while with a passion that expelled every other form of consciousness— even the memory of the grievance that had caused it. As at last the sobs were getting quieter and the grinding less fierce, a sudden beam of sunshine, falling through the wire lattice across the worm-eaten shelves, made her throw away the Fetish and run to the window.[52]

Maggie enacts a preemptive version of play-therapy, using a toy that is a mere battered remnant to articulate her bitter and frustrated feeling. In the Tullivers' attic, as in the later Kleinian playroom, the wooden figure allows the unac-ceptable "ill-humours" of the child to be "fretted out." She moves between inflicting "pain" on and "poulticing" the object in a cycle of aggressive and reparative play. The Fetish's symbolic capacities—to stand in for Aunt Glegg, for example—are noted, but what is dwelled on is the violent self-soothing that we are told has become a habitual practice. The "grinding and beating" of the wooden doll keep time with the rhythm of the child's violent sobs and gradually modulate them.

Maggie's brutal actions exceed the mild damage wrought by the child pup-peteer Wilhelm Meister: indeed they are not far removed from the fierce play of the minor character Quilp with his defaced wooden figurehead, its "face horribly seared by the frequent application of the red-hot poker, and further ornamented by the insertion in the tip of the nose of a tenpenny nail."[53] And the violence of the childish feeling they divulge unbalances her Bildungsroman. Some pages later, as Maggie again cries passionately in humiliated angry sor-row, Eliot describes the inaccessibility to the adult self of the intensity of child-hood envy, defiance, and grief:

> Is there any one who can recover the experience of his childhood, not merely with a memory of what he did and what happened to him, of what he liked and disliked when he was in frock and trousers, but with an intimate penetration, a revived consciousness of what he felt then— when it was so long from one Midsummer to another?—what he felt when his school fellows shut him out of their game because he would pitch the ball wrong out of mere wilfulness; or on a rainy day in the holidays when he didn't know how to amuse himself and fell from idleness into mischief, from mischief into defiance, and from defiance into sulkiness; or when his mother absolutely refused to let him have a

tailed coat that "half," although every other boy of his age had gone
into tails already? Surely if we could recall that early bitterness, and
the dim guesses, the strangely perspectiveless conception of life that
gave the bitterness its intensity, we should not pooh-pooh the griefs of
our children. (122–23)

As Eliot observes, "Every one of those keen moments has left its trace and lives
in us still, but such traces have blent themselves irrecoverably with the firmer
texture of our youth and manhood; and so it comes that we can look at the
troubles of our children with a smiling disbelief in the reality of their pain"
(122). Eliot adumbrates here a paradox, not just for adult retrospection but for
Bildung. Childish feeling is formative; its residues contribute to the finished
perspectives of adulthood. Yet this same process of maturation requires a re-
linquishment that reduces the poignant moment to teleological instance. In
order to do justice to the feelings played out in the schoolfellows' game, the
adult would need to enter it, not merely remember it. To do so, however, would
be to lose oneself in "perspectiveless conception," sacrificing the Bildungsroman's forward momentum. It is the Kleinian child therapist, of course, who
would come to "look at the troubles of our children" with a soothing absence
of "disbelief in the reality of their pain," entering into their games, and according to their feelings of "defiance," "sulkiness," and envy the recognition of
engaged play. But Eliot, even as she models this kind of attentiveness to childish
woe, feared she had risked narrative satisfaction by dallying too long in the
world of the child: "My love of the childhood scenes made me linger over
them; so that I could not develop as fully as I wished the concluding 'Book' in
which the tragedy occurs, and which I had looked forward to with much attention and premeditation from the beginning."[54]

Eliot's "love of the childhood scenes" is a problem to which criticism of the
novel repeatedly returns. The characterization of Maggie, weighted toward
infantile perception rather than maturation, is widely regarded as failing to
deliver the ethical and emotional satisfactions typically channeled by a Bil-
dungsheld. An early review in *MacMillian's Magazine* had complained that
"It is *not* right to paint *Maggie* only as she is in her strong, unsatisfied, erring
youth—and leave her there, her doubts unresolved, her passions unregulated";
another from the *Guardian* highlighted the "clear dislocation in the story,
between Maggie's girlhood and Maggie's great temptation."[55] F. R. Leavis de-
nounced *The Mill on the Floss*'s "immaturity," arguing that Eliot presents her
heroine's childishness as an object of sympathy rather than achieved understanding: "To understand immaturity would be to 'place' it, with however subtle
an implication, by relating it to mature experience."[56] Jerome Thrale mentions

"a certain disproportionate fullness in the account of the early years"; Barbara Hardy comments on the novel's failure to deliver "personal evolutions"; Gillian Beer notes that "Maggie's *Bildung* takes her only to the point where she knows that there is no place for her in her own community."[57] Others have suggested ways in which *The Mill on the Floss*'s "backward turning reverence," to requote Dames out of context, might be seen to critique or expand the category of the Bildungsroman.[58] Charlotte Goodman sees the novel as exemplifying a "male-female double *Bildungsroman*," suggesting that such versions of Bildung, which establish a childhood experience of gender equality and unity, necessarily conclude with "a turning away from mature adult experience and a reaffirmation of the childhood world in which the male and female protagonist were undivided."[59] Susan Fraiman rightly takes issue with any idealization of the novel's early scenes, highlighting the "radical discontent," "anger and resistance" of Maggie's childhood, and proposing that we "move from the perception that Maggie has trouble growing up to argue that George Eliot's text has trouble with the story of growing up and begins to call it into question."[60] Jed Esty also suggests that *The Mill on the Floss* undermines the narrative of individual progress, claiming that "[t]he novel's immaturity is neither accident nor flaw, but the necessary formal premise and thematic goal of its entire operation."[61] In rejecting the marriage plot, Esty argues, *The Mill on the Floss* "represents Maggie's childhood in and of itself, not as mere prelude to the demands of full Victorian womanhood."[62]

Eliot's undeveloped Bildungsheldin seems to exemplify Franco Moretti's distinction between the European Bildungsroman, which depends on the hero breaking with, rather than remaining faithful to, youthful impressions, and the English version, where "the most significant experiences are not those that alter but those which *confirm* the choices made by childhood 'innocence.'"[63] And Eliot's phrase "I could not develop as fully as I wished" implicitly equates her novelistic practice with broader principles of failed development exemplified in Maggie's history. But the notion that a novel might linger with the child also looks forward to Klein's reweighting of psychic development toward early childhood and its objects, in a radical rewriting of the Oedipal Bildungsroman. Maggie's "grinding and beating" of her toy emerges startlingly from a context of realist quotidian and object-oriented description, painting, as Meira Likierman would write of Klein's early case studies, "a picture of childhood sadism that is unprecedented in its ferocity, and that seems out of keeping with ordinary expectations."[64] The Fetish scene anticipates Klein's little patient Rita, who occupied her therapy session "grinding and beating" a triangular wooden block she referred to as "'a little woman'" with "a 'little hammer,' as she called another long-shaped brick."[65] Rita's brick-as-doll is a block in a doubled sense, marking an impediment in the progress of her maturation. It is comparable to Maggie's doll part-object in its solidity: there is no interior to be investigated here by the purportedly knowledge-seeking developing child described by an Edgeworth or a Goethe. Maggie has another doll, made of wax, recipient of her equally taxing love. She is described as "lavishing so many warm kisses on it that the waxen cheeks had a wasted unhealthy appearance" (68), and later holding it "topsy-turvy and crush[ing] its nose against the wood of the chair" (73).[66] As the loved-to-death toy is also aggressed, so too Maggie evinces a subsequent impulse to make reparation to the battered wooden doll remnant: an urge to "comfort [the Fetish], and make believe to poultice it when her fury had abated." Eliot makes clear that such actions are not conclusive: the attic is a site of habitual return for Maggie, and the wooden toy has endured "a long career of vicarious suffering."

Maggie's Fetish has rarely been considered primarily a toy, or even a childish object. Peter Logan reads it as an ethnographic artifact, generated by Eliot's reading in contemporary anthropology, and extrapolates contradictions between her aim of depicting a Victorian "domestic primitivism" and the imperatives of her own realist aesthetic.[67] Both Logan and Sally Shuttleworth map the Fetish scene onto Comte's framework of social development, and Shuttleworth further argues that the Fetish anticipates E. B. Tylor's analogy between the idol and the doll.[68] Brabro Norbelie suggests that it represents "the oppressive and life-denying traits in the Dodson ideology," while John Plotz uses it to illustrate a capacity of nineteenth-century portable objects to bridge the gap between fungibility and sentiment.[69] Nina Auerbach sees it as a Gothic intrusion into a world otherwise evoked with "sympathetic naturalism."[70] Its capitalized title might, alternatively, beg us to read the Fetish as Freudian supplement or Marxist commodity; its unsettling at-homeness in the wooden world of the attic as Uncanny. Yet this Fetish is wholly familiar, emphatically unsexed, and without exchange value: a mere trunk, worm eaten rather than appendaged. A "trunk" in the attic, not "in a trunk in the attic," its story lies on its "defaced" surface rather than a revealed interior. Its simultaneous inscrutability and hyper-interpretability anticipate Kafka's Odradek, favorite plaything of philosophers from Benjamin through Adorno to Butler and Agamben. Benjamin equates the creature/toy/thing Odradek, who, Kafka writes, "stays alternately in the attic, on the staircase, the corridors, and in the hall," primarily with the space of the attic, "place [. . .] of discarded, forgotten objects," and invokes the "feeling with which one approaches trunks in the attic which have been locked up for years."[71] Odradek is for Benjamin "the form which things assume in oblivion. They are distorted."[72] Maggie's doll, by contrast, is held in mind, if only at times of need, and pressed into the service of an active and expressive "distortion."

In Kleinian terms, the beating of the Fetish is an urgent communication. What counts is not what the object signifies as such, but the mechanism of projective identification it inaugurates. Over the course of the novel, the fort/da of grinding and poulticing, aggression and reparation, shifts from the toy in the attic to Maggie's relations with her fellow characters.

Maggie's violent play in the attic is preempted by a scene in which, as Mrs. Tulliver brushes out her daughter's "reluctant black crop," Maggie suddenly rushes "from under her hands," and douses her head in water "in the vindictive determination that there should be no more curls that day" (78). Her recourse, immediately afterward, to the scarcely doll-like doll is an appropriate "re-dress" for her mother's attempts to coif and costume her daughter into an object resembling her doll-like cousin Lucy.[73] In one of a number of parental conversations on the ironies of inheritance in the early part of the novel, Mrs. Tulliver compares Maggie's unruly thatch with Lucy's curls, and complains that "[i]t seems hard as my sister Deane should have that pretty child; I'm sure Lucy takes more after me nor my own child does" (61). Later she confesses of Lucy, "I can't help loving the child as if she was my own, and I'm sure she's more like *my* child than sister Deane's, for she'd allays a very poor color for one of our family, sister Deane had" (96). Maggie's assaults on her own appearance, which amplify the mortifications of genetic inheritance, are astutely interpreted by Mrs. Tulliver as an attack on her maternal self: "Folks 'ull think it's a judgment on me as I've got such a child—they'll think I've done summat wicked" (78). Maggie bastes a handed down dress and bonnet of her Aunt Glegg's with juices from the Sunday roast (115), and pouts and writhes under an "exasperating tucker," only just refraining from tearing it off (146). Her hair is a particular source of aggression. On another occasion, when querulously urged to brush it, she fetches a "large pair of scissors" and crops her black locks "in a jagged, uneven manner" (120). This "irrevocable" piece of "play" occurs soon after yet another disparaging comparison with Lucy:

> Mrs Tulliver had to look on with a silent pang while Lucy's blond curls were adjusted. It was quite unaccountable that Mrs Deane, the thinnest and sallowest of all the Miss Dodsons, should have had this child who might have been taken for Mrs Tulliver's any day. And Maggie always looked twice as dark as usual when she was by the side of Lucy. (116)

In this instance Mrs. Tulliver's reiterated complaint has shifted from reported speech to free indirect discourse, her particular view threatening to leak beyond her into third-person narration, and requiring drastic action. Maggie's preemptive attack on her appearance leaves her initially "with a sense of clearness and freedom" (120); however, in the mirror her newly unimpeded vision allows her to observe only that the repudiated part is more firmly attached than ever: "She could see clearly enough now the thing was done that it was very foolish, and that she should have to hear and think more about her hair than ever" (121). She has succeeded only in turning herself into the antithesis of the charming Lucy, an object closer to the Fetish: "What a queer thing you look," Tom tells her (120).[74]

The "queer thing" eventually retaliates by transforming her rival, Lucy, into an equally Fetish-like "unprecedented apparition" (161). The door to the parlor of Lucy's home opens to reveal "an object so startling that both Mrs Pullet and Mrs Tulliver gave a scream" (160). The narrative subsequently tracks back to account for the metamorphosis of "pink-and-white" Lucy into startling object, "with one side of her person, from her small foot to her bonnet-crown, wet and discoloured with mud, holding out two tiny blackened hands and making a very piteous face" (161). Eliot thus reverses the transformation of Maggie into "queer thing"; gradual is replaced by achieved transmutation, and phenomenon precedes explanation. Having established Lucy's defining neatness ("everything about her was neat" [117]), "natty completeness,"[75] and apparently charmed immunity to accident ("no accidents ever happened to her clothes" [146]), the narrative must pause to register that this soiled and damaged object is "no other than little Lucy" (161). Eliot's use of the noun "object" is particularly insistent in this episode, bridging the gap between two chapters, where it is reiterated with only slight variation ("object so startling" [160] becoming "the startling object" [161]). When the narrative reverts to the moment of Lucy's appearance, she has again become "so dirty an object" (165). Between these instances, however, a different sense of the term obtrudes as Eliot registers the aggression and envy that have propelled Maggie to become the agent of Lucy's first "accident." Mrs. Tulliver has ushered Maggie, Tom, and Lucy to "play out of doors," "foreseeing nothing but misbehavior" while the children remain inside (155). Maggie, who has already clumsily upset Tom's card "pagoda" (147), knocked over his glass of cowslip wine, and trodden cake into the carpet, is excluded by Tom from the all too symbolic outdoor games of tickling a fat toad and viewing a water snake. She nonetheless follows her brother and cousin, because, we are told in a sentence that might have been written by Klein, "anger and jealousy can no more bear to lose sight of their objects than love" (163). As she observes the pair, Maggie relinquishes her feeling that "she could never be cross with pretty little Lucy," a kittenish thing she has been used to "pet and make much of," and gives way to an envious sadism: "she should like to make Lucy cry, by slapping or pinching her" (162). Ultimately her "grinding and beating" here take the form of pushing "poor little pink-and-white Lucy into the cow-trodden mud" with "a fierce thrust of her small brown arm" (164).

Maggie renders the Dodson complexion that Lucy shares with Tom, earlier described as a "pink-and-white bit of masculinity" (85), unrecognizable, soiling her with mud that matches the palette of her own "brown arm."

After the muddying of Lucy, Maggie conceives that the only appropriate reparation for the transformation of her former idol to startling object is to run away with the gypsies. The escapade, which has the lineaments of the Freudian family romance,[76] resonates with an earlier "fancy" of merging with the object of her disavowed envy: "She was fond of fancying a world where the people never got any larger than children of their own age, and she made the queen of it just like Lucy with a little crown on her head and a little sceptre in her hand . . . only the queen was Maggie herself in Lucy's form" (117). She imagines herself assuming the role of gypsy queen, passing on the benefits of her relative education to her people and receiving their homage. However, her experience in the gypsy encampment instead reenacts the humiliations of the haircutting episode, providing her with numerous reflections of her appearance, not as arrested child-queen, but as "queer thing." While the gypsy mother proves indeed "really something like what she used to see in the glass before she cut her hair off" (172), the children she encounters are perceived as partial, scruffy, and menacing: "she caught sight of a small pair of bare legs sticking up, feet uppermost, by the side of a hillock; they seemed something hideously preternatural, [. . .] she was too much agitated to see the ragged clothes and the dark shaggy head attached to them." It is this type of dismembered, Fetish-like part-object with which she must resist a persistent sense of kinship: "Tom had said that her cropped hair made her look like an idiot, and it was too painful an idea to be readily forgotten" (169).

Maggie's uncertain progress along the Bildungsheldin's trajectory is accompanied by oscillations between self-beating and self-soothing. With reflexive qualms, she negotiates the mixed entitlement conferred by a developmental narrative form whose ramifications include damage to characters relegated to the status of minor. Like Lucy, Philip, the other friend of Maggie's and Tom's early years, is repeatedly referred to as an "object" in early scenes. However, if Lucy is the perfect plaything, characterized by her wax-doll complexion and "natty completeness," the disabled Philip's description recalls, in uncomfortable ways, Maggie's other toy-object, the wooden Fetish. To Tom, Philip is "simply a humpback" (233), the "hump" summoning up the "trunk" that is Maggie's misshapen plaything. His fourteen years of "suffering and sad privation" (258) further align Philip with the Fetish and its "long career of vicarious suffering." Philip is the toy that Tom inadvertently "grinds and beats" and Maggie attempts reparatively to "poultice":

> Tom was an excellent bovine lad, who ran at questionable objects in
> a truly ingenious bovine manner; but he had blundered on Philip's
> tenderest point. [. . .] Maggie [. . .] had rather a tenderness for deformed
> things; [. . .] and she was especially fond of petting objects that would
> think it very delightful to be petted by her. (251–52)

When Maggie reencounters Philip in early adulthood, she sees him as a living connection with childish feeling; "she put out her hand and looked down at the lower deformed figure before her with frank eyes, filled for the moment with nothing but the memory of her child's feelings—a memory that was always strong in her" (394). However, she fails to appreciate the distinction the narrator has early drawn between "memory *of*" and "an intimate penetration, a revived consciousness." The relationship she attempts to reenter with Philip is founded on prevarication, and the "child's feelings" she enacts with him are both pitying and punishing (poulticing and grinding). When Tom discovers their meetings and repudiates the phantasy of Philip's "puny, miserable body" uniting with a "fine girl" (448)—Fetish with doll—Maggie's rage vents itself in a self-beratement that again takes us back to her childhood attic: "Her heart bled for Philip—she went on recalling the insults that had been flung at him with so vivid a conception of what he had felt under them, that it was almost like a sharp bodily pain to her, making her beat the floor with her foot, and tighten her fingers on her palm." Yet while she assures Tom that the more he abuses Philip's warped trunk, the more she will seek to poultice it—"The deformity you insult would make me cling to him and care for him the more"—her anger gives way to an immediately repudiated consciousness "of a certain dim background of relief in the forced separation from Philip" (450–51).

In childhood, Maggie's envy of Lucy manifests, as we have seen, not just as play-aggression, but in a "fancy" of merging with the object of her disavowed bad feeling. Her adult dealings with her cousin return her to that unresolved "child's feeling," reworking her early phantasy of a protean infantile queenliness. Maggie's maturing beauty is described in fairy-tale terms: she is at last the gypsy queen "showing a queenly head above her old frocks" (388); Lucy observes that "some witchery" makes Maggie continue to "look best in shabby clothes" (480). While Lucy nonetheless retains her status as "acknowledged queen" (558) of the St. Ogg's social scene, she also colludes in the transformation of her cousin into a version of herself. When Maggie comes to visit her, Lucy dresses her like a favorite doll, attempting to "fancy" her in fine clothing before settling for pinning her own large jet brooch onto her cousin's dress (480). Where Maggie's mother formerly reprimanded her for casting off her bonnet or refusing to wear her frock, Lucy now calls her a "naughty child" for "looking as if you were ready to dress for a ball" at bedtime (495). Maggie graduates to "an object of some envy" among the women of St. Ogg's, with "several young ladies' proposing to imitate her costume" (512).

If we consider *Mill on the Floss* not as Bildungsroman but as toy story, narrating recursion rather than development, then the final sections of the novel act out a story of envy and gratitude, love, guilt, and reparation, that has been adumbrated in the object relations of the childhood scenes.[77] Maggie's capacity simultaneously to know and not to know what she does in her intimate equivocations with Philip and Lucy displays a fundamental ambivalence, which only becomes intolerable when it shifts from an unconscious realm of play to conscious articulation. Philip and Lucy, in adulthood as in childhood, are beaten and poulticed, petted and pinched. Maggie is fleetingly aware of her own envious aggression (termed by Eliot "cruel selfishness"), asking herself "why should not Lucy—why should not Philip suffer?" (582). Publicly, though, she rejects such acknowledgment, as when she tells Philip, albeit haltingly, "if I behave as if I had forgotten all about you, it is not out of envy or pride—or—or any bad feeling" (396). Knowing both the difference and the commensurability between toy story and real-world referent is for Klein "the basis of the subject's relation to the outside world and to reality in general."[78] But Maggie seems unable to remaster that flexible symbolism she demonstrated with the Fetish, whereby sadism can be relegated to the world of phantasy (played out), and real-world anxiety assuaged or tolerated. Philip observes that she is rendered anxious, to the extent of losing her capacity for play, if parallels are drawn between phantasy and reality. When he teasingly predicts that she may "carry away all the love from your cousin Lucy," Maggie is "hurt" by his words, telling him that it "is not pretty of you, to apply my nonsense to anything real." Philip comments with surprise that "it is not like you to take playfulness literally" (433).

Maggie's adult relationships reiterate the projections of her brutal play in the attic, directing aggressive envy onto fellow characters. Perhaps the dissatisfactions expressed first by Eliot and then by her critics that the novel lingers too long in childhood in part speak, not simply to the extensiveness of the childhood scenes, but to this regressive momentum, and to the precarity of Maggie's concluding reparative gestures; their failure, to recall Elizabeth Wilson's words, to "abolish sadism itself."[79] The realist novel, unlike the Dickensian object world, requires an understanding of character as person that abjures the therapeutic brutality of the toy story. Aggressed characters, successfully rounded by the realist narrator, will be understood as human casualties: victims of harm. Maggie's recuperative efforts at the novel's conclusion take the form of Anna

Freud's altruistic surrender, with the hope of self-constitution contingent on acts of self-abnegation. Yet toy stories disrupt her efforts. She battles daily, like the Brontës at play, with emotional avatars, "the old shadowy enemies that were forever slain and rising again" (644). For the Bildungsheldin, the specter of the Fetish as much as the resurrection of psychic demons undermines the attempt to embody an achieved moral plenitude. Her final, self-constituting act of reparation on the swollen waters of the Floss sees her take on the form of the punished, broken doll: with "weary, beaten face" (654), submerged by "huge fragments" of the novel's "wooden machinery" (655).

Next to wooden toys, Klein found water "the most important" medium of childish play expression, and always ensured that a "wash-basin with running water" was present in her therapy room. Her patient Erna, whom we met in Chapter 2 playing violently with Punch-like wooden figures, acted out other aggressive phantasies with water. "A small piece of paper floating in the basin was a captain whose ship had gone down." Though this paper captain was initially declared able to save himself, Erna "then tore off his head and announced: "His head's gone; now he's drowned."'[80] Like Erna's play, Quilp's demise, and Maggie's self-sacrifice, *Villette* too concludes with wreckage and drowning, attacking its own reparative ending. M. Paul, the "ugly plaything" who was at first perceived as Quilp-like: "dreadful: a mere sprite of caprice and, ubiquity: one never knew either his whim or his whereabout" (270); "harsh and strange; the low stature, the wiry make, the angles, the darkness, the manner" which had "displeased," has become "preferred [. . .] before all humanity" (542). But Charlotte Brontë, as in her childhood "plays," tires of resolved toy stories. Gratitude can form no end point; female Bildung unmoors itself from marriages of true minds. The vexed "finis" of *Villette* sees the beloved object broken beyond repair: outgrown by a narrator who has written her tale and chooses, in conclusion, to use shipwreck and its emotional lumber to play with the feelings of her audience.

Conclusion: Toy Stories

Throughout this book, the term "toy stories" has been applied to scenes and subplots within canonical works of nineteenth-century literature in which children display aggression, destructiveness, or an urge to make amends in their play that seems out of kilter with conventional nineteenth-century versions of childhood, anticipating instead the kind of fraught object relating that would eventually be disclosed by twentieth-century play-therapy. I have suggested that we might refresh our conceptions of both nineteenth-century childhood and the literary forms through which it is represented by paying attention to such moments. I have argued that key features of what is understood as the novel's development—interiorized psychology, mimetic realism, and Bildung—are redistributed to therapeutic effect in toy stories whose affective complexity remains contingent on the blunt dynamics of wooden characters, unrealistic and abruptly play-like transitions and scenarios, and regressed plotlines. But "toy story" is more familiarly understood as a form of children's tale in which the toy is the animate protagonist.[1] Over the course of the nineteenth century, this genre kept up a conversation with the novel about the child and its toys. Maggie's wooden doll, the broken Fetish that can be soothingly abused, and her other doll of wax, easily damaged; Polly Home's, Jenny Wren's, and Bertha Plummer's miniature work-boxes; the wooden soldiers of the Brontë "plays" and of Tackleton's toy shop; Lucy Snowe's dollhouse; Quilp's Punch and Tilly Slowboy's Judy: all find their counterparts in the pages of children's books that trotted alongside adult fiction, refashioning its toy stories for minors. Those "little books," which also engage with Rousseau's and Edgeworth's pedagogical theories, and their rational toys and object lessons, flip the novelistic hierarchy of person and character, offering memoirs and Bildungsromane of dolls and puppets predicated on the fantasy that toys are secretly living objects.

In other ways, too, these books speak back to, rather than simply mimic, literary depictions of child and toy. In the preface to Julie Gouraud's *Memoirs of a Doll* (1854), for example, the author begins in Rousseauian mode to extol the doll as model for the maturing child. However, here the doll's correlate is not the adult female but the man-child. The little girl prepares herself for maternity by nursing her doll, and the child is mother to the man: "Happy the man, who, seeking the companion of his life, is privileged to choose her from among those he formerly heard chat to their dolls! To him the past reveals and guarantees the future; he alone has seen his wife before he espouses her—the doll! It was himself in the past!"[2] Gouraud goes on to parody Rousseau's anxious stipulations regarding wet nursing, reminding her reader that "Plutarch tells us that he judged of the goodness of his daughter's heart, from hearing her beg her nurse to give the breast not only to the other children who played with her, but also to their dolls" (vi). And should the satire on *Émile* not be sufficiently clear, she later confesses that she "once had an idea of a fine parallel between the Memoirs of *Vermeille* and the 'Emile' of Rousseau" (ix–x). She has ultimately rejected Rousseau's model, for "Emile is only a puppet, *Vermeille* is a doll. Emile never existed, he is an impossibility: it is the conception of a diseased mind. Who ever saw an Emile? and who has not seen a doll?" (ix–x). Gouraud uses a hierarchized toy-poetics to refute conceptions of lifelike characterization that prioritize notional person over clearly depicted thing.

The *Memoirs of a Doll*, "adapted from the French by Mrs Besset" the year after *Villette* was published, is a lengthy picaresque memoir in which the narrating doll changes hands many times, experiencing life with a variety of exemplary children, both naughty and nice. In each of its episodes, which include a *Paul et Virginie*–style shipwreck and sojourn in Barbados, the doll's material constitution remains a primary focus. As her family sets out for the West Indies, Vermeille (translated as Violet in the English edition, a name that sacrifices the original's sentimental connotations) claims to be "in no fear of sea sickness," yet, like Lucy Snowe, is seized with forebodings. Where Lucy's apprehensions intimate the impending sacrifice of the novel's "little man" M. Paul, whose West-Indian sojourn commenced ominously with his departure on the *Paul et Virginie*, Violet's fears are for a self that is also an object: of being thrown into the hold like a package, and that "my head would undoubtedly have been smashed" during the wreck (140). Cast up on the island shore "my face was crystalised; I had saline stalactites hanging from my ears like ear-rings, and round my throat a necklace of the same kind: my whole person was slightly salted, which for some minutes deprived me of my usual suppleness" (144).

Later this salting preserves her from dissolution in the tropic-island climate. Violet finally expires after catching fire, leaving her memoir to be discovered, along with a will, in her wardrobe. Her remains "consisted only of a patch of wax burnt into the carpet" (169). Her demise is attributed to a young child's confusion of her material character with personhood (the very elision on which such living-doll stories rely): "On returning from a walk Miss Ellen Ainsworth, wishing to warm the feet of her cousin's doll, placed it on a chair so near the fire, that by some means [. . .] both it and the chair were upset into the fender" (168).

An abruptly picaresque children's narrative whose unrepentant brutality is predicated on the material affordances of a toy: this encapsulation of the nineteenth-century doll-memoir might equally serve for the toy stories of Erna or Dick or any of the other infants who assembled violent analogs in Klein's consultation rooms. And as in Klein's toy-work, wood becomes the ideal medium of their aggression. In *Memoirs of a London Doll* (1852), which is clearly influenced by Dickens, the doll speaks of its "birth" in the workshop of the doll-maker Sprat. Birth is here reimagined as the assemblage of dismembered parts: "little wooden legs and arms, and wooden heads without hair, and small bodies, and half legs and half arms."[3] Mrs. Sprat's "department," like Bertha Plummer's in *The Cricket on the Hearth* (1845), is "entirely that of the *eyes*," which are fitted in glass, rather than painted on wood, "for the superior class of dolls" (3). Although Sprat makes the occasional wax doll, the wooden is his specialty, and the appositeness of wood for channeling affect while deflecting harm becomes apparent as the story continues. When one of the doll's subsequent owners, a child milliner, begins to cut out clothing for her with a little friend they insist on cambric muslin underclothes "in order to be soft to the skin of such a little creature as I was" (39). The doll "could not help laughing to myself" at these Anna Freudian doll's dressmakers, "because I was made all of wood, and my skin was only the fine hard polished varnish of the celebrated Mr. Sprat. I was not quite so tender as they fancied" (39). While the premise of doll memoirs is that the wooden object conceals an animate interior, its role as a vector of "tender feeling" derives precisely from its absence of tenderness. When the London doll falls in the fire, or is mauled by a dog, its hard core is preserved and it can be repaired with a coat of varnish and a new wig. One of its adventures even sees it at a Punch show at that crucial moment, whose script we encountered in Chapter 2, when "Mr Punch declared he would have nothing to do with such a cross child, and would throw it out of the window" (94). As "Punch actually did what he had threatened, and tossed the Wooden doll out upon the heads of the crowd," the doll, too, is jostled by its mistress's pet dog "with such a jerk that he knocked me out of her arms, and I fell down among the crowd!" (94). Doll is mistaken for baby and Punch child for doll, in an explicit toy story enactment of the reciprocity that characterizes doll-Nell's relationship with Punch-like Quilp.

The puppet figures in these doll memoirs as a lower species of toy: beneath the doll in its verisimilitude, heft and capacity to serve as a proxy in family stories; the bad character counterpart to the almost human, secretly sentient doll.[4] Yet the most enduring of nineteenth-century toy stories is Pinocchio's: a tale in which the toy comes alive not merely as lively object of the child's hand and mind, but by itself transforming into a human child. Like Goethe's puppet-child Mignon, Carlo Collodi's Pinocchio is fashioned in violence and born destructive. The carpenter Master Cherry selects "a regular woodpile log" to fashion into a table leg, to be taken aback when the wood protests "Ouch! You hurt me!" Forced to wonder whether "this piece of wood [has] somehow learned to cry and complain like a little boy?" Master Cherry responds, not with sympathy for its boyish voice, but with redoubled brutality, "whacking it mercilessly against the walls of the room."[5] Its next owner, Geppetto, more responsive to its childish cries, gives it a child's shape, but wooden vindictiveness only increases when it takes anthropomorphic form. Carved a mouth, the puppet laughs and mocks its creator; crafted hands, it steals his wig; once legs are added it runs away, and when Geppetto threatens punishment, he is himself imprisoned as an abuser. Advised by the talking cricket that Disney would call Jiminy to go to school or earn an honest trade, Pinocchio flings a wooden mallet, squashing the insect against the wall.[6] The toy's relentless rebellion against paternal injunction, in human or insect form, upends the tale's phantasy of motherless procreation.

Collodi's *Pinocchio*, serialized from 1881 to 1883, overlapped the date of Klein's birth in 1882, and is the only child's tale discussed here that would likely have been read by both Klein and Anna Freud. Its German translation appeared in 1905, when Klein was raising her young children and Anna was ten years old. In the puppet's Bildung, the tensions between their eventual theories are played out in advance. The puppet's maturation into "a boy like other boys" is achieved by its eventual embrace of the domestic example.[7] Giving up an affiliation to the toy world that involved repeatedly running away—joining "wooden brothers" in the circus, or escaping to Toyland, a sinisterly seductive land of pure play, where children who seek to escape education are transformed into donkeys and sold at market—Pinocchio instead tends to the injured Geppetto, working to procure him a glass of warm milk every day and fashioning him a wheelchair. The puppet achieves normative personhood by becoming a therapeutic object. Yet so he has always been. His maturation into full humanity is as much perversely ratified by his initial free-wheeling aggression as by his education into an equivocal ethics of reciprocal reparation. The striking violence of Collodi's tale is legitimated by the notion of the puppet as wooden object that neither feels nor understands what it inflicts ("Luckily, the puppet was made of very hard wood indeed, which explains why both blades had shattered into a thousand pieces"; "wooden puppets, you see, have the advantage of falling ill only rarely and of then healing quite quickly").[8] Pinocchio's reformation is underwritten by a phantasy of omnipotence as much as development. As both toy and boy, Pinocchio represents the havoc and repair that are the twinned powers through which the toy forms the child subject.

In 1865, the year of publication of the chronologically final major novel (*Our Mutual Friend*) examined in this study, Mrs. Alfred Gatty published *Aunt Sally's Life*, a book-length version of a tale that had appeared in her collection *Aunt Judy's Letters* in 1862. Its preface promises not just the picaresque adventures of a doll refashioned for different owners and scenes, but the downward spiraling narrative of a revenant toy: "the boys have dug up mother's old doll again"; "she has been buried and dug up again three times at least."[9] As this doll is passed from hand to childish hand across generations, its burial and exhumation, both literal and figurative, serves a variety of reparative purposes. Its first little mistress plies her nurse with "grave" and "graver" questions about whether toy objects survive "the end of the world": "whether dolls, and books, and all the pretty things she liked so much, would be destroyed" (12). She eventually answers herself with a Little-Nell-esque death-driven object lesson: "This is a doll. It was once a tree, and lived in a wood. [. . .] Then came carpenters and cut it down, and made it into a doll, and (perhaps) a coffin as well. So when the doll's mistress is grown old enough to die, there will be the coffin ready for both" (13). The child's unsurprising death delivers, in what feels like a parody of Edgeworth's somewhat callous hyper-rationality, the lesson "that dolls are made of apple-wood and coffins of elm" (18). Some time later, the child's mother disinters the doll from the closet to serve a set of replacement children: her adopted nieces. On becoming a mother, the youngest niece in turn recalls "my old doll" from the "garret" (38) where it has languished, and it passes between her daughters. It is then taken up by her male children for *Practical Education*–style experimentation. Its wig is burned in a candle flame; it is "bathed in the mill-dam with a rope tied round [its] neck"; and diagnosed with a spine complaint that necessitates its being driven around in a fast carriage from which it is regularly thrown. These accidents leave it in a state similar to Maggie's Fetish: a mere "trunk": "The old stump was thrown into a rubbish closet" (58), then retrieved again "*sans* arms, *sans* legs, *sans* everything almost, but the old solid stump" (60). It is interred in the garden and then exhumed three times, recast as "a noble scarecrow" (66), enlisted in a Brontëesque trial and hanging "play," before finishing the book as an Aunt Sally, "scrubbed and painted up, and dressed and fixed on the stump of a tree for my new character" (83).

Early in the tale, as it is locked away in a "dark closet" after the death of its little mistress (19), the doll processes feelings of "ill-use" by framing an Edgeworthian counter-ethos of utility that is repeatedly invoked as the narrative proceeds: "every place is a good place if you can be of use in it" (20). Use-value becomes its principle of revivification, galvanizing the doll's many "life" changes: "being of use [. . .] was the only thing worth living for. Those words became the text-book of my life!" (23). The doll's material constitution sustains this ethos of serviceable endurance: "Wood wears out less than flesh" (8), Aunt Sally states at the beginning of her narrative. It also enables it to morph from primarily girl's to boy's toy, farewelling any Rousseauian ideal of the doll as template for adult femininity. The doll boasts that "her solidity was a match even for the boys. They might cut off her wig, scratch her cheeks, break her legs, and poke holes in her arms; but armless, legless, wigless, and scratched, she could always be repaired. New legs, new arms, new wigs, new paint, and the old stump came out as fresh as ever" (46). The "altruistic surrender" of its sacrificial dedication to usefulness, however, is prompted by a more Kleinian doll-envy. When new dolls are purchased, "Aunt Sally" acknowledges "a jealous feeling about my position in life, and the supposed superiority of others. So I wished the new dolls out of the house, [and] felt very angry" (28). Its bouts of envious feeling are primarily directed at "little Waxy" (42), a wax doll with "those eyes that opened and shut, what a trial they have been to me more than once! No matter what a doll is made of or like, if she has only eyes that open and shut, children rave about her" (41). (We might recall here Bertha Plummer's unsighted work with doll's eyes, and her envious gripping of her father's arm when he began to talk of the beauty of May Fielding's eyes.) The doll phantasizes the destruction of its rivals, channeling wounded feeling into materially specific dreams of toy abuse: "when once the elegant creatures' eyes are poked in, and their noses pinched off, and their necks have been melted white at the fire, the miserable remains of their bran-filled bodies are cared for by nobody" (45–46). Its own "good downright bodily solidity" and "good hard head [. . .] full of solid wood" offer hard "comfort" (35, 38), reminding the wooden toy of its durability and capacity to survive (indeed reverse) those changes of fashion where "wood gives way to wax, no matter how brittle it may be, or how liable to melt" and children only have eyes for blinking dolls (34). Its shift to masculine play-object is legitimized by the same envious feeling: "Not a doll that ever came into the house could rival me in general favour; no, not even Waxys with eyes that opened and shut! They might be very elegant, but wanted solidity, you see; and only let anything wanting solidity come near a boy, and you'll see how long it lasts" (45). Sally's narrative is a bizarre marriage plot, in which the doll graduates from confidant of a circle of girls to the courted favorite of little men: an enviable object of abuse.

Although the use-motivated doll's enduring desire is to serve as object lesson, even in its final incarnation given to advising children to "go home and learn Mangnall's questions, and find out where wood comes from," it comes to understand that it serves best as therapeutic object within scenarios of violent and aggressive play (8). When the boys decide to burn its wig because they have discovered how deliciously disgusting is the smell of burnt hair, the doll acknowledges that there is no rationale behind the experiment—"(here comes the reason without sense)"—just the "gleam of delight" (48). Where Edgeworth warned parents who "tremble for their furniture" of hostile childish attacks "upon inanimate objects,"[10] this doll reflects "on my broken limbs and battered frame with great comfort, for, thought I, 'I have saved my mistress's furniture, and that's something'" (57). Its repeated interment cannot but recall Esther Summerson's burial of her doll in the early pages of *Bleak House*, offering insight into the perverse comfort offered by the toy in scenarios of mimic harm. As embodied damage control, "degenerated into a sort of object of universal fun, everybody's favourite to do whatever they liked with," the doll is no longer the clearly defined topic of the object lesson, but a "sort of object" whose functionality is determined purely by the play in which it is wielded. Its physical degeneration is understood as a corollary to the child's development: a parallel anti-Bildungsroman that is equally necessary to subject formation.

Clara Bradford's *Ethel's Adventures in the Doll Country* (1880) delivers the kind of girl-child such therapeutic toys would eventually enable. Before going to bed one night, Ethel, a veteran toy destroyer, searches for a lost doll that she has recently allowed her brothers to court-martial. Nurse opines that the doll may have run away "because she cannot forgive you for punishing her."[11] As Ethel tries to sleep, she slips into "a funny train of speculation" that is clearly an extrapolation of her sadistic doll-play: phantasizing how "people would look lying in bed *asleep*, with wide-open eyes! just like great big dolls!" (3). Identifying her own open eyes with those of the ever-alert doll, she envisages a world in which humans must cooperate to close one another's eyes at night, and devises from this a form of reciprocal punishment for the brothers who have disciplined her doll. She would refuse to close her brothers' eyes: "with tears they would beseech me to relent, but I would remain firm" (4). Sliding into a dream-work whose borders are indistinguishable from the projected landscape of play, Ethel imagines she follows that archetypal novelistic protagonist the "Crusoe doll" on a journey that passes through the Toy Kingdom, before gaining admission to the Doll Country. As she travels, she is reprimanded by the toys she has incapacitated in her robust games, with the tale culminating in a lengthy trial in which the lost doll, "a poor old doll, with bandaged head, soiled pink and white dress, and only one boot on" brings its own case against its callous owner (116). The doll introduces its history by recounting its purchase by Ethel's father, "a nice, kind-looking gentleman, who handled me as carefully as though I had been a baby" (120). It has been selected, it seems, with the aim of inculcating a comparable sentiment in his daughter, for as the doll explains, as well as being "considered a great beauty, though your majesty would scarce think so now, judging by my appearance," it was "educated," and "could say in a pretty manner, 'Ma-ma—Pa-pa'" (120). If this is Rousseau's doll, modeling self-adornment and activating maternal impulse, it is, as Edgeworth declared, the kind of beguiling automaton that the child must have "sense and courage to destroy."[12]

The reproaches of what are understood to be injured toys throughout Ethel's journey into the Doll Country and lengthy trial seek to stimulate a sentimentalized guilt that she resolutely resists.[13] Marshaled along by a Rod that constantly threatens her with a whipping, Ethel reaches a spot where she can observe the arrival of hundreds of dolls at a garden party held by the Fairy Queen. Although the narrative seeks to frame these as disabled subjects, worthy of sympathy: "some without arms, or hair, and some without eyes—these were led by their companions—others had bandages round their heads to keep them together," the dolls that lead the blind fail to soften the child who phantasized torturing her brothers by leaving their doll-like eyes open (79). "Just fancy those wretched objects going to a garden party!" Ethel exclaims (79). Repeatedly she insists on maintaining the distinction between person and thing that the doll-autobiography and other enlivened-toy stories seek to dissolve, reminding herself, "It's only to be done to a doll, and dolls can't feel" (139). When the Rod tries to shame her for the toys' dilapidation, "'I shall just whip those disagreeable dolls to-morrow,' muttered Ethel, 'for coming here—showing off their forlorn condition—to excite pity, I suppose'" (83). Sentimentalization of the object is the real crime this "mutter" (incidentally the German word for mother) castigates. When the Rod then accuses her of cruelty: "'How would you like to be whipped because some one had broken your nose, and you tried to forget your troubles by going out and enjoying yourself a little?'" she blithely replies, "'Not at all, [. . .] that would be, as my papa says, adding insult to injury—but then, I am not a doll!'" (84). The emphatic "I" underlines Ethel's brisk insistence on maintaining the distinction between object and feeling subject; an understanding inculcated through her violent play. She shifts, as the trial continues, between laughter at recounts of her former sadistic toy-play and boredom as the doll details its woes. And she cuts through to the envy that underpins sentimentalized replacement doll narratives such as Aunt Sally's. When her doll claims, "Little girls have no idea what unhappiness is caused through the advent of a new doll" (161–62), she observes with proto-analytic acuity: "what an encouragement to jealousy," her commentary again relayed via a "mutter" (162). Ethel has learned through play what Klein would soon demonstrate to her infant patients with her robust toys: an imperviousness to shaming and guilt for what is clearly understood to have been, not harm, but object relating.

In these children's stories, where the dolls and puppets and toy soldiers that have been my focus across this book come to life only to meditate on the affordances of the wood and wax and cloth that constitute them, we witness the encounter between phantasy and materiality that would impel Klein's formulation of her play-technique. Children's literature exposes the workings of canonical fiction's toy stories, assisting in the formation of a wider cultural understanding that maturation is not innocence relinquished and regretted, but aggression acknowledged, and repair understood as ongoing effort rather than attainment. Children's and adult fictions across the nineteenth century registered, hand over hand, perturbations to sentimentalized narratives of developmental conduct in the interactions they depicted between children and their objects. This composite literary repository would in turn ensure that child therapy, in the following century, could introduce a recognizable cast of sadistic, envious, or shamed child characters narrating stories of fractured development through the medium of broken, cherished, and discarded toys. In the countenanced violence of these surprisingly brutal tales, the tussle between Anna Freud and Melanie Klein preemptively plays out. Toys and their children come to understand that their best use is not as domestic surrogate or educative tool, but as object of cyclical destruction and restoration, deployed to register and alleviate infantile feeling.

Acknowledgments

Much of this book was written over a period in which the usual circuits of personal and intellectual exchange were broken or rendered virtual. I am forever grateful to those whose conversation, critique, and companionship, real or mediated, sustained me as I assembled my thoughts on the therapeutic work of damage and repair.

The incisive comments and warm encouragement of many brilliant colleagues and interlocutors have helped my "wild analysis" grow into an argument, and then a manuscript. My heartfelt thanks to Ellis Avery, Nancy Armstrong, Gillian Beer, William Cohen, Guy Davidson, Rod Edmond, Sara Fernandes, John Frow, Sarah Hackenberg, Melissa Hardie, Yoon Sun Lee, Kate Lilley, Lana Lin, Deidre Lynch, Sharon Marcus, Megan Nash, Julie Park, John Plotz, Monique Rooney, Janet Sayers, Liam Semler, Nick Smith, Jim Telfer, and Katie Trumpener. Joe Litvak's exceptionally generous critical engagement during the late stages of writing has been transformative. Jan Gottwald animated my understanding of the toy model. Vivian and Sybille Smith's loving interest nurtures everything I do.

My special thanks to two people who were the making of this book. Elizabeth Wilson, ever a guiding light, enabled and invigorated my work at every turn. Her expansive, unstintingly shared erudition and energizing conversation kindled my appreciation of psychoanalysis, and crucially shaped and sharpened my thinking. Gabrielle Smith encountered both Klein and Anna Freud well before I did, during her master's studies, and inspired me, as she so often has, to understand what interested her. I treasure her gift of a set of Klein toys, and her insight into Klein's often-missed compassion.

Saven Morris and Joanne Halford at the British Psychoanalytical Society Library gave valuable assistance with my early archival research. My sincere thanks to Richard Morrison at Fordham University Press for his sustained enthusiasm for the project, to Mark Lerner for making my cover image into art, and to Eric Newman and the editorial team at Fordham for their work on the book's production.

I'm indebted to the organizers of the following conferences and colloquiums, where I found hospitable first audiences for chapters in progress: Interdisciplinary Nineteenth-Century Studies (U.S. and Europe); the Brandeis Department of English literature seminar; the Eighteenth-Century Objects symposium, Mahindra Humanities Centre; the Society for the Study of Narrative; the Interdisciplinary Nineteenth-Century Study Group, University of Sydney; the Centre for Victorian Studies, Royal Holloway; and the Novel Theory seminar, Harvard. A very early version of Chapter 4's discussion of *The Mill on the Floss* was published as "Toy Stories" in *Novel* 50 (2017): 35–55, and a good chunk of Chapter 2 appeared as "Possible Persons: Dickensian Character, Violent Play" in *PMLA* 137 (2022): 215–29.

Through every stage of writing, my home life has been my greatest good fortune. This book is for Georg Gottwald and Leo Smith: my lockdown playfellows, and my beloved objects.

Notes

Preface: A Toy Is Being Broken

1. John Locke, *Some Thoughts Concerning Education* (Mineola, NY: Dover, 2007), 31.

2. Jean-Jacques Rousseau, *Émile or On Education*, trans. Allan Bloom (London: Penguin, 1991), 90.

3. Virginia Blum, *Hide and Seek: The Child Between Psychoanalysis and Fiction* (Urbana: University of Illinois Press, 1995), 3–4. For childhood's conceptual timeline, see also Phillippe Ariès, *Centuries of Childhood: A Social History of Family Life*, trans. Robert Baldick (New York: Knopf, 1962); Ivy Pinchbeck and Margaret Hewitt, *Children in English Society*, vol. 1, *From Tudor Times to the Eighteenth Century*, and vol. 2, *From the Eighteenth-Century to the Children's Act 1948* (London: Routledge and Kegan Paul, 1969 and 1973); Lawrence Stone, *The Family, Sex and Marriage in England 1500–1800* (London: Weidenfeld and Nicolson, 1977).

4. Teresa Michals, "Experiments before Breakfast: Toys, Education and Middle-Class Childhood," in *The Nineteenth-Century Child and Consumer Culture*, ed. Dennis Denisoff (Aldershot: Ashgate, 2008), 29.

5. Michals, "Experiments before Breakfast," 30.

6. Antonia Fraser, *A History of Toys* (London: Spring Books, 1972), 90.

7. Rousseau, in the world of toys as in his politics, reversed this model, advocating a return to the primitive and simple toy and a rejection of the complex and artificial (see Chapter 1).

8. William Cowper, "Hope," *Eighteenth-Century Poetry Archive*, lines, 187–90, accessed May 2022, https://www.eighteenthcenturypoetry.org/works/o3794-w0050 .shtml. Cowper's poem is also cited by Fraser, *History of Toys*, 13.

9. To register this dominant narrative of the child is not, of course, to ignore a growing body of work which challenges its formulations. Elisabeth Thiel's

examination of what she terms "transnormative family units": those "headed by single parents, step-parents, aunts, uncles, grandparents, siblings or the state that exists [sic] in opposition to the 'natural' and 'complete' family of the husband, wife and children . . . " is only the most recent study to question a Victorian ideology "that privileged the concept of the idyllic family group." *The Fantasy of Family: Nineteenth-Century Literature and the Myth of the Domestic Ideal* (London: Routledge, 2008), 8, 9. See also John R. Gillis's groundbreaking A *World of Their Own Making: Myth, Ritual and the Quest for Family Values* (Cambridge, MA: Harvard University Press, 1996) and Karen Chase and Michael Levenson, *The Spectacle of Intimacy: A Public Life for the Victorian Family* (Princeton, NJ: Princeton University Press, 2000). Where such research questions the normative model by highlighting often class-based counter examples or analyzing the pressures of ideological formations, toy-damaging, as I have indicated, cuts across social and economic categories.

10. For work that deconstructs the figure of the child, see foundationally Jacqueline Rose, *The Case of Peter Pan, or the Impossibility of Children's Fiction* (Philadelphia: University of Pennsylvania Press, 1984); James Kincaid, *Child-Loving: The Erotic Child and Victorian Culture* (New York: Routledge, 1994); Carolyn Steedman, *Strange Dislocations: Childhood and the Idea of Interiority, 1780–1930* (Cambridge, MA: Harvard University Press, 1995); Lee Edelman, *No Future: Queer Theory and the Death Drive* (Durham, NC: Duke University Press, 2004). For a cogent critique of the impasse created by Rose's and Kincaid's early focus on "adults' instrumental use of children," and the different ways in which Steedman and Edelman address this, see Laurie Langbauer, "Marjorie Fleming and Child Authors: The Total Depravity of Inanimate Things," *Romanticism and Victorianism on the Net* 56 (November 2009), https://id.erudit.org/iderudit/1001092ar. For children's literature and the formation of versions of the child, see Martin Green, *Dreams of Adventure, Deeds of Empire* (New York: Basic Books, 1979); Joseph Bristow, *Empire Boys* (London: Routledge, 2017); Katie Trumpener, "The Making of Child Readers," in *The Cambridge History of British Romanticism*, ed. James Chandler (Cambridge: Cambridge University Press, 2009); Edel Lamb, *Reading Children in Early Modern Culture* (London: Palgrave Macmillan, 2018); Michelle Beissel Heath, *Nineteenth-Century Fictions of Childhood and the Politics of Play* (London: Routledge, 2017). Historicist work, which is attentive to the social conditions within which childhood began to be imagined, includes Thomas E. Jordan, *Victorian Childhood: Themes and Variations* (Albany: SUNY Press, 1987); Hugh Cunningham, *Children of the Poor: Representations of Childhood since the Seventeenth Century* (Oxford: Blackwell, 1991); Lionel Rose, *The Erosion of Childhood: Child Oppression in Britain 1860–1918* (London: Routledge, 1991); Priscilla Ferguson Clement, *Growing Pains: Children in the Industrial Age, 1850–1890* (New York: Twain, 1997); Andrew O'Malley, *The Making of the Modern Child: Children's Literature and Childhood in the Late Eighteenth Century* (Hove, UK: Psychology Press, 2003).

11. An exception here is Ruth Y. Jenkins's work, which considers "the relationship between Victorian children's literature, its readers and their psychic development"

using Kristevan theory. See Jenkins, *Victorian Children's Literature: Experiencing Abjection, Empathy, and the Power of Love* (London: Palgrave, 2016), 2.

12. Sally Shuttleworth, *The Mind of the Child: Child Development in Literature, Science, and Medicine, 1840–1900* (Oxford: Oxford University Press, 2010), 3.

13. Shuttleworth's coedited anthology *Embodies Selves* is a key reference work here. Jenny Bourne Taylor and Sally Shuttleworth, eds., *Embodies Selves: An Anthology of Psychological Texts 1830–1890* (Oxford: Oxford University Press, 1998). See also Rick Rylance, *Victorian Psychology and British Culture: 1850–1880* (Oxford: Oxford University Press, 2000); Jill Matus, *Shock, Memory and the Unconscious in Victorian Fiction* (Cambridge: Cambridge University Press, 2011); and Daniel Pick, *Faces of Degeneration: A European Disorder, c. 1848–1918* (Cambridge: Cambridge University Press, 1989).

14. Sharon Marcus, *Between Women: Friendship, Desire, and Marriage in Victorian England* (Princeton, NJ: Princeton University Press, 2007), 169–70.

15. Sigmund Freud, "Analysis of a Phobia in a Five-Year-Old Boy," in *Case Histories 1. "Dora" and "Little Hans*," trans. Alix and James Strachey, vol. 8, *Pelican Freud Library* (Harmondsworth, UK: Penguin, 1977), 169.

16. Freud, "Phobia in a Five-Year-Old Boy," 170. Freud, of course, meditated on the formative role of childhood experience across his oeuvre. He also turns occasionally to children's play, notably in "Creative Writers and Daydreaming" (1908) and *Beyond the Pleasure Principle* (1920), both of which I shall turn to in more detail in subsequent chapters.

17. The phrase is Anne Stiles's, whose article "Victorian Psychology and the Novel" takes a strong stand against the purported "anachronism" of applying modern psychological paradigms to Victorian literature. Attempting to counter the argument that "Freud himself came of age during the late nineteenth century," Stiles claims that literary texts should be "pair[ed]" with contemporaneous or earlier psychological studies as "we thereby gain a clearer idea of what psychological ideas the literary author might have read about or absorbed from the ambient culture." *Literature Compass* 5, no. 3 (2008): 678n1. Stiles exemplifies a mode of historicist criticism that can only understand literature as reactive. My proposal in this book is that the literary at times outstrips the scientific (or as Stiles insists of psychology, the "pseudo-scientific") in its understanding of both psychic and psychoanalytic processes.

Introduction: Child's Play

1. Melanie Klein, "The Development of a Child (1921)," in *Love, Guilt and Reparation and Other Works 1921–1945* (London: Vintage, 1998), 32. Erich appears under the pseudonym Fritz in this and other early papers.

2. Melanie Klein, *The Psycho-Analysis of Children*, trans. Alix Strachey (London: Vintage, 1997), 16.

3. Melanie Klein, "The Psychological Principles of Early Analysis (1926)," in *Love, Guilt and Reparation*, 134.

4. Klein, "Psychological Principles," 134.

5. Melanie Klein, "The Psycho-Analytic Play Technique; Its History and Significance (1955)," in *Envy and Gratitude and Other Works 1946–1963* (London: Vintage, 1997), 126.

6. Melanie Klein, *Narrative of a Child Analysis: The Conduct of the Psycho-Analysis of Children as Seen in the Treatment of a Ten-Year-Old Boy* (London: Vintage, 1998), 67.

7. Introjection was a concept first used by Klein's early mentor Ferenczi, who contrasted the paranoiac who projects negative impulses outward and the neurotic who internalizes objects from the outside world in phantasy. He correlated oral impulses with introjection and anal expulsion with projection. Freud formulated projection in relation to paranoia and to narcissistic object choice. Klein's later mentor Abraham linked the notion to the fear of losing the object in melancholia, and followed Ferenczi in connecting this to the impulse for anal expulsion. Klein's notion of part-objects arose from the understanding that, in its limited perception, the very young infant is only able to apprehend part of the object or mother, so that, for example, a bodily part rather than the whole being might become the object of cathexis. Elizabeth Bott Spillius et al., *The New Dictionary of Kleinian Thought* (London: Routledge, 2011), 374, 453–54, 434–35, 375.

8. Klein, "Play Technique," 128.

9. Klein, "Play Technique," 127.

10. Bott Spillius et al., *New Dictionary*, 63.

11. Klein, "Play Technique," 127.

12. Klein, "Play Technique," 133. Cf. "Weaning," in Klein, *Love, Guilt and Reparation*, 293–94.

13. Klein, "Play Technique," 132. Albeit significantly less grudging, this is not so far from Anna Freud's recognition that "even unintelligent children [. . .] did not fail in dream interpretation." Anna Freud, "Introduction to the Technique of the Analysis of Children (1926)," in *The Psycho-Analytical Treatment of Children: Technical Lectures and Essays*, trans. Nancy Proctor-Gregg (London: Imago Publishing, 1946), 19. Subsequent in-text references are to this edition.

14. Klein, *Narrative*, 99.

15. Klein, *Psycho-Analysis of Children*, 53.

16. Pearl King, "Background and Development of the Freud-Klein Controversies in the British Psycho-Analytical Society," in *The Freud-Klein Controversies 1941–45*, ed. Pearl King and Riccardo Steiner (London: Routledge, 1991), 18, 19.

17. Meira Likiermann, *Melanie Klein: Her Work in Context* (London: Continuum, 2001), 9.

18. Quoted in Phyllis Grosskurth, *Melanie Klein; Her World and Her Work* (London: Hodder and Stoughton, 1986), 138. Grosskurth notes that while Jones was indeed enthusiastic about Klein's work, his initial invitation to London came at her prompting (134).

19. Throughout this book, I have alternated between using "phantasy" and "fantasy" depending on context, and on whether the work of Klein or Anna

Freud is at the forefront of my discussion. The concept of phantasy is central to Klein's thinking. Sigmund Freud had used the term "unconscious phantasy" inconsistently in work that predated Klein's. She broadened phantasy's remit considerably, to encompass both the conscious and unconscious psychic processes of very small children. Klein's expanded use of the Freudian term was one of the many aspects of her work that Anna Freud and her followers resisted. Anna Freud continued to use "fantasy" in relation to the mental activities of children.

20. Patrizia Cupelloni, "Anna and Her Father," *JEP: European Journal of Psychoanalysis* (Winter/Fall 2000): 10–11, http://www.psychomedia.it/jep/number10-11/cupelloni.htm.

21. Hereafter referred to as "Analysis of Children."

22. Klein, "Symposium on Child Analysis (1927)," in *Love, Guilt and Reparation*, 139–69.

23. Meira Likiermann, "The Debate between Anna Freud and Melanie Klein: An Historical Survey," *Journal of Child Psychotherapy* 21, no. 3 (1995): 318.

24. Klein, "Symposium," 142, 167.

25. Elisabeth Young-Bruehl, "Anna Freud and Dorothy Burlingham at Hempstead [*sic*]: The Origins of Psychoanalytic Parent-Infant Observation," *Annual of Psychoanalysis* 32 (2004): 185–97.

26. Elisabeth Young-Bruehl, *Anna Freud*, 2nd ed. (New Haven, CT: Yale University Press, 2008), 221.

27. A clear and balanced appraisal of the differences between the two analysts can be found in Alex Holder, *Anna Freud, Melanie Klein, and the Psychoanalysis of Children and Adolescents* (London: Karnac, 2005).

28. Anna Freud, *The Ego and the Mechanisms of Defence*, trans. Cecil Baines (London: Hogarth Press and the Institute of Psychoanalysis, 1966), 121, 133, 140.

29. While Klein had become a naturalized British citizen by the outbreak of war, the Freuds remained refugees in London.

30. King, "Freud-Klein Controversies," 23.

31. In a careful reappraisal of the controversial discussions, which notes that Melanie Klein and Anna Freud never themselves engaged in really virulent or acrimonious criticism of one another, Luiz Eduardo Prado de Oliveira argues that the "myth" of a battle between these two innovators in child analysis served nonetheless to entrench their, and in particular Klein's, theories and to assert the importance of the child analytic field. "The Nature of the Transference between Anna Freud and Melanie Klein: Learning from the Controversies," *International Forum of Psychoanalysis* 10 (2001): 247–58.

32. Donald Winnicott, "Transitional Objects and Transitional Phenomena," in *Playing and Reality* (Abingdon, UK: Routledge, 2005), 7.

33. Donald Winnicott, "The Use of an Object and Relating through Identifications," in *Playing and Reality*, 118.

34. Klein, "Play Technique," 123.

35. Bott Spillius et al., *New Dictionary*, 25, 23, 27.

36. Subsequently retranslated as "breaking the child in." Anna Freud, *Introduction to Psychoanalysis: Lectures for Child Analysts and Teachers 1922–1935* (London: Hogarth Press and Institute of Psycho-Analysis, 1974), 7.

37. Klein, "Symposium," 150.

38. Klein, "Psychological Principles," 137.

39. Klein, "Psychological Principles," 137.

40. Klein, "Symposium," 155, 149.

41. Alternatively, Mary Jacobus characterizes Klein's interpretative facility, disturbing to other analysts (she is referring here to Lacan), as a different type of literalism: her ability to "[move] with untroubled literalness between phantasy and its objects." Jacobus, *First Things: The Maternal Imaginary in Literature, Art, and Psychoanalysis* (New York: Routledge, 1995), 129.

42. Klein, "Psychological Principles," 132, 136.

43. Klein, "Psychological Principles," 138.

44. Anna Freud, "The Theory of Child Analysis," in *Introduction to Psychoanalysis*, 173.

45. Freud, "Theory of Child Analysis," 175.

46. Freud, "Theory of Child Analysis," 174.

47. Jacqueline Rose, *The Case of Peter Pan, or the Impossibility of Children's Fiction* (Philadelphia: University of Pennsylvania Press, 1984), 60.

48. Peter Brooks, *Realist Vision* (New Haven, CT: Yale University Press, 2005), 1, 2.

49. Brooks, *Realist Vision*, 2.

50. Brooks, *Realist Vision*, 1, 5.

51. Brooks, *Realist Vision*, 3.

52. Young-Bruehl, *Anna Freud*, 50.

53. Young-Bruehl, *Anna Freud*, 50.

54. Gottfried Keller's Bildungsroman *Grüne Heinrich* (1855, revised 1879) might have provided inspiration for the name of the titular character.

55. Young-Bruehl, *Anna Freud*, 87. For a discussion of Anna Freud as writer, see Monique Vanneufville, "The theme of Writing in the Letters between Lou Andreas, Anna Freud, and Sigmund Freud," *Savoirs et Clinique* 1, no. 15 (2012): 118–27.

56. Grosskurth, *Melanie Klein*, 66. For an analysis of Klein's literary references, which span Aeschylus, Coleridge, and Henry Green, and their relationship to her theory, see Mary Jacobus, *The Poetics of Psychoanalysis: In the Wake of Klein* (Oxford: Oxford University Press, 2005), 62–87.

57. Freud, *Introduction to Psychoanalysis*, 12.

58. Sigmund Freud, "'A Child Is Being Beaten': A Contribution to the Study of the Origin of Sexual Perversions," in *An Infantile Neurosis and Other Works*, vol. 17, *Standard Edition of the Complete Psychological Works of Sigmund Freud*, ed. and trans. James Strachey (London: Vintage Books, Hogarth Press, and the Institute of Psychoanalysis, 2001), 195–96.

59. Freud, "'A Child Is Being Beaten,'" 190.

60. Freud, "'A Child Is Being Beaten,'" 191.

61. Anna Freud, "Beating Fantasies and Daydreams," in *Introduction to Psychoanalysis*, 139, 140.

62. Freud, "Beating Fantasies," 142.

63. Freud, "Beating Fantasies," 142.

64. Freud, "Beating Fantasies," 143.

65. Freud, "Beating Fantasies," 144, 145.

66. Quoted by Klein in "Psychological Principles," 135. The reference is to Freud's *History of an Infantile Neurosis (The "Wolfman")* (1918).

67. For a searing and brilliant critique of academic and public tendencies to denounce interpretative sophistication, which has implications for my discussion of Klein's reception, see Joseph Litvak, *Strange Gourmets: Sophistication, Theory, and the Novel* (Durham, NC: Duke University Press, 1997).

68. Klein, "Personification in the Play of Children (1929)," in *Love, Guilt and Reparation*, 205.

69. Carolyn Laubender, in an impressive essay on Klein's uptake within feminist theory, shows a tendency to repeat Anna Freud's literalism in her understanding of the real-world harm that the analytic play-technique risks by purportedly abrogating the authority both to delimit injury and "to select (and exclude) the always already political objects worthy of repair in the first place." Laubender's reservations are again expressed as a critique of Kleinian hyperinterpretation: she amplifies Anna Freud's insinuation in "Analysis of Children" that Klein crosses the line "from interpretation to out-and-out suggestion." Carolyn Laubender, "Beyond Repair: Interpretation, Reparation, and Melanie Klein's Clinical Play-Technique," *Studies in Gender and Sexuality* 20, no. 1 (2019): 57, 56.

70. Klein saw herself as Freud's true analytic inheritor: bold enough to develop his insights to their fullest consequences rather than merely repeat and enshrine the theories of the father. A number of commentators have understood the two child analysts to have been engaging in "sibling" rivalry over the Freudian legacy. See, for example, King and Steiner, "Freud-Klein Controversies," 28. Luiz Eduardo Prado de Oliveira argues that "between Anna Freud and Melanie Klein, there seems to have been a repressed transferential and countertransferential element" ("Nature of the Transference," 257).

71. Holder recognizes the link between Anna Freud's resistance to the notion of infant transference and her refusal to interpret: "For Klein, it is precisely the interpretation of negative transference manifestations that is of central importance, whereas Anna Freud considered them to be 'disturbing,' and did her best to reduce and weaken them as quickly as possible, i.e., without interpreting them." *Anna Freud, Melanie Klein*, 75. For Klein's also relatively limited engagement with the notion of the counter-transference, see R. D. Hinshelwood, "Melanie Klein and Countertransference: A Note on Some Archival Material," *Psychoanalysis and History* 10, no. 1 (2008): 95–113.

72. For the complexities of the term "wild analysis," coined by Sigmund Freud to denote "interpretative shooting from the hip," and deployed in different contexts as

a term of opprobrium or respect, see Roy Schaffer, "Wild Analysis," *Journal of the American Psychoanalytic Association* 33, no. 2 (1985): 281.

73. Anna Freud to Ernst Simmel, December 27, 1927. Quoted in Young-Bruehl, *Anna Freud*, 179. Anna Freud compared such brilliant and premature analytic interpretation with her own model of child therapy in "Analysis of Children." Noting that "technical precepts warn us, as you know, against interpreting dreams too early," she nonetheless acknowledges that there are instances where "we may be glad to be able to offer [the patient] an especially happy and impressive dream-interpretation. Thereby we interest him and satisfy his exacting intellectual demands—and at bottom we are doing nothing else but what the children's analyst does, when he shows a boy that he can do much cleverer tricks with a piece of string than he can himself" (16). Trump card or cat's cradle, Anna Freud's terminology cannot help converting hermeneutics into the language of play. In her essay "Envy and Gratitude (1957)," which I look at in Chapter 4, Klein provides a number of instances of patient envy of or gratitude for her virtuoso analysis. Mary Jacobus speculates that these fasten onto Klein's literary stylistics, in particular her use of "allegory, personification and punning." *Poetics of Psychoanalysis*, 71.

74. Anna Freud to Max Eitingon, October 4, 1927. Quoted in Young-Bruehl, *Anna Freud*, 179.

75. Stephen Best and Sharon Marcus, "Surface Reading: An Introduction," *Representations* 108 (Fall 2009): 3, 1. Amanda Anderson correlates such reading practice specifically with Kleinian analysis: "The structural pathology of Kleinian psychoanalysis is parallel to the systemic pathology posited by paranoid theory—or by the hermeneutics of suspicion broadly conceived—which sees power and violence as ineluctable and pervasive." *Psyche and Ethos: Moral Life After Psychology* (Oxford: Oxford University Press, 2018), 66.

76. Heather Love, "Close but not Deep: Literary Ethics and the Descriptive Turn," *New Literary History* 41, no. 2 (Spring 2010): 381.

77. Love, "Close but not Deep," 374, 375, 378–79.

78. Love, "Close but not Deep," 376.

79. In a number of seminars, Jacques Lacan acknowledged his interest in and debt to, and also attacked, the work of Klein, particularly with regards to her formulations of ego-constitution and the object. Some of the confluences and antipathies within their thinking are carefully unpacked in Amy Allen and Mari Ruti, *Critical Theory Between Klein and Lacan: A Dialogue* (London: Bloomsbury, 2019). See also Julia Barossa, ed., *The New Klein-Lacan Dialogues* (Boca Raton, FL: Routledge, 2018), especially the chapters by Lionel Bailly ("Klein-Lacan Ego," "The Object," "The Symbolic") and Roberto Ileyassoff ("The Object in Klein and Lacan").

80. Jacqueline Rose, *Why War? Psychoanalysis, Politics and the Return to Melanie Klein* (Oxford: Blackwell, 1993). The overlaps between key figures of (in particular Bloomsbury) modernist literary culture and the cast of the interwar British

Psychoanalytical Society are well established. See also Lyndsey Stonebridge, *The Destructive Element: British Psychoanalysis and Modernism* (New York: Routledge, 1998) which, like Rose's book, takes its historical cue in part from Denise Riley's groundbreaking *War in the Nursery: Theories of the Child and the Mother* (London: Virago, 1983), and Esther Sanchez-Pardo, *Cultures of the Death Drive: Melanie Klein and Modernist Melancholia* (Durham, NC: Duke University Press, 2003).

81. Jacobus, *Poetics of Psychoanalysis*, 9–10. Jacobus is much more acknowledging of the foundational importance of Klein's thinking for subsequent theorists than other post-Kleinian critics I go on to discuss here. See also her *First Things* and *Psychoanalysis and the Scene of Reading* (Oxford: Oxford University Press, 1999).

82. Carolyn Dever, *Death and the Mother from Dickens to Freud: Victorian Fiction and the Anxiety of Origins* (Cambridge: Cambridge University Press, 1998).

83. Adam Frank, *Transferential Poetics, from Poe to Warhol* (New York: Fordham University Press, 2014), 8.

84. Eve Kosofsky Sedgwick, "Melanie Klein and the Difference Affect Makes," in *The Weather in Proust*, ed. Jonathan Goldberg (Durham, NC: Duke University Press, 2011), 124, 126. Of course, Klein also put the "relations" in object relations.

85. Eve Kosofsky Sedgwick, "Paranoid Reading and Reparative Reading; or, You're so Paranoid, You Probably Think This Essay Is About You," in *Touching Feeling: Affect, Pedagogy, Performativity* (Durham, NC: Duke University Press, 2003).

86. Robyn Wiegman, "The Times We're In: Queer Feminist Criticism and the Reparative 'Turn,'" *Feminist Theory* 15, no. 1 (2014): 17, 7.

87. Barbara Johnson, *Persons and Things* (Cambridge, MA: Harvard University Press, 2008), 94–105; Carol Mavor, *Reading Boyishly: Roland Barthes, J. M. Barrie, Jacques Henri Lartigue, Marcel Proust, and D. W. Winnicott* (Durham, NC: Duke University Press, 2007), esp. 57–75; Anderson, *Psyche and Ethos*. Anderson exempts Winnicott from the latter critique.

88. Naomi Morgenstern, *Wild Child: Intensive Parenting and Posthumanist Ethics* (Minneapolis: University of Minnesota Press, 2018); David Russell, *Tact: Aesthetic Liberalism and the Essay Form in Nineteenth-Century Britain* (Princeton, NJ: Princeton University Press, 2017); Alicia Christoff, *Novel Relations: Victorian Fiction and British Psychoanalysis* (Princeton, NJ: Princeton University Press, 2019); Alison Bechdel, *Are You My Mother? A Comic Drama* (Boston: Houghton Mifflin Harcourt, 2012).

89. Kuznets's brief mention of Klein is based solely on secondary studies of her work. Lois R. Kuznets, *When Toys Come Alive: Narratives of Animation, Metamorphosis and Development* (New Haven, CT: Yale University Press, 1994), 38, 62.

90. Martha C. Nussbaum, "Winnicott on the Surprises of the Self," *The Massachusetts Review* 47, no. 2 (Summer 2006): 375.

91. Anderson, *Psyche and Ethos*, 62. Anderson twice uses the term "hinge" to describe Klein's contribution to object relations. She, like many of the critics discussed here, focuses her critique on Klein-as-formulated-by-Sedgwick, rather than on Klein's original essays.

92. Anderson, *Psyche and Ethos*, 62.

93. Mavor, *Reading Boyishly*, 122.

94. Mavor, *Reading Boyishly*, 473.

95. Mavor, *Reading Boyishly*, 123. See also Adam Phillips, *Winnicott* (London: Penguin, 2007).

96. Nussbaum, "Winnicott," 384.

97. Nussbaum, "Winnicott," 384. By contrast Bott Spillius et al. consistently refer to the depressive position as entailing an innate morality, based on psychically acknowledged guilt at the injuries inflicted on the other, both real and in phantasy. *New Dictionary*, 94.

98. Winnicott, "Use of an Object," 118. That Anna Freud's attention to the shared reality of the domestic environment underwrites the concept of object use is something that both Winnicott and his early expositor Adam Phillips acknowledge, but that seems to have been suppressed in the recent literary critical uptake of Winnicott's work. Winnicott, "Use of an Object," 54; Phillips, *Winnicott*, 44.

99. Christoff, *Novel Relations*, 209. Christoff writes of Sedgwick's previously discussed comments on the "chunky affordances" of Kleinian thought.

100. J. B. Pontalis, *Frontiers in Psychoanalysis: Between the Dream and Psychic Pain*, trans. Catherine and Phillip Cullen (London: Hogarth Press and the Institute of Psychoanalysis, 1981), 138.

101. Julie Park, *The Self and the It: Novel Objects in Eighteenth-Century England* (Stanford, CA: Stanford University Press, 2010).

102. Susan Stewart, *On Longing: Narratives of the Miniature, the Gigantic, the Souvenir, the Collection* (Durham, NC: Duke University Press, 1992); Brooks, *Realist Vision*; Daniel Tiffany, *Toy Medium: Materialism and Modern Lyric* (Berkeley: University of California Press, 2000).

103. I briefly discuss a number of thing theorists in Chapter 1. Matthew Kaiser, *The World in Play: Portraits of a Victorian Concept* (Stanford, CA: Stanford University Press, 2012).

104. William Makepeace Thackeray, *Vanity Fair: A Novel Without a Hero* (London: Penguin, 2001), 6.

105. Quoted in Michael Ragussis, *Acts of Naming: The Family Plot in Fiction* (Oxford: Oxford University Press, 1986), 36.

1. Proper Objects

1. Sigmund Freud, "Beyond the Pleasure Principle," in *Beyond the Pleasure Principle, Group Psychology and Other Works*, vol. 18, *The Standard Edition of the Complete Psychological Works of Sigmund Freud*, translated and edited by James Strachey (London: Vintage Books, Hogarth Press, and the Institute of Psycho-analysis, 2001), 14, 15. Subsequent in-text references are to this volume.

2. Jean-Jacques Rousseau, *Émile or On Education*, trans. Allan Bloom (London: Penguin, 1991), 97. Subsequent in-text references are to this edition.

3. Maria Edgeworth and Richard Lovell Edgeworth, *Practical Education* (London: J. Johnson, 1798), 1. Subsequent in-text references are to this edition.

4. Charles Baudelaire, *The Painter of Modern Life and Other Essays*, trans. Jonathan Mayne (London: Phaidon, 1964), 5.

5. Baudelaire, *Painter of Modern Life*, 5.

6. Mark Blackwell, "Introduction: The It-Narrative and Eighteenth-Century Thing Theory," in *The Secret Life of Things: Animals, Objects and It-Narratives in Eighteenth-Century England*, ed. Mark Blackwell (Lewisburg, PA: Bucknell University Press, 2007), 9, 10.

7. Lynn Festa, "The Moral Ends of Eighteenth- and Nineteenth-Century Object Narratives," in Blackwell, *The Secret Life of Things*, 314.

8. Melanie Klein, "The Psycho-Analytic Play Technique; Its History and Significance (1955)," in *Envy and Gratitude and Other Works 1946–1963* (London: Vintage, 1997), 128.

9. Festa, "Moral Ends," 315.

10. Melanie Klein, "Weaning (1936)," in *Love, Guilt and Reparation and Other Works 1921–1945* (London: Vintage, 1998), 290–305, 290, 291.

11. Klein, "Weaning," 292.

12. As Katie Trumpener observes, Rousseau is one of the first to argue that "wet-nursing weakens the state in its foundation by preventing the consolidation of the family." Trumpener argues that the banishment of the wet-nurse after 1800 "gave rise to new anxieties, with far-reaching effects on the bourgeois psyche." Katie Trumpener, *Bardic Nationalism: The Romantic Novel and the British Empire* (Princeton, NJ: Princeton University Press, 1997), 194, 195.

13. Rousseau's own confusion of part object and whole and his latent hostility toward the mother-figure resonates, despite its sophistry, with the rage of the Kleinian infant. A number of critics of Klein focus their objections around her concept of the "bad breast," reading this, with surprising literalism, as a critique of maternal capacity rather than an exposition of infant phantasy. Carol Mavor is typical here, writing "arguably, though a mother herself, Klein seems to fear the maternal." Figuring Klein's symbolic interpretation as dismemberment, Mavor in turn sees her own project as "an attempt to *unmake* [Klein's] mistake of not positively recognizing the maternal." Carol Mavor, *Reading Boyishly: Roland Barthes, J. M. Barrie, Jacques Henri Lartigue, Marcel Proust, and D. W. Winnicott* (Durham, NC: Duke University Press, 2007), 122. There is a tellingly parallel critical tendency to judge Rousseau's elevation of the maternal breast in *Émile*. His glorification of mother's milk is understood to be inconsistent with his own abandonment of his children: see, for example, Mary Jacobus, *First Things: The Maternal Imaginary in Literature, Art, and Psychoanalysis* (New York: Routledge, 1995), 211.

14. Klein, "Weaning," 293.

15. Klein, "Weaning," 294.

16. Sarah Anne Carter, "An Object Lesson, or Don't Eat the Evidence," *The Journal of the History of Childhood and Youth* 3, no. 1 (2010): 8, 11.

17. I refer here to the famous automaton of Vaucanson, also known as the "digesting duck," which caused a sensation at the French court during Rousseau's lifetime. See Jessica Riskind, "The Defecating Duck, or, the Ambiguous Origins of Artificial Life," in *Things*, ed. Bill Brown (Chicago: Chicago University Press, 2004), 99–133. For work on the automaton as Enlightenment phenomenon, see Simon Schaffer, "Enlightened Automata," in *The Sciences in Enlightenment Europe*, ed. William Clark, Jan Golinski, and Simon Schaffer (Chicago: University of Chicago Press, 1999), 125–65 and Minsoo Kang, *Sublime Dreams of Living Machines: The Automaton in the European Imagination* (Cambridge, MA: Harvard University Press, 2011).

18. Jacques Derrida, *Of Grammatology*, trans. Gayatri Spivak (Baltimore: Johns Hopkins University Press, 1976), 97–316.

19. Bill Brown regards the turn toward things to be a peculiarly twentieth-century phenomenon, speaking to the longing for "someplace of origin unmediated by the sign." Yet the quotations he assembles from Rilke ("'Only things speak to me'"), Pessoa ("'what we see of things are the things'") and Ponge ("'Ideas give me a queasy feeling, nausea, [. . .] objects in the external world, on the other hand, delight me'") all sound like Rousseau. Brown, *Things*, 1–2.

20. *Robinson Crusoe* is positioned as inaugural novel by Ian Watt, *The Rise of the Novel: Studies in Defoe, Richardson and Fielding* (Berkeley: University of California Press, 2001). This is a rank Lennard J. Davis robustly contests in *Factual Fictions: The Origins of the English Novel* (Philadelphia: University of Pennsylvania Press, 1996), 102–22.

21. In a complex analysis of Rousseau's use of Crusoe, Brian McGrath suggests that "Émile will learn from *Robinson Crusoe* to relate even to language as a tool, as if it were a thing." "Rousseau's Crusoe: Or, On Learning to Read as Not Myself," *Eighteenth-Century Fiction* 23, no. 1 (2010): 131.

22. Teresa Michals, *Books for Children, Books for Adults: Age and the Novel from Defoe to James* (Cambridge: Cambridge University Press, 2014), 41.

23. Joachim Heinrich Campe, *The New Robinson Crusoe* (London: John Stockdale, 1789), 12–18. Quoted in Michals, *Books for Children*, 46–47.

24. Michals, *Books for Children*, 46.

25. Mitzi Myers suggests that *Robinson Crusoe*'s appeal from a child's point of view" lies in the fact that (quoting G. K. Chesterton), it "'celebrates the poetry of limits [. . .]. The best thing in the book is simply the list of things saved from the wreck. The greatest of poems is an inventory.'" Mitzi Myers, "'Anecdotes from the Nursery' in Maria Edgeworth's *Practical Education* (1798): Learning from Children 'Abroad and at Home,'" *The Princeton Library Chronical* 60, no. 2 (1999): 224.

26. Michals, *Books for Children*, 56, 58.

27. See "Froebel Archive Digital Collection," University of Roehampton, London, accessed May 2022, http://urweb.roehampton.ac.uk/digital-collection /froebel-archive/. In the 1880s Richter blocks, manufactured in Germany and very successfully marketed in Britain, were used by children to construct fantasy houses,

castles, and cemeteries. As with foundational object relations psycholoanalysis, the history of the development of wooden play objects is an intertwined British/ Germanic one. See Brenda and Robert Vale, *Architecture on the Carpet: The Curious Tale of Construction Toys and the Genesis of Modern Buildings* (London: Thames and Hudson, 2013).

28. Klein, "Psycho-Analytic Play Technique," 123; Melanie Klein, *The Psycho-Analysis of Children*, trans. Alix Strachey (London: Vintage, 1997), 9.

29. To take just one example, from the "Children's Corner" section of *The Londoner*, entitled "The Doll as Teacher": "How many mothers realise what a prominent factor in a little girl's education a doll may be? Through love of her little inanimate playmate, a child may become learned in all the intricate problems of housekeeping." July 2, 1897, 7. Sharon Marcus offers an exemplary excursus of this kind, though without reference to Rousseau. *Between Women: Friendship, Desire, and Marriage in Victorian England* (Princeton, NJ: Princeton University Press, 2007).

30. Rita appears in many of Klein's papers, including her essay "Weaning."

31. Claudia Frank, *Melanie Klein in Berlin: Her First Psychoanalyses of Children*, trans. Sophie Leighton and Sue Young (London: Routledge, 2009), 117.

32. Klein, *Psycho-Analysis of Children*, 31.

33. Marilyn Butler, "Edgeworth's Stern Father: Escaping Thomas Day, 1795–1801," in *Tradition in Transition: Women Writers, Marginal Texts, and the Eighteenth-Century Canon*, ed. Alvaro Ribiero and James G. Basker (Oxford: Oxford University Press, 1996), 78.

34. Richard Lovell Edgeworth, "Preface," in *Practical Education; Or, The History of Harry and Lucy*, vol. 2, ed. Honora Sneyd Edgeworth and Richard Lovell Edgeworth (Lichfield, UK: J. Jackson, 1780), iii–v. Quoted in Myers, "'Anecdotes from the Nursery,'" 223.

35. Myers, "'Anecdotes from the Nursery,'" 223.

36. If Butler's account of the tensions between Maria and Honora is correct, then this is, rather, a fantasy of female mentoring.

37. Caroline Gonda, *Reading Daughters' Fictions 1709–1834* (Cambridge: Cambridge University Press, 1996), 206–7.

38. Myers, "'Anecdotes from the Nursery,'" 223.

39. Tony Lyons gets this categorically wrong in his article "Play and Toys in the Educational Work of Richard Lovell Edgeworth 1744–1817," attributing the authorship of the chapter to Richard Lovell. *Irish Educational Studies* 20, no. 1 (2001): 310–20.

40. In figuring the child as incipient scientist or laborer, Edgeworth diverges from the sentimental tradition that saw the destructive child as father to the impractical poet. Henry Mackenzie's *The Man of Feeling* (1771), for example, includes an anecdote of a boy whose "poetic inclination" is evident from infancy, "for his nurse will tell you, that when he was a child, he broke his rattle, to discover what it was that sounded within it; and burnt the sticks of his go-cart, because he

liked to see the sparkling of timber in the fire" (Oxford: Oxford University Press, 1987), 61.

41. Edgeworth's notion of common-sense violence as a deflection of harm here again resonates with Anna Freud, who advised "harmless explanations" of rational play subtexts over what she regarded as Klein's overly intricate interpretative performances.

42. We might recall here Freud's grandson's preference for a simple wooden reel as object of emotionally expressive play, and his refusal to "pull it along the floor behind him, for instance, and play at its being a carriage." *Beyond the Pleasure Principle*, 15.

43. Maria Edgeworth, *Moral Tales: By Maria Edgeworth; with Original Designs by Darley* (Philadelphia: Ashmead and Evans, 1865), 411. Subsequent in-text references are to this edition.

44. Klein, "Weaning," 294.

45. Carol Strauss Sotiropoulos has compared *Practical Education* with "The Good French Governess," arguing that in the fictional text Edgeworth fails to manage the swerve of readerly sympathy toward unexemplary characters, such as the undisciplined and undisciplining servant Grace. Grace's discourse of wounded feeling exposes an emotional deficit in the rationality that Madame de Rosier inculcates in the children, which has left them immune to earlier sentimental ties. "Where Words Fail: Rational Education Unravels in Maria Edgeworth's 'The Good French Governess,'" *Children's Literature in Education* 32 (2001): 305–21.

46. See, for example, Julia Douthwaite, "Experimental Child-Rearing After Rousseau: Maria Edgeworth, *Practical Education* and *Belinda*," *Irish Journal of Feminist Studies* 2 (1997): 35–56 and Annette Wheeler Cafarelli, "Rousseau and British Romanticism: Women and British Romanticism," in *Cultural Interactions in the Romantic Age: Critical Essays in Comparative Literature*, ed. Gregory Maertz (Albany: State University of New York Press, 1998), 125–56.

47. Gary Cross, *Kids' Stuff: Toys and the Changing World of American Childhood* (Cambridge, MA: Harvard University Press, 1997), 129.

48. Festa, "Moral Ends," 310, 317–18.

49. Walter Benjamin, "Russian Toys," in *Moscow Diary*, ed. Gary Smith, trans. Richard Sieburth (Cambridge, MA: Harvard University Press, 1986), 123. Gary Cross links educational toys to the growth of Arts and Crafts and argues more broadly that they "represented a 'do-it-yourself' movement on behalf of children that rose in reaction to the instant gratification of manufactured goods." *Kids' Stuff*, 137.

50. Roland Barthes, *Mythologies*, trans. Annette Lavers (London: Vintage, 1993), 54.

51. Klein, *Psycho-Analysis of Children*, 32.

52. Klein, "Psycho-Analytic Play Technique," 126.

53. Klein, *Psycho-Analysis of Children*, 16.

54. It is worth recalling here that, despite her opposition to Klein's decontextualized toy-room, Anna Freud relied similarly on "simple, unpainted

wooden toys" as advocated by Maria Montessori when she set up the Jackson nursery in Vienna in the 1930s. Elisabeth Young-Bruehl, *Anna Freud*, 2nd ed. (New Haven, CT: Yale University Press, 2008), 224.

55. Barthes, *Mythologies*, 54.

56. Catharine Macaulay, *Letters on Education. With Observations on Religious and Metaphysical Subjects. By Catharine Macaulay Graham* (London: C. Dilly, 1790), esp. 210–13. An alternative contender for the subject of Edgeworth's veiled reference is Mary Wollstonecraft, who pays particular attention to the education of Sophie in her extended critique of Rousseau in chapter 5 of A *Vindication of the Rights of Woman* (1792). Like Macaulay, she was (just) "a late female writer" by the time of *Practical Education*'s publication. Mary Wollstonecraft, *Vindication of the Rights of Woman: With Strictures on Moral and Political Subjects* (Auckland: The Floating Press, 2010), 139–64.

57. Richard Lovell Edgeworth and Maria Edgeworth, *Memoirs of Richard Lovell Edgeworth Esq. Begun by Himself and Concluded by his Daughter Maria Edgeworth* (London: Richard Bentley, 1844), 112, 164, 165.

58. For example, Douthwaite, "Experimental Child-Rearing"; Catherine Toal, "Control Experiment: Edgeworth's Critique of Rousseau's Educational Theory," in *An Uncomfortable Authority: Maria Edgeworth and her Contexts*, ed. Heidi Kaufman and Chris Fauske (Cranbury, NJ: Associated University Presses, 2004), 212–31.

59. Maria Edgeworth, *Belinda* (Oxford: Oxford University Press, 2008), 3. Subsequent in-text references are to this edition.

60. One of the maturational subplots of the novel, not pursued here despite its too overt Kleinian resonances, involves Lady Delacour's gradual reinterpretation of what she has understood to be a terminally cancerous breast as merely wounded and capable of healing—a plot development which is synchronized with the reinvigoration of her maternal feeling. My resistance to tracing this trope reflects my interest, across this book, in attending to play-therapy as praxis rather than hermeneutic. Articles that take the breast as starting point for an analysis of, in turn, Lady Delacour's wit, maternal failure, or lesbian attraction, are Jordana Rosenberg, "The Bosom of the Bourgeoisie: Edgeworth's *Belinda*," *ELH* 70, no. 2 (2003): 575–96; Leah Larson, "Breast Cancer and the 'Unnatural' Woman in Edgeworth's *Belinda*," *The Explicator* 67, no. 3 (2009): 195–98; and Ula Klein, "Bosom Friends and the Sapphic Breasts of *Belinda*," *Aphra Behn Online: Interactive Journal for Women in the Arts, 1640–1830* 3, no. 2 (2013). A more psychoanalytically inflected interpretation of the politics of the breast, focusing on *Ennui*, is Bonnie Blackwell's "War in the Nursery, 1798: The Persecuting Breast and the Melancholy Babe in Maria Edgeworth's *Ennui*," *Women's Studies* 31, no. 3 (2002): 349–97. Although the title adopts Kleinian terminology, the article makes no mention of her work.

61. Heinrich von Kleist, "On the Marionette Theatre," in *On Dolls*, ed. Kenneth Gross (London: Notting Hill Editions, 2012), 1, 3, 4–5, 7, 6.

62. In this sense, she allegorizes Edgeworth's own gradual emergence as an author of novels of affect as well as education from what was regarded by one reviewer as the

potentially pernicious "guidance of her mechanical father." *London Magazine*, June 1820. Quoted in Gonda, *Reading Daughters' Fictions*, 208.

63. Benjamin Franklin, *Experiments and Observations on Electricity, Made at Philadelphia in America, by Mr. Benjamin Franklin, and Communicated in Several Letters to Mr. P. Collinson, of London, F. R. S.* (London: E. Cave, 1751), 16–17. The link to Franklin is not fanciful. Franklin was a regular visitor, when in England, to the "Lunar Society" of Birmingham, a group of experimental enthusiasts of which Richard Lovell Edgeworth and Thomas Day were key members. Maria attended a meeting of the Lunar Society in 1799, shortly before beginning *Belinda*. James Chandler, "Edgeworth and the Lunar Enlightenment," *Eighteenth-Century Studies* 45, no. 1 (2011): 89, 92.

64. Yoon Sun Lee, "Bad Plots and Objectivity in Maria Edgeworth," *Representations* 139 (2017): 35, 36, 40.

65. E. T. A. Hoffmann, "The Sandman," in *Tales of Hoffman*, trans. R. J. Hollingdale with assistance of Stella and Vernon Humphries and Sally Hayward (London: Penguin, 1982), 106.

66. Sigmund Freud, "The 'Uncanny,'" in *An Infantile Neurosis and Other Works*. Vol. 17, *The Standard Edition of the Complete Psychological Works of Sigmund Freud*, translated and edited by James Strachey (London: Hogarth Press and The Institute of Psychoanalysis, 2001), 233. In a brilliant reading of Freud reading Hoffman, Julie Park "considers Freud as an epiphenomenon of the eighteenth-century." Her attempt to "show that the ideas and visions of the eighteenth century remain very much with us as post-Freudian subjects" resonates with this book's efforts to understand long-nineteenth-century texts and twentieth-century child analysis as on a continuum in their discernment about the psychic import of play with toy objects. *The Self and the It: Novel Objects in Eighteenth-Century England* (Stanford, CA: Stanford University Press, 2010), 190.

2. Possible Persons

1. Charles Dickens, "*The Cricket on the Hearth*: A Fairy Tale of Home," in *A Christmas Carol and Other Christmas Books* (Oxford: Oxford University Press, 2006), 180. Subsequent in-text references are to this edition.

2. Anna Freud, "Introduction to the Technique of the Analysis of Children," in *The Psycho-Analytical Treatment of Children: Technical Lectures and Essays*, trans. Nancy Proctor-Gregg (London: Imago Publishing, 1946), 34. Quoted in the Introduction.

3. A point made differently by Frances Armstrong, who reads Dot, along with *Martin Chuzzlewit*'s Ruth Pinch and *Our Mutual Friend*'s Bella Wilfer, as women involved in "making a game of housekeeping." *Dickens and the Concept of Home* (Ann Arbor, MI: UMI Research Press, 1990), 55.

4. Henry Mayhew, *London Labour and the London Poor*, vol. 3, *The London Street-Folk* (London: Griffin, Bohn, 1861), 55.

5. Mary Ann O'Farrell notes the "betraying willfulness of things" in this tale, meditating, following Thad Logan, on "the thingy nature of the Victorian parlor."

"Blindness Envy: Victorians in the Parlors of the Blind," *PMLA* (2012): 517, 514. Catherine Waters, on the other hand, reads the objects of the Peerybingle household as domestic testimonies: "Mrs Peerybingle's virtue is most clearly shown in her superintendence of the 'small snug home and the crisp fire'" and other "wifely ministrations." *Dickens and the Politics of the Family* (Cambridge: Cambridge University Press, 1997), 78.

6. G. K. Chesterton, *Appreciations and Criticisms of the Work of Charles Dickens* (London: E. P. Dutton, 1921), 63.

7. Dorothy Van Ghent, "The Dickens World: A View from Todgers's," *Sewanee Review* 58, no. 3 (1950): 420.

8. Van Ghent, "Dickens World," 426.

9. George Orwell, "Charles Dickens," in *Essays* (London: Penguin, 1994), 35–78, 74; J. Hillis Miller, *Victorian Subjects* (Durham, NC: Duke University Press, 1991), 128.

10. Herbert Sussman and Gerhard Joseph, "Prefiguring the Posthuman: Dickens and Prosthesis," *Victorian Literature and Culture* (2004), 617; Tamara Ketabgian, *The Lives of Machines: The Industrial Imaginary in Victorian Literature and Culture* (Ann Arbor: University of Michigan Press, 2011), 167.

11. Elisabeth Gitter wittily characterizes the tale as "dotted with eyes," and connects this descriptive emphasis with the Hoffmanesque delivery of "a whole box full of eyes [. . .] to Bertha so that she, a blind oculist, can give sight to the dolls she makes." Elisabeth G. Gitter, "The Blind Daughter in Dickens's 'Cricket on the Hearth,'" *Studies in English Literature, 1500–1900* 39, no. 4 (Autumn 1999): 678. Gitter lists "the dark, 'penetrating' eyes of the bespectacled Stranger; the dull, 'wandering' eyes of Caleb, the staring eyes of the dolls; the glittering, half-shut, little eye of Tackleton; the beautiful, downcast eyes of May Fielding; the 'twinkling of an eye' in which story time passes" (678).

12. My argument here touches on and departs from Ketabgian's impressive critique of the consensus that "industrial character" in the Victorian novel is "dull, wooden, and emotionally undeveloped" (*Lives of Machines*, 8). Ketabgian proposes that figures of mechanical power and force pervade the realist novel, modeling a version of affect as force-impelled and "rooted in the non-human" (167). She, too, regards such representation as prefigurative, particularly of early psychoanalytic thought, registering how "Freud consistently likens the psyche's conflict to the hydrodynamic processes of a steam engine—its energy conversion, circulation, storage and release" (165). However, whereas Ketabgian's mechanical model leaves a primarily metaphoric Freudian trace, the fictional play dynamics unfolded in this chapter are reiterated by Klein's psychoanalytic *practice*.

13. According to the Oxford English Dictionary, "under coram" means "under discipline or correction" ("Coram," def. b).

14. Charles Dickens, *Little Dorrit* (London: Penguin, 1985), 142, 143, 130.

15. Alex Woloch, *The One vs. the Many: Minor Characters and the Space of the Protagonist in the Novel* (Princeton, NJ: Princeton University Press, 2004), 125; John Frow, *Character and Person* (Oxford: Oxford University Press, 2014), 143.

16. It is worth underlining here the difference between my approach and those evident in the few critical texts that couple Dickens's novels with the work of Klein. Both Carolyn Dever's *Death and the Mother from Dickens to Freud* (Cambridge: Cambridge University Press, 1998) and Lynn Cain's *Dickens, Family, Authorship: Psychoanalytic Perspectives on Kinship and Creativity* (London: Routledge, 2016), mention Klein's work in relation to *Bleak House* in particular, though in Cain's case the references are glancing and heavily mediated by the work of Julia Kristeva. Both works focus on the Kleinian theoretical apparatus as hermeneutic key, rather than the relationship between her praxis and formal aspects of Dickens's fiction.

17. Charles Dickens, *Great Expectations* (London: Penguin, 1996), 59; Charles Dickens, *Bleak House* (London: Penguin, 1985), 70. Charles Dickens, *The Old Curiosity Shop* (London: Penguin, 2000), 274–75. Subsequent in-text references are to this edition. One of a number of examples illustrating Sally's "legal childhood" (274), the execution in question may be either a seizure of goods or an infliction of capital punishment on her dolls. Sharon Marcus's virtuoso reading of Pip as a dildo played between Miss Havisham and Estella offers an alternative (sex-) toy story for *Great Expectations'* child's play. *Between Women: Friendship, Desire, and Marriage in Victorian England* (Princeton, NJ: Princeton University Press, 2007), 167–90. The doll's burial, inexplicable in terms of Esther's character, yet rich in its psychic symbolism, has received greater critical attention than other Dickensian scenes of destructive play: however, while it has been interpreted as uncanny, transitional, as magical thinking, or as acting out a poignantly inverted maternity, its quiet violence has gone unrecognized. This reflects the widespread preference for viewing Dickens's work in Freudian and Winnicottean rather than Kleinian terms. See Dever, *Death and the Mother*, 87–88; Robyn L. Schiffman, "Wax-Work, Clock-Work, and Puppet-Shews: *Bleak House* and the Uncanny," *Dickens Studies Annual* 30 (2001): 159–71; Richard A. Currie, "Surviving Maternal Loss: Transitional Relatedness in Dickens's Esther Summerson," *Dickens Quarterly* 6, no. 2 (June 1989): 60–66; Christopher Pittard, "The Travelling Doll Wonder: Dickens, Secular Magic, and *Bleak House*," *Studies in the Novel* 48, no. 3 (Fall 2016): 279–300; and Brianna Behler, "The Doll's Gift: Ventriloquizing *Bleak House*," *Nineteenth-Century Literature* 75, no. 1 (2020): 24–49.

18. Charles Dickens, *David Copperfield* (Oxford: Oxford University Press, 2008), 12. Among Melanie Klein's papers is a cutting from the *Observer* of an article by Edwin Muir on rereading Proust, which includes a reference to *David Copperfield*. Muir suggests that, in contrast to Proust, who shows the world of Combray through a young boy's eyes, "In 'David Copperfield' Dickens describes a boy growing up, very convincingly," but only as viewed "from the outside." Edwin Muir, "The Famous Madeleine," *The Observer*, September 14, 1958, Wellcome Collection, London, accessed May 2022, https://wellcomecollection.org/works/mkfkpv8c/items. David's memory retracings are in fact quite specifically rendered in terms of the infant's gradual acquisition of visual focus (see my discussion of Klein's essay "Weaning" in Chapter 1).

19. Charles Dickens, *Hard Times*, ed. Paul Schlicke (Oxford: Oxford World's Classics, 2008), 98. Matthew Kaiser argues that Dickens's notion of ameliorative play, as exemplified by the counter examples of Louisa and Tom Gradgrind, "masks its own normalising violence." *The World in Play: Portraits of a Victorian Concept* (Stanford, CA: Stanford University Press, 2012), 31. My very different understanding of Dickens's reparative play dynamics is predicated on a recognition of the anarchic and critiquing violence that underpins the toy story.

20. Dickens, *Hard Times*, 39–44. Joseph Litvak traces a similarly paradoxical tension between Sleary-esque ludic theatricality and the evocation of psychological interiority across Dickens's fiction. *Caught in the Act: Theatricality in the Nineteenth-Century English Novel* (Berkeley: University of California Press, 1992), 109–28.

21. A not exhaustive list would include Peter Coveney, "The Child in Dickens," in *The Image of Childhood*, rev. ed. (Baltimore: Penguin, 1967), 111–61; Arthur A. Adrian, *Dickens and the Parent-Child Relationship* (Athens: Ohio University Press, 1984); Catarina Ericsson, *A Child Is a Child, You Know: the Inversion of Father and Daughter in Dickens's Novels* (Stockholm: Almqvist and Wiksell, 1986); Badro Raina, *Dickens and the Dialectic of Growth* (Madison: University of Wisconsin Press, 1986); Malcolm Andrews, *Dickens and the Grown-Up Child* (Basingstoke, UK: Macmillan, 1994); Hilary M. Schor, *Dickens and the Daughter of the House* (Cambridge: Cambridge University Press, 1999); Laura C. Berry, *The Child, the State and the Victorian Novel* (Charlottesville: University of Virginia Press, 1999), 1–92; Robert Newsome, "Fictions of Childhood," in *The Cambridge Companion to Charles Dickens*, ed. John O. Jordan (Cambridge: Cambridge University Press, 2001); the essays in Laura Peters, ed., *Dickens and Childhood: A Library of Essays on Charles Dickens* (Aldershot, UK: Ashgate, 2012); Amberyl Malkovich, *Charles Dickens and the Victorian Child: Romanticizing and Socializing the Imperfect Child* (New York: Routledge, 2013); and the essays in Peter Merchant and Catherine Waters, eds., *Dickens and the Imagined Child* (Farnham, UK: Ashgate, 2015).

22. Rosemary Bodenheimer, "Dickens and the Knowing Child," in Merchant and Waters, *Dickens and the Imagined Child*, 13.

23. Bodenheimer, "Knowing Child," 15. Bodenheimer's insistence on these characters' proper names, rather than their preferred diminutives, forces us to measure the degree to which acknowledging the woman in the child registers as a form of violation.

24. John Kucich, *Repression in Victorian Fiction: Charlotte Brontë, George Eliot, and Charles Dickens* (Berkeley: University of California Press, 1987), 219.

25. Laurie Langbauer, "Ethics and Theory: Suffering Children in Dickens, Dostoevsky, and Le Guin," *ELH* 75, no. 1 (Spring 2007): 92.

26. Lauren Byler, "Dickens's Little Women; or, Cute as the Dickens," *Victorian Literature and Culture* 41 (2013): 224.

27. Algernon Charles Swinburne, "The Greatness of Dickens," in *Charles Dickens: A Bookman Extra Number, 1914* (London: Hodder and Stoughton, 1914), 183.

28. Henry James, "Our Mutual Friend," *The Nation*, December 21, 1865, 787.

29. James, "Mutual Friend," 787.

30. The description here is Ben Moore's. "The Doll's Dressmaker Re(ad)dressed: Jenny Wren's Critique of Childhood, Femininity, and Appearance," *Victorian Literature and Culture* 44 (2016): 473. The terms of such dismissals were reiterated by John Carey in venomous cadences that echo James's: "We recall Dickens' [*sic*] affection for dwarves like Little Dorrit, who has a child's body but is really a woman. As dwarfs, they have close affinities with the modern garden gnome. [. . .] Like Dickens' plastic children, the gnome is a cheery, middle-class version of an alien and menacing species of being—the race of deities, who used to be worshipped in churches, but are now stuck in gardens, as they were before churches were thought of." Carey's adamant iconoclasm sits squarely within a nineteenth-century tradition of resistance to Dickens's miniaturized effects. John Carey, *The Violent Effigy: A Study of Dickens' Imagination* (London: Faber and Faber, 1973), 136–37.

31. Deirdre Shauna Lynch, *The Economy of Character: Novels, Market Culture, and the Business of Inner Meaning* (Chicago: University of Chicago Press, 1998), 1.

32. Lynch, *Economy of Character*, 18.

33. Woloch, *One vs. the Many*, 125, 128.

34. Woloch, *One vs. the Many*, 127.

35. Frow, *Character and Person*, 24.

36. Frow, *Character and Person*, 107, 2.

37. Toril Moi, "Rethinking Character," in *Character: Three Inquiries in Literary Studies*, by Amanda Anderson, Rita Felski, and Toril Moi (Chicago: Chicago University Press, 2019), 29.

38. Moi, "Rethinking Character," 58.

39. Frow, *Character and Person*, 2, 36.

40. Melanie Klein, *The Psycho-Analysis of Children*, trans. Alix Strachey (London: Vintage, 1997), 16.

41. The figuration of Tilly Slowboy, not as a new Crusoe, but as the notched "wooden calendar" upon which that prototypical character "marked the days" is a telling case in point. In *Martin Chuzzlewit*, Dickens classifies *Robinson Crusoe* as a children's book whose "impress" on "boyish memory" is dependent on the co-presence of the isolated central character's objects: "dog and hatchet, goat-skin cap and fowling-pieces." Charles Dickens, *Martin Chuzzlewit* (London: Penguin, 1999), 78.

42. Lynch, *Economy of Character*, 6, 12.

43. Rachel Bennet, "Punch versus Christian in *The Old Curiosity Shop*," *The Review of English Studies* 22, no. 88 (November 1971): 423–34; Paul Schlicke, *Dickens and Popular Entertainment* (London: Routledge, 2016), 125–31. Robert Leach considers Quilp to embody only "the worser parts of Punch, not, as has been argued, a new embodiment of him." *The Punch and Judy Show: History, Tradition and Meaning* (London: Batsford Academic and Educational, 1985), 68–69. For alternative considerations of Quilp as a pantomimic figure, see Edwin M. Eigner, *The Dickens Pantomime* (Berkeley: University of California Press, 1989) and

Jonathan Buckmaster, *Dickens's Clowns: Charles Dickens, Joseph Grimaldi and the Pantomime of Life* (Edinburgh: Edinburgh University Press, 2019), 145–71.

44. George Speaight, *The History of the English Puppet Theatre* (London: Robert Hale, 1990), 73. Julie Park also uses Speaight as a launching point for her analysis of eighteenth-century puppetry/fictional synergies. Park argues that "a poetics of puppetry in eighteenth-century England informed not just textual productions of narrative, but also the ability for narrative to reconstruct the human subject as a character to create and manipulate across the page." *The Self and the It: Novel Objects in Eighteenth-Century England* (Stanford, CA: Stanford University Press, 2010), 164.

45. Heinrich von Kleist, "On the Marionette Theatre," in *On Dolls*, ed. Kenneth Gross (London: Notting Hill Editions, 2012), 6.

46. Katherine Inglis has analogized character in *The Old Curiosity Shop* to a different toy model, the automaton. She takes a number of the features I have isolated here as puppet-like ("Quilp's habit of bursting from concealed niches" [14], the frozen expression of his face [15–16] and his capacity to subject "his small frame to gustative ordeals" [16]) as evidence of "mechanical affinities" that "Clockwork Quilp" is said to share with Little Nell. However, my focus on the psychic compensations of toy character leads me to concur with Bennet in understanding Quilp as belonging to the wooden toy world of the puppet theater rather than the mechanized realm of the automaton. Katherine Inglis, "Becoming Automatous: Automata in *The Old Curiosity Shop* and *Our Mutual Friend*," 19: *Interdisciplinary Studies in the Long Nineteenth Century* 6 (2008): 14, 15, 16, 13, 2, https://19.bbk.ac.uk/article/id/1726/; Bennet, "Punch versus Christian."

47. My identification of this repetition compulsion contradicts James Kincaid, who argues for the freshness of each of Quilp's acts of domestic cruelty: he "must, over and over again, come up with new tricks and new devices, new torments for his wife" to satirize the "regularity and redundancy in Kit's sit-com plot." *Annoying the Victorians* (New York: Routledge, 2013), 44.

48. Rachel Bennet suggests that the violent slapstick of Quilp's interactions shows "all the exaggeration of handheld puppets" ("Punch versus Christian," 432); however, the constant evocations of his hard, impenetrable interior imply that he is a composite figure. Beryl Gray, while acknowledging Quilp's resemblance to "a range of fairy-tale monsters or lawless vice figures, pre-eminently Punch," focuses her analysis of the woodcuts for *The Old Curiosity Shop* on a perceived animalism, which she regards as eclipsing his puppet-like qualities: "to whatever extent he owes his origin to Punch, [. . .] the source of his animality is not the puppet, whose body can only dangle 'all loose and limp and shapeless.'" Yet the puppet's brief depiction in the graveyard scene as unmotivated is in the context of its removal from public activity: it otherwise functions with a rebarbative vitality, as a supremely animated but provokingly material object. Beryl Gray, "Man and Dog: Text and Illustration in Dickens's *The Old Curiosity Shop*," in *The Lure of Illustration in the Nineteenth Century*, ed. L. Brake et al. (London: Palgrave Macmillan, 2009), 97, 98.

49. David Amigoni, *Victorian Literature* (Edinburgh: Edinburgh University Press, 2011), 49–50.

50. Kenneth Gross, *Puppet: An Essay on Uncanny Life* (Chicago: University of Chicago Press, 2011), 69.

51. Gross, *Puppet*, 70.

52. Gross, *Puppet*, 70.

53. Rosalind Crone, *Violent Victorians: Popular Entertainment in Nineteenth-Century London* (Manchester: Manchester University Press, 2012), 56.

54. Melanie Klein, "The Psycho-Analytic Play Technique; Its History and Significance (1955)," in *Envy and Gratitude and Other Works 1946–1963* (London: Vintage, 1997), 127.

55. Charles Dickens, "Letter to Mary Tyler, 6 November 1849," in *1847–1849*, vol. 5, *The British Academy/Pilgrim Edition of the Letters of Charles Dickens*, ed. Graham Storey and K. J. Fielding (Oxford: Oxford University Press, 1980), 640. The letter was written some eight years after the publication of *The Old Curiosity Shop*.

56. The harmlessness Dickens adduces here was also a key term in Anna Freud's later attack on Klein's toy therapy: "Instead of being invested with symbolic meaning [child's play] may sometimes admit of a *harmless* explanation" (*Psycho-Analytical Treatment of Children*, 29; emphasis mine). However Anna Freud infers that it is analytic interpretation which has the capacity to injure. The common ground here is perhaps an implicit belief that adult interpretation alone can warp violent play toward psychic harm.

57. Melanie Klein, "Symposium on Child Analysis (1927)," in *Love, Guilt and Reparation and Other Works 1921–1945* (London: Vintage, 1998), 150.

58. Klein, "Symposium," 150, 149.

59. Melanie Klein, "The Psychological Principles of Early Analysis (1926)," in *Love, Guilt and Reparation*, 137.

60. Klein, "Psychological Principles," 137. Compare to the Introduction.

61. Gross, *Puppet*, 69.

62. Mayhew, *London Labour*, 54–55.

63. Klein, *Psycho-Analysis of Children*, 36.

64. Klein, *Psycho-Analysis of Children*, 54.

65. Klein, *Psycho-Analysis of Children*, 54.

66. Armstrong, *Concept of Home*, 51, 50.

67. This figure will be reconceived more tragically in Louisa Gradgrind of *Hard Times*, whose playless education has left her fit only for marriage to Bounderby, and more ambivalently in the "child-wife" Dora of *David Copperfield*. Quilp also likes to figure Nell as growing up into marriage, over the body of the current Mrs. Quilp: "'To be Mrs Quilp the second, when Mrs Quilp the first is dead, sweet Nell,' said Quilp, wrinkling up his eyes and luring her towards him with his bent forefinger, 'to be my wife, my little cherry-cheeked, red-lipped wife. Say that Mrs Quilp lives five year, or only four, you'll be just the proper age for me'" (53).

68. Newsome, "Fictions of Childhood," 94.

69. Langbauer, "Ethics and Theory," 95.

70. Anna Freud, *The Ego and the Mechanisms of Defence*, trans. Cecil Baines (London: Hogarth Press and The Institute of Psychoanalysis, 1966), 134. As I noted in the Introduction, this self-erasure is understood by Anna Freud to be perversely self-constituting. In *The Old Curiosity Shop* it underpins Nell's status as central minor.

71. Freud, *Mechanisms of Defence*, 135.

72. Byler, "Dickens's Little Women," 237, 231, 239.

73. James Kincaid has been the main exponent of the abuse, particularly pedophilic, manifest in and (by his argument) enabled by Dickens's fiction. Kincaid proposes that Quilp "parodies the Nell plot; that is, he energizes that plot by setting himself up as its opposite" (*Annoying the Victorians*, 43). Catherine Robson also notes the "dangerous—and seemingly inappropriate—eroticism around the figure of Nell": a product, she speculates, of "pushing the ideal girl into the position of the abused child of the working class." *Men in Wonderland: The Lost Girlhood of the Victorian Gentleman* (Princeton, NJ: Princeton University Press, 2001). See also John A. Stoler, "Affection and Lust in The Old Curiosity Shop: Dickens and Mary—Again," *McNeese Review* 53 (1997): 90–102; Mark Spilka, "Little Nell—Revisited," *Papers of the Michigan Academy of Science, Arts, and Letters* 45 (1960): 427–37; and Michael Steig, "The Central Action of *The Old Curiosity Shop*; or, Little Nell Revisited Again," *Literature and Psychology* 13, no. 3 (Summer 1965): 163–70.

74. While this sobriquet refers to Nell's work in advertising Mrs. Jarley's waxwork show, it also highlights the malleability and vulnerability of her form. I discuss the alternative associations of wooden and wax dolls in my reading of *The Mill on the Floss* in Chapter 4 and in the Conclusion.

75. Klein, "Psycho-Analytic Play Technique," 127.

76. Dickens, *David Copperfield*, 450

77. Dickens, *David Copperfield*, 447.

78. Klein, "Psycho-Analytic Play Technique," 128; see Introduction.

79. Klein, "Psycho-Analytic Play Technique," 127.

80. Dickens, *Letters of Charles Dickens*, 5:674n5.

81. Julia Miele Rodas, "Tiny Tim, Blind Bertha, and the Resistance of Mrs Mowcher: Charles Dickens and the Uses of Disability," *Dickens Studies Annual* 34 (2004): 90.

82. Elizabeth A. Wilson, *Gut Feminism* (Durham, NC: Duke University Press, 2015), 71.

83. Wilson, *Gut Feminism*, 71.

84. Wilson, 71. See also Carolyn Laubender, "Empty Space: Creativity, Femininity, Reparation, Justice," *Free Associations: Psychoanalysis and Culture, Media, Groups, Politics* 75 (June 2019): 29.

85. Gitter, "Blind Daughter," 679, 680.

86. Gitter, 679, 675, 686. See also Rodas, "Uses of Disability," 71–78. Other critics interpret Bertha as passive object of a misguided care, rather than victim of unarticulated aggression. See Heather Tilley, *Blindness and Writing: From*

Wordsworth to Gissing (Cambridge: Cambridge University Press, 2018), 159–60; O'Farrell, "Blindness Envy," 517–18; and John Paul M. Kanwit, "'People Mutht Be Amuthed': Work, Play, and the Dickensian Disabled Child," *Dickens Studies Annual* 47 (2016): 42.

87. As Freud had observed in "Beyond the Pleasure Principle," "if a child has been told a nice story, he will insist on hearing it over and over again rather than a new one; and he will remorselessly stipulate that the repetition shall be an identical one and will correct any alterations of which the narrator may be guilty—though they may actually have been made in the hope of gaining fresh approval." Sigmund Freud, "Beyond the Pleasure Principle," in *Beyond the Pleasure Principle, Group Psychology and Other Works*, vol. 18, *The Standard Edition of the Complete Psychological Works of Sigmund Freud*, trans. and ed. James Strachey (London: Vintage Books, Hogarth Press, and the Institute of Psychoanalysis, 2001), 35

88. There is, of course, another kind of toy-work that Jenny Wren more immediately exemplifies: that of Victorian child labor. For discussions of doll-work and its relationship to exploitation in *Our Mutual Friend*, see Kanwit, "Dickensian Disabled Child" and Marah Gubar, *Artful Dodgers: Reconceiving the Golden Age of Children's Literature* (Oxford: Oxford University Press, 2009), 152–53.

89. Inglis, "Becoming Automatous," 19; Helena Michie, "'Who is this in Pain?': Scarring, Disfigurement, and Female Identity in *Bleak House* and *Our Mutual Friend*," *NOVEL: A Forum on Fiction* 22, no. 2 (Winter 1989): 209.

90. Schor, *Daughter of the House*, 198; Moore, "Doll's Dressmaker Re(ad)-dressed," 477.

91. Charles Dickens, *Our Mutual Friend* (London: Penguin, 1997), 222, 228. Subsequent in-text references are to this edition.

92. Susan Zieger argues that the queerness of Dickensian children inheres in their scrambling of the "normative temporal sequence of childhood, maturity and parenthood." She lists Jenny Wren in this context but does not include Jenny in her more detailed discussion of examples of the "wizened child damaged by market forces" that, across Dickens's oeuvre, become "a queer source of radical class and social reorganization." "Dickens's Queer Children," *Literature, Interpretation, Theory* 20, nos. 1–2 (2009): 144, 145, 146, 155.

93. Klein, *Psycho-Analysis of Children*, 34.

94. Klein, "Weaning," 294.

95. Mark M. Hennelly Jr., "'Toy Wonders' in *Our Mutual Friend* (Part One)," *Dickens Quarterly* 12, no. 2 (1995): 65.

96. Freud, *Psycho-Analytical Treatment of Children*, 10.

97. Inglis and Michie each make a version of this argument, hinged upon the term "articulation," and comparing Jenny with the taxidermist Mr. Venus. Inglis argues that "Jenny, like Venus, is an accomplished reconstituent of the human frame" ("Becoming Automatous," 20), while Michie proposes that "Jenny, like Venus, 'articulates' hidden parts" ("Scarring, Disfigurement, and Female Identity," 211). However, the wordplay here relies on their elision of Jenny's dressmaking with Mr.

Venus's "articulating" (*Our Mutual Friend*, 86) of skeletons. As Inglis subsequently acknowledges, "Jenny works principally with costume: there is no evidence" that she has a hand in making or assembling her dolls ("Becoming Automatous," 20).

3. Our Plays

1. Charlotte Brontë, *The Glass Town Saga, 1826–1832*, vol. 1, *The Early Writings of Charlotte Brontë*, ed. Christine Alexander (Oxford: Basil Blackwell, 1987), 5. Subsequent in-text references are to this volume.

2. Fannie Elizabeth Ratchford, *The Brontës' Web of Childhood* (New York: Columbia University Press, 1941), 6.

3. As Kenneth D. Brown explains, while metal toy soldiers were widely available across Europe from the beginning of the nineteenth century, "they were not popular in Britain, where such toy soldiers as were available tended in the main to be made of wood." "Modelling for War? Toy Soldiers in Late Victorian and Edwardian Britain," *Journal of Social History* 24, no. 2 (Winter 1990): 238.

4. Patrick Branwell Brontë, *The Works of Patrick Branwell Brontë*. Vol. 1, 1827–33, ed. Victor Neufeldt (London: Routledge, 1997), 138.

5. Carol Bock, "'Our Plays': The Brontë Juvenilia," in *The Cambridge Companion to the Brontës*, ed. Heather Glen (Cambridge: Cambridge University Press, 2002), 39.

6. As Robin St John Conover documents, Charlotte seems to have introduced the Genii, and she and Branwell took turns in disposing of them once they had moved to their separate collaboration, the Angria sequence. Branwell sought to eliminate these self-reflexive characters in 1832, but he then returned to them after Charlotte finally abandoned them in 1833. Robin St John Conover, "Creating Angria: Charlotte and Branwell Brontë's Collaboration," *Brontë Society Transactions* 24, no. 1 (April 1999): 22–23. The dynamics of claim and repudiation evident in the two accounts of "The Twelve," then, are reiterated in this collaborative dynamic.

7. Deborah Lutz, *The Brontë Cabinet: Three Lives in Nine Objects* (New York: Norton, 2015), 37, 2–33.

8. Kate E. Brown, "Beloved Objects: Mourning, Materiality, and Charlotte Brontë's 'Never-Ending Story'," *ELH* 65 (1998): 395, 399. Their biographer Juliet Barker does register that the Brontës' childhoods were toy-filled: that in addition to the soldiers, "they had plenty of toys. They had painted wooden alphabet blocks, a wooden lion, a toy barrel and a set of ninepins. For the girls there were wax-headed dolls with hats and frocks, a wickerwork doll's cradle, a children's tea service and even a tiny working model of an iron in brass." However, she is explicitly resistant to understanding their play, as I shall in this chapter, as a form of psychic work, sounding somewhat like Anna Freud in her insistence on the straightforwardness of play dynamics: "like any normal children, the Brontës played with their toys, gave them characters and invented stories around then." Juliet Barker, *The Brontës, Wild Genius on the Moors: The Story of a Literary Family* (New York: Pegasus, 2010), 174, 175.

9. Sigmund Freud, "Creative Writers and Daydreaming," in *Jensen's "Gradiva"*; *And Other Works*, vol. 9, *The Standard Edition of the Complete Psychological Works of Sigmund Freud*, trans. James Strachey (London: Vintage Books, Hogarth Press and the Institute of Psychoanalysis, 2001), 144.

10. Freud, "Creative Writers," 25.

11. Kenneth D. Brown notes that English children's wooden toy soldiers "usually came from Germany," since (as with child therapists) "there were very few toymakers at all in Britain" ("Modelling for War," 238). I surmised in Chapter 1 that the intertwining of British and Germanic toy culture and object relations psychoanalysis may not have been accidental.

12. Conover characterizes the relationship between the collaborators benignly, as an "intimate, intertextual working alliance," punctuated by "good natured volleys of bantering." Conover, "Creating Angria," 16, 24. As will become clear, I see the family dynamics here as more subject to envy and aggression than Conover concedes.

13. Michael Moon, *Darger's Resources* (Durham, NC: Duke University Press, 2012), 52, 53, 52.

14. Branwell Brontë, *Works*, 1:153n25.

15. Branwell Brontë, *Works*, 1:153.

16. Melanie Klein, "The Psycho-Analytic Play Technique; Its History and Significance (1955)," in *Envy and Gratitude and Other Works 1946–1963* (London: Vintage, 1997), 128.

17. Branwell Brontë, *Works*, 138–39. My emphases.

18. Moon, *Darger's Resources*, 47.

19. Meg Harris Williams, "Book Magic: Aesthetic Conflicts in Charlotte Brontë's Juvenilia," *Nineteenth-Century Literature* 42, no. 1 (June 1987): 41; Conover, "Creating Angria," 18; Bock, "'Our Plays,'" 39.

20. Charlotte Brontë, *The Professor* (London: Penguin, 1989), 37. Subsequent in-text references are to this edition.

21. Williams, "Book Magic," 30.

22. Brown, "Beloved Objects," 397.

23. Charlotte's spelling. Charlotte Brontë, "The Roe Head Journal," *Tales of Glass Town, Angria, and Gondal: Selected Writings*, ed. Christine Alexander (Oxford: Oxford University Press, 2010), 165. Subsequent in-text references are to this edition.

24. Elizabeth Gaskell, *The Letters of Mrs Gaskell*, ed. J. A. V. Chapple and Arthur Pollard (Manchester: Manchester University Press, 1997), 398. Gaskell reserved these comments for private correspondence, only mentioning the formal oddities of the juvenile archive in her biography of Charlotte Brontë (1857), where she refers to "an immense amount of manuscript, in an inconceivably small space, [. . .] written [. . .] in a hand which it is almost impossible to decipher without the aid of a magnifying glass." Elizabeth Gaskell, *The Life of Charlotte Brontë* (London: Penguin, 1997), 64.

25. Brown, "Beloved Objects," 396.

26. For the idea of juvenile complexity generally see the essays collected in *The Child Writer from Austen to Woolf*, ed. Christine Alexander and Juliet McMaster (Cambridge: Cambridge University Press, 2005) and Laurie Langbauer, *The Juvenile Tradition: Young Writers and Prolepsis, 1750–1835* (Oxford: Oxford University Press, 2016). For its application to the Brontës, see Christine Alexander, "Autobiography and Juvenilia: The Fractured Self in Charlotte Brontë's Early Manuscripts," and Victor Neufeldt, "The Child is Parent to the Author: Branwell Brontë," both in Alexander and McMaster, *Child Writer*. For the Gothic and Byronic, see Sandra M. Gilbert and Susan Gubar, *The Madwoman in the Attic: The Woman Writer and the Nineteenth-Century Literary Imagination*, 2nd ed. (New Haven, CT: Yale University Press, 2000), 248–371; and Deborah Lutz, *The Dangerous Lover: Gothic Villains, Byronism, and the Nineteenth-Century Seduction Narrative* (Athens: Ohio University Press, 2006), 48–67.

27. Examples of such diagnostic critique include Brown, who sees the juvenilia as attesting to the siblings' incomplete mourning for their two older sisters ("Beloved Objects"), and Moon, who reads Branwell's destructive poetics as evidence of possible epilepsy, as well as his phantastical investment in unreciprocating love objects (*Darger's Resources*).

28. This way of re-envisaging Charlotte's work brings it closer to the widespread understanding of Branwell's authorship. Branwell never "left" the Angrian world: his adult compositions are all framed by the context of the "plays." Moon argues that Branwell's regressive creativity is not symptomatic of individual incapacity— his "spoiled" precocity and "wasted" talent—but reflects the anxiously disabled condition of masculine youth in a century of recurrent violent conflict. For a detailed study of the Brontë juvenilia in the context of warfare, see Emma Butcher, *The Brontës and War: Fantasy and Conflict in Charlotte and Branwell Brontë's Youthful Writings* (Cham, Switzerland: Palgrave, 2019).

29. Marianne Thormählen contests any equation of the educative with Bildung for the Brontë oeuvre, arguing that whereas, "in view of the importance of education in the Brontë fiction, it might have seemed natural to discuss these works as Bildungsromane, [. . .] none of the terms offered by the relevant conceptual arsenal fits even the majority of the novels well enough to form a useful terminological implement." Thormählen understands the Brontë novels to be informed by an ethos of self-education that is distinct from "the process of maturation." *The Brontës and Education* (Cambridge: Cambridge University Press, 2007), 4.

30. Moon, *Darger's Resources*, 60.

31. Conover argues that, under the mutual influence of their collaboration, Charlotte "gives increasing weight in her stories to [. . .] civil strife," while Branwell shifts focus "from the domain of the battlefield to that of the drawing room" ("Creating Angria," 17). Her gendered conclusion that "Charlotte domesticated Branwell's narrative while he politicized hers" feels a little too neat: my suggestion is

that violent play and its narrativization enable both children to understand the domestic as a battlefield (17).

32. For the overlap between real-world events and fantastical narrative in this and other Brontë tales, see Barker, *Wild Genius*, 181–84.

33. Charlotte Brontë, "The Silver Cup: A Tale," unpublished manuscript, Oct. 1829, Houghton Library, MS Lowell 1 (5), accessed May 2022, https://iiif.lib.harvard .edu/manifests/view/drs:6131695$2i.

34. Julie-Marie Strange, "Fairy Tales of Fertility: Bodies, Sex and the Life-Cycle, c. 1750–2000," in *The Routledge History of Sex and the Body 1500 to the Present*, ed. Sarah Toulalin and Kate Fisher (Abingdon: Routledge, 2013), 300.

35. Maria Edgeworth, *The Purple Jar, and Other Tales* (London: Routledge, Warne and Routledge, 1860), 16.

36. Mary Jacobus, *First Things: The Maternal Imaginary in Literature, Art, and Psychoanalysis* (New York: Routledge, 1995), 129.

37. Melanie Klein, *Narrative of a Child Analysis: The Conduct of the Psycho-Analysis of Children as Seen in the Treatment of a Ten-Year-Old Boy* (London: Vintage, 1998), 64. Subsequent in-text references are to this edition.

38. Carolyn Laubender, "Beyond Repair: Interpretation, Reparation, and Melanie Klein's Clinical Play-Technique," *Studies in Gender and Sexuality* 20, no. 1 (2019): 59.

39. Laubender, "Beyond Repair," 59.

40. Laubender, "Beyond Repair," 59.

41. Anna Freud, "The Theory of Child Analysis," in *Introduction to Psychoanalysis: Lectures for Child Analysts and Teachers 1922–1935* (London: Hogarth Press and The Institute of Psycho-Analysis, 1974), 165.

42. Claire Harman, *Charlotte Brontë: A Fiery Heart* (Toronto: Alfred A. Knopf, 2015), 62. While the little books rather than the toy soldiers are once again the focus here, Harman represents these in toy-like terms, as props co-opted from the everyday into the world of play.

43. Emily and Anne Brontë, "Appendix A: Diary Papers," in Alexander, *Tales of Glass Town*, 485.

44. Deborah Lutz further observes a drawing of a long tress belonging to "lady Julet [*sic*]," a Gondal figure, at the side of the diary entry, "as if she is sitting next to them in the kitchen, her locks sweeping the paper" (*Brontë Cabinet*, 38).

45. Emily and Anne Brontë, "Diary Papers," 487.

46. Emily and Anne Brontë, "Diary Papers," 487.

47. Gilbert and Gubar, *Madwoman*, 258.

48. Lutz generously reads the "lack of punctuation and experimental style" as precocious: "a kind of stream-of-consciousness, a term not yet invented" (*Brontë Cabinet*, 38). Juliet Barker is stricter in her assessment, highlighting the siblings' "slap-dash writing, appalling spelling and non-existent punctuation well into their late teenage years" (*Wild Genius*, 178). Perhaps these stylistic traits, whether understood as flaws or virtues, are themselves simply material vestiges: indices of working in miniature.

49. Emily and Anne Brontë, "Diary Papers," 492.

50. Emily and Anne Brontë, "Diary Papers," 492.

51. Emily and Anne Brontë, "Diary Papers," 492–93.

52. Jan B. Gordon suspects that Anne and Emily's relationship "underwent a sea change" between the final diary entry and their deaths, prompted by Charlotte and Anne's disclosure of the identities behind the novelist's pseudonyms to Charlotte's publisher. Charlotte subsequently claimed that "Ellis Bell will not endure to be alluded to under any appellation than the nom de plume. I committed a grand error in betraying her identity." Jan B. Gordon, "Gossip, Diary, Letter, Text: Anne Brontë's Narrative Tenant and the Problematic of the Gothic Sequel," *ELH* 51, no. 4 (Winter 1984): 739, 744n22.

53. Klein's term for the pedagogic influences she believed pressed Anna Freud's analytic work into the service "of the repressing faculties." Melanie Klein, "Symposium on Child Analysis (1927)," in *Love, Guilt and Reparation and Other Works 1921–1945* (London: Vintage, 1998); see the Introduction.

54. Charlotte Brontë, "Farewell to Angria," in Alexander, *Tales of Glass Town*, 314.

55. Brontë, "Farewell to Angria," 314.

56. Emily Brontë, *Wuthering Heights*, ed. Richard J. Dunn (New York: Norton, 2003), 29.

57. Brontë, *Wuthering Heights*, 29, 30.

58. Brontë, *Wuthering Heights*, 30.

59. Brontë, *Wuthering Heights*, 30.

60. Brontë, *Wuthering Heights*, 30.

61. Anne Brontë, *Agnes Grey* (Oxford: Oxford World's Classics, 1988), 34.

62. Brontë, *Agnes Grey*, 28.

63. Brontë, *Agnes Grey*, 9.

64. Cates Baldridge makes a very different, more effectively Anna Freudian argument for the failure of Bildung in *Agnes Grey*, referencing what he terms "the soul-sculpting hearth." Baldridge suggests that Agnes's bourgeois domestic education proves so comprehensive that there is no room for maturation or improvement over the course of the novel. He argues that a Victorian "rigid, unconditional belief in the middle class hearth's nearly exclusive responsibility for molding—and its unmatched ability to mold—a child into a virtuous adult poses [problems] for character development, especially in the context of a *Bildungsroman*. [. . .] The bourgeois heroine must go forth from her parents' house essentially completed, thereby short-circuiting any chance for genuine character development and rendering the idea of a *Bildungsroman* all but impossible." "'Agnes Grey': Brontë's 'Bildungsroman' That Isn't," *The Journal of Narrative Technique* 23, no. 1 (Winter 1993): 33, 32–33. In my reading the hearth exerts a different anti-maturational pull, as site of regression rather than achieved formation.

65. J. Hillis Miller, "*Wuthering Heights*: Repetition and the Uncanny," in *Fiction and Repetition: Seven English Novels* (Cambridge, MA: Harvard University Press, 1982), 42–72; Katherine Hallemeier, "Anne Brontë's Shameful *Agnes Grey*," *Victorian*

Literature and Culture 41 (2013): 251; Catherine Paula Han, "The Myth of Anne Brontë," *Brontë Studies* 42, no. 1 (2017): 50.

66. Marianne Thormählen, "Introduction," in *The Brontës in Context*, ed. Marianne Thormählen (Cambridge: Cambridge University Press, 2012), 3.

67. Beth Newman, "Big Sister," *Victorian Review* 42, no. 2 (Fall 2016): 259. For critique of Charlotte's actual editing of her sisters' novels and poems, see Irene Wiltshire, "Speech in *Wuthering Heights*: Joseph's Dialect and Charlotte's Emendations," *Brontë Studies Journal* 30, no. 1 (2005): 19–29; and Robert Inglesfield, "Introduction," *Agnes Grey*, xi. An exception to the negative trend is Carol Bock, who regards the prefaces as displaying "a savvy ability to purvey constructed identities for her sisters," and argues that "we are indebted to this admittedly needy yet pushy older sister, who energetically prodded Emily into publishing and facilitated Anne's career as well." Carol A. Bock, "Authorship, the Brontës, and 'Fraser's Magazine': 'Coming Forward' as an Author in Early Victorian England," *Victorian Literature and Culture* 19, no. 2 (2001): 255, 263.

68. Charlotte Brontë, "To Sydney Dobell, 8 December 1850," reprinted in Emily Brontë, *Wuthering Heights*, 306.

69. Sydney Dobell, "*Palladium*, September 1850," reprinted in Emily Brontë, *Wuthering Heights*, 295.

70. Charlotte Brontë, "Biographical Notice of Ellis and Acton Bell (1850)," reprinted in Emily Brontë, *Wuthering Heights*, 309.

71. Brontë, "Biographical Notice," 308.

72. Brontë, "Biographical Notice," 312, 311.

73. Brontë, "Biographical Notice," 307.

74. Anna Freud, "Introduction to the Technique of the Analysis of Children (1926)" *The Psycho-Analytical Treatment of Children: Technical Lectures and Essays*, trans. Nancy Proctor-Gregg (London: Imago Publishing, 1946), 29.

75. Brontë, "Biographical Notice," 311, 310.

76. Charlotte Brontë, "Editor's Preface to the New Edition of *Wuthering Heights* (1850)," reprinted in Emily Brontë, *Wuthering Heights*, 313, 315, 316.

77. Brontë, "Editor's Preface," 313, 316.

78. Brontë, "Biographical Notice," 307.

79. Brontë, "Editor's Preface," 316.

80. Brontë, "Farewell to Angria," 314.

81. Robert Keefe, *Charlotte Brontë's World of Death* (Austin: University of Texas Press, 1979), 77; Stevie Davies, "'Three Distinct and Unconnected Tales': *The Professor, Agnes Grey* and *Wuthering Heights*," in Glen, *Cambridge Companion*, 77.

82. William Cohen, *Embodied: Victorian Literature and the Senses* (Minneapolis: University of Minnesota Press, 2009), 40.

83. Heather Glen, ed., "Introduction," in Charlotte Brontë, *The Professor*, 7.

84. See for example Davies, "Unconnected Tales," 74, 76, 80. William Cohen notes the temptation to read *The Professor* as a channeling of "erotic blockage into fiction" (*Embodied*, 40). Historicist approaches instead use the negative affect the

novel provokes and enshrines as a way to understand its perverse memorability, figuring it as a window into Victorian understandings of scientistic surveillance, the sensing body, or the phrenological gaze. See Sally Shuttleworth, *Charlotte Brontë and Victorian Psychology* (Cambridge: Cambridge University Press, 1996), 124–47; Cohen, *Embodied*, 40–64; Nicholas Dames, *Amnesiac Selves: Nostalgia, Forgetting, and British Fiction, 1810–1870* (Oxford: Oxford University Press, 2001), 102–12.

85. Terry Eagleton, *Myths of Power: A Marxist Study of the Brontës* (London: Macmillan, 1975), 34; Keefe, *World of Death*, 77; Barker, *Wild Genius*, 591.

86. This is, of course, Jane Eyre's passionate self-description.

87. Manuscript studies have revealed that Charlotte's original title for the novel was *The Master*. See Janet Butler, "Charlotte Brontë's Manuscripts: Two Sketches and Her Holograph Preface to *The Professor*," *Studies in Bibliography* 40 (1987): 203.

88. Cohen, *Embodied*, 43.

89. Dames suggests that "Crimsworth usually compels submission through a phrenologically tinged gaze that at once exposes his students and masks himself" (*Amnesiac Selves*, 109). Shuttleworth proposes that "phrenology [. . .] supplies the validating authority for his judgments" (*Victorian Psychology*, 133). Cohen convincingly contests the tendency to trace "the line of influence from psychological science to literary work," arguing instead for the particular and primary ways in which Brontë's literary imagination renders interiority (*Embodied*, 44–45). Beth Tressler also critiques the "alliance of her novels with [phrenological] theories" and instead understands Charlotte's opus (though without reference to *The Professor*) as mocking and inverting nineteenth-century psychology. "Illegible Minds: Charlotte Brontë's Early Writings and the Psychology of Moral Management in *Jane Eyre* and *Villette*," *Studies in the Novel* 47, no. 1 (Spring 2015): 1.

90. In *Wuthering Heights* Heathcliff's repugnance for Isabella Linton is similarly depicted as a repudiation of the waxen doll: "You'd hear of odd things, if I lived alone with that mawkish, waxen face." Like the Kleinian child, Heathcliff phantasizes beating the toy object into the real: "painting on its white the colours of the rainbow, and turning the blue eyes black, every day or two." Brontë, *Wuthering Heights*, 84.

91. Indeed, the phrenological discourse that informs the novel might be adduced to this same thesis, with the narrator's aggressive reading of the bumpy features of hard-surfaced characters substituting for the child's beating of wooden toy heads: both acts of sadism against domestic avatars.

92. Cohen, *Embodied*, 49–51.

93. Glen understands Crimsworth as embodying Charlotte Brontë's critique of the Victorian ethos of self-help. "Introduction," 9–11.

94. Anna Freud, "Beating Fantasies and Daydreams," in *Introduction to Psychoanalysis*, 142. Subsequent in-text references are to this edition.

95. Dare one ask whether these associations were sublimated in Anna Freud's later allegiance to therapy as pedagogy?

4. Bildung Blocks

1. Johann Wolfgang Goethe, *Wilhelm Meister's Apprenticeship*, trans. Eleanor Grove (Leipzig: Tauchniz, 1873), 13. Subsequent in-text references are to this edition.

2. Maria Edgeworth and Richard Lovell Edgeworth, *Practical Education* (London: J. Johnson, 1798), 1–2. See Chapter 1.

3. In an alternative interpretation of the Oedipal synergies between Wilhelm's childhood and adult play, Katie Trumpener observes that the puppet theater "was erected between the legs of a table—thus perhaps already taking on associations which will reach consummation in his later sexual and theatrical involvement with Marianne." "Actors, Puppets, *Girls*: Little Women and the Collective Bildungsroman," in *The Bildungsroman: Form and Transformations*, ed. John Frow, Melissa Hardie, and Vanessa Smith, special issue, *Textual Practice* 34, no. 12 (2020): 1913.

4. Stefanie Bach, "Musical Gypsies and Anti-Classical Aesthetics: The Romantic Reception of Goethe's Mignon Character in Brentano's *Die mehreren Wehmüller und ungarische Nationalgesichter*," in *Music and Literature in German Romanticism*, ed. Siobhán Donovan and Robin Elliott (Suffolk, UK: Camden House/Boydell and Brewer, 2004), 111.

5. As noted in Chapter 2, the eighteenth-century Punch was a marionette.

6. Sperata's reparative impulse is further mimicked and inverted by the history of the book in which Mignon came to life. In *Wilhelm Meister's Theatrical Mission*, the belatedly discovered first version of the novel, Mignon is spared death: it is only in the final version that the aggression that underpins the relationship between "real" child and toy avatar becomes manifest in her brutal destruction. Johann Wolfgang Goethe, *Wilhelm Meister's Theatrical Mission*, trans. Gregory A. Page (New York: Brentano, 1913).

7. Bach, "Musical Gypsies and Anti-Classical Aesthetics," 111; Terence Cave, *Mignon's Afterlives: Crossing Cultures from Goethe to the Twenty-First Century* (Oxford: Oxford University Press, 2011), 6; Marc Redfield, *Phantom Formations: Aesthetic Ideology and the Bildungsroman* (Ithaca, NY: Cornell University Press, 1996), 89.

8. Redfield, *Phantom Formations*, 90–91.

9. Redfield, 91.

10. Carolyn Steedman, *Strange Dislocations: Childhood and the Idea of Human Interiority, 1780–1930* (Cambridge, MA: Harvard University Press, 1995), 156–57, 96, 5.

11. Michael Bell, *Open Secrets: Literature, Education and Authority from J. J. Rousseau to J. M. Coetzee* (Oxford: Oxford University Press, 2007), 105, 90.

12. Redfield, *Phantom Formations*, 91.

13. Melanie Klein, "The Psychological Principles of Early Analysis (1926)," in *Love, Guilt and Reparation and Other Works 1921–1945* (London: Vintage, 1998), 137.

14. Alternative interpretations of what Elisha Cohn terms the "anti-developmental stakes" (42) of nineteenth-century female Bildungsromane include her *Still Life: Suspended Development in the Victorian Novel* (Oxford: Oxford University Press, 2016) and Stephanie Insley Hershinow's *Born Yesterday: Inexperience and the Early Realist Novel* (Baltimore: Johns Hopkins University Press, 2019). Cohn is interested in

states of suspension or reverie that halt forward momentum; Hershinow focuses on inexperience through the figure of the female novice.

15. Christopher Lane, *Hatred and Civility: The Anti-Social Life in Victorian England* (New York: Columbia University Press, 2004), 86, 87.

16. I want at the outset to distinguish my recognition, in this chapter, of Lucy's envious aggression from the valorization of anger that Elisha Cohn has censured in twentieth-century interpretations of *Villette*. Cohn suggests that, in rewriting Lucy's "cynicism [. . .] and hostility" as proto-feminist critique, such scholarship "recruit[s] to the novel as a whole [a] critical stance often, if not wholly, unavailable to Lucy herself." Cohn chooses instead to hold her focus on "the novel's recourse to moments of unconsciousness, helplessness, and non-reflectiveness" (*Still Life*, 33). The models of envy and therapeutic play that are my analytic correlates here obviate such an either/or, allowing for attention to both aggression and the unconscious.

17. Gretchen Braun summarizes this position, observing that *Villette* "draws upon the established narrative forms of the marriage plot [. . .] and the male ambition plot [. . .]. But it disappoints the reader who expects the steady progress and satisfying closure common to these models." Gretchen Braun, "'A Great Break in the Common Course of Confession': Narrating Loss in Charlotte Brontë's *Villette*," *ELH* 78, no. 1 (Spring 2011): 196.

18. Charlotte Brontë, *Villette* (London: Penguin, 2004), 28. Subsequent in-text references are to this edition.

19. Melanie Klein, *The Psycho-Analysis of Children*, trans. Alix Strachey (London: Vintage, 1997), 35.

20. Klein, *Psycho-Analysis of Children*, 53.

21. Figured as "little woman" and "queer" child, Polly has shades of both Jenny Wren and Little Nell (20, 21). Her stabbing needle recalls Jenny's scissors; when Graham lifts her, toy-like, into the air she responds with a similarly phrased sense of injury to Jenny's: "'I wonder what you would think of me if I were to treat you in that way, lifting you with my hand' (raising that mighty member)" (21). Swinburne, we might recall, would castigate Little Nell as "the child [that] has never a touch of childhood about her." Algernon Charles Swinburne, "The Greatness of Dickens," in *Charles Dickens: A Bookman Extra Number, 1914* (London: Hodder and Stoughton, 1914), 183. See Chapter 2.

22. Nicholas Dames, *Amnesiac Selves: Nostalgia, Forgetting, and British Fiction, 1810–1870* (Oxford: Oxford University Press, 2001), 117. Dames makes what is apparently a telling typo at this point, writing Lucy "can only look enviably on Polly's physical charms" (117). His slip converts Lucy from envious spectator to envied subject, granting the wish informing her scrutiny of the doll-child-woman.

23. Melanie Klein, "Envy and Gratitude (1957)," in *Envy and Gratitude and Other Works 1946–1963* (London: Vintage, 1997), 181. While envy has not been the focus of critical interpretation of *Villette*, William Cohen has convincingly illustrated the analytic possibilities offered for the Victorian novel by this affect, invoking Klein. "Envy and Victorian Fiction," *NOVEL: A Forum on Fiction* 42, no. 2 (Summer 2009): 297–303.

24. Klein, "Envy and Gratitude," 180.

25. Klein, "Envy and Gratitude," 184.

26. Joseph Litvak, on the other hand, provides a dazzling reading of *Villette*'s fluctuations between concealment and self-exposure as a fort/da toggle between the theatrical and the pedagogic that unhinges both terms. *Caught in the Act: Theatricality in the Nineteenth-Century English Novel* (Berkeley: University of California Press, 1992), 75–107.

27. Braun, "Narrating Loss," 196.

28. Braun, "Narrating Loss," 196.

29. Rachel Ablow, *Victorian Pain* (Princeton, NJ: Princeton University Press, 2017), 74.

30. Ablow, *Victorian Pain*, 81, 85.

31. Kate E. Brown, "Catastrophe and the City: Charlotte Brontë as Urban Novelist," *Nineteenth-Century Literature* 57, no. 3 (December 2002): 352, 380.

32. Melanie Klein, "The Importance of Symbol-Formation in the Development of the Ego (1930)," in *Love, Guilt and Reparation*, 224. Subsequent in-text references are to this edition.

33. M. Paul's repeated imperative anticipates Miss Havisham's perverse injunction to Pip and Estella, "play, play, play!" but equally its reparative reworking in Jenny Wren's dream: "They call: 'Come and play with us!' When I said 'I never play! I can't play!' they swept about me and took me up." Charles Dickens, *Great Expectations* (London: Penguin, 1996), 59; Charles Dickens, *Our Mutual Friend* (London: Penguin, 1997), 238. His refusal to accommodate Lucy's resistance to play is in part, like Klein's engagement with Dick, a healing strategy.

34. Litvak, *Caught in the Act*, 94.

35. In Marcus's powerful reading, Lucy's performance, and the feelings that inform it, bespeak an "erotic heat" between Ginevra and Lucy that "dissipates into what each sees as a more primary contest over men"; a contest she also sees played out between Lucy and Paulina de Bassompierre. Marcus identifies a version of doll-play as integral to the erotics she observes here, situating them within a broader argument that the female child learns to commodify and fetishize femininity "by idolizing, caressing or tormenting, her female doll." Sharon Marcus, *Between Women: Friendship, Desire, and Marriage in Victorian England* (Princeton, NJ: Princeton University Press, 2007), 105, 113.

36. Eva Badowska, "Choseville: Brontë's *Villette* and the Art of Bourgeois Interiority," *PMLA* 120, no. 5 (October 2005): 1515.

37. Badowska, "Choseville," 1516.

38. Benton Jay Komins, for example, misconstrues Lucy's earlier sarcastically granted permission to the reader to picture her post-Bretton years as a time of "plump happiness" as describing a reality that she seeks to recover. "Godaffiliation: Lucy Snowe's Thwarted Development in Charlotte Brontë's *Villette*," *Journal of Literary Studies* 16, no. 2 (2000): 43. Rachel Ablow misunderstands the resumed relationship with the man she terms "Graham Bretton, her childhood playmate" as

one in which Lucy "has every reason to expect kindness" (*Victorian Pain*, 77). Graham and Lucy were never "the playmates": Lucy noted, in the chapter of that title, that Graham and Polly amused one another "a great deal more than [. . .] Lucy Snowe" (31). Their lack of "kindness" in registering their play-preference for one another has, I am arguing, long staged the later relationship between the three; one in which Lucy is soon again to be erased by their mutual, playful fascination.

39. Badowska, however, is emphatic that, in her estimation, "there is no straightforward equivalence between psychology and material being" ("Chose-ville," 1518).

40. Badowska, "Choseville," 1511.

41. Badowska's article takes its title from this abandoned term.

42. For an analysis of Charlotte's editing of *Villette* as scissor-work (though without reference to the novel's altered title), see Ileana Marin, "Charlotte Brontë's Busy Scissors Revising *Villette*," *Brontë Studies* 39, no. 1 (2014): 42–53.

43. We might also, more tenuously, invoke here the Freudian term *Das Ding*, which surfaced most significantly in his work in relation to the fort/da game in *Beyond the Pleasure Principle* (the text that spurred Melanie Klein's thinking around child's play). *Das Ding* would translate in French as "*la chose*." In Lacan's seminar "L'Éthique de la Psychanalyse" (1958–59), in which he discusses the Freudian term, *la chose* and *das Ding* are used interchangeably. Jacques Lacan, *The Seminar, Book VII: The Ethics of Psychoanalysis*, 1959–60, trans. Dennis Porter (London: Routledge, 1992), esp. 54–55.

44. Klein, "Envy and Gratitude," 206.

45. Juliet Barker, *The Brontës, Wild Genius on the Moors: The Story of a Literary Family* (New York: Pegasus, 2010), 834.

46. Barker, *Wild Genius*, 836.

47. Klein, "Envy and Gratitude," 198.

48. Klein, "Envy and Gratitude," 208.

49. Klein, "Envy and Gratitude," 208.

50. Badowska identifies Lucy's final home as "a dollhouse," and acknowledges, mixing her toy metaphors, that "Villette, with its miniaturized title (little City), could well be read as a novel about life in a dollhouse, where Lucy is the puppet master, pulling the strings of her collection of dolls" ("Choseville," 1520). Yet she persists in understanding the dollhouse as "locus of the nostalgic mode" rather than the therapeutic, thus plumping for the *Wunderkammer* analogy for the novel's world of things (1520). Cabinet to dollhouse is as Rousseau's enlightened child to Klein's envious and angry one: it evacuates the complexity of the novel's object relating.

51. My analysis of Lucy and M. Paul's child-therapeutic relationship contradicts Nicholas Dames's. Focusing on M. Paul's examination of Lucy phrenologically, Dames also suggests that M. Paul is able to interpret Lucy rightly, but argues that his understanding of her "is crucially not founded on childhood cathexes but rather on an adult process of reading, counter-reading, attribution, and denial." Dames, *Amnesiac Selves*, 116.

52. George Eliot, *The Mill on the Floss* (London: Penguin, 1979), 78–79. Subsequent in-text references are to this edition.

53. Charles Dickens, *The Old Curiosity Shop* (London: Penguin, 2000), 505.

54. George Eliot, *The George Eliot Letters*, vol. 3, *1859–1861*, ed. Gordon S. Haight (New Haven. CT: Yale University Press, 1954), 374.

55. David Carroll, *George Eliot: The Critical Heritage* (London: Routledge and Kegan Paul, 1971), 160, 168.

56. F. R. Leavis, *The Great Tradition* (London: Chatto and Windus, 1948), 56.

57. R. P. Draper, ed., *George Eliot* The Mill on the Floss *and* Silas Marner: A Casebook (London: Macmillan, 1977), 125–26, 181; Gillian Beer, *George Eliot* (Brighton, UK: Harvester Press, 1986), 99.

58. Dames, *Amnesiac Selves*, 117.

59. Charlotte Goodman, "The Lost Brother, the Twin: Women Novelists and The Male-Female Double *Bildungsroman*," *NOVEL: A Forum on Fiction* 17, no. 1 (Autumn 1983): 30, 30–31.

60. Susan Fraiman, "*The Mill on the Floss*, the Critics, and the Bildungsroman," *PMLA* 108, no. 1 (Jan 1993): 137, 138.

61. Jed Esty, *Unseasonable Youth: Modernism, Colonialism, and the Fiction of Development* (Oxford: Oxford University Press, 2012), 63.

62. Esty, *Unseasonable Youth*, 63.

63. Franco Moretti, *The Way of the World: The* Bildungsroman *and European Culture*, trans. Albert Sbragia (London: Verso, 2000), 182.

64. Meira Likiermann, *Melanie Klein: Her Work in Context* (London: Continuum, 2001), 65. In reading Maggie's actions in terms of Klein's work with her small patients, my focus remains, as it has throughout the book, on play-therapy as praxis rather than on its symbolic content. For the opposite approach (for the most part deploying the theory of post-Kleinian analysts), from which I'd want categorically to distinguish my own work, see Peggy Fitzhugh Johnstone, *The Transformation of Rage: Mourning and Creativity in George Eliot's Fiction* (New York: New York University Press, 1994), 41–67.

65. Klein, *Psycho-Analysis of Children*, 32.

66. Wax was not always the medium of deflected aggression: see my discussion of doll autobiographies in the Conclusion. The foundational toy story of Donald Winnicott's autobiographical Bildungsroman is a far from soothing wax doll play, narrated with the cadences of Eliot describing Maggie's toy-damaging: "It was on that slope I took my own private croquet mallet (handle about a foot long because I was only three years old) and I bashed flat the nose of the wax doll that belonged to my sisters and that had become a source of irritation in my life because it was over that doll that my father used to tease me." Like Eliot, the infant Winnicott betrays, in 1899, a proto-Kleinian understanding that toy-damaging is predicated on family dynamics, and is real and symbolic at once: "I knew the doll had to be altered for the worse, and much of my life has been founded on the undoubted fact that I did

this deed, not merely wished it and planned it." Clare Winnicott, "D. W. Winnicott: A Reflection," quoted in Adam Phillips, *Winnicott* (London: Penguin, 2007), 156.

67. Peter Melville Logan, *Victorian Fetishism: Intellectuals and Primitives* (Albany: State University of New York Press, 2009), 68.

68. Logan, *Victorian Fetishism*, 69–72; Sally Shuttleworth, *The Mind of the Child: Child Development in Literature, Science, and Medicine, 1840–1900* (Oxford: Oxford University Press, 2010), 98–99.

69. Barbro Almqvist Norbelie, *"Oppressive Narrowness": A Study of the Female Community in George Eliot's Early Writings* (Uppsala: Almqvist and Wiksell, 1992), 124; John Plotz, *Portable Property: Victorian Culture on the Move* (Princeton, NJ: Princeton University Press, 2008), 8.

70. Nina Auerbach, "The Power of Hunger: Demonism and Maggie Tulliver," *Nineteenth-Century Fiction* 30, no. 2 (Sep 1975): 159, 155.

71. Franz Kafka, quoted in Walter Benjamin, *Illuminations*, trans. Harry Zohn (New York: Schocken, 1986), 133.

72. Benjamin, *Illuminations*, 133.

73. Klein's Rita, who obsessively dressed and undressed her dolls as well as subjecting them to sadistic attacks, also "constantly and repeatedly changed her own clothes in the treatment sessions," displaying great anxiety in the process. Claudia Frank, *Melanie Klein in Berlin: Her First Psychoanalyses of Children* (New York: Routledge, 2009), 127.

74. Sarah E. Maier sees Maggie's recourse to the Fetish as a violent response to the social imperative to "look [. . .] like an angelic doll": "Literally acting out her mother's accusations that she is 'like a Bedlam creature' Maggie sadistically enacts her vengeance against her doll's brain" (325). "Portraits of the Girl-Child: Female *Bildungsroman* in Victorian Fiction," *Literature Compass* 4, no. 1 (2007): 324, 325. The odd conception of a "doll's brain" here is illustrative of a conflation of material objecthood and human subjectivity that is repeatedly evidenced in critical discussion of scenes of violent play, and that Klein's analysis directly addresses.

75. Eliot seems to be groping for the word "cute," which was just coming into use in its sense of slightly suspect, infantile attractiveness in the United States at the time she was writing, to describe Lucy; "cute" in the alternative sense of perceptive is the adjective with which Mr. Tulliver claims a primary kinship with Maggie.

76. "Family romance" describes the child's fantasy of discovering that she is a stepchild or adopted child, one typically acted out in the play world. Freud initially notes the aggression the fantasy discloses (with its motives of revenge and retaliation, which he links to Oedipal revelations). However he modifies this insight, rereading "these works of fiction, which seem so full of hostility," as preserving "the child's original affection for his parents" and ultimately disclosing a desire to exalt rather than annihilate their bond. Sigmund Freud, "Family Romances," in *Jensen's "Gradiva"; And Other Works*, vol. 9, *The Standard Edition of the Complete Psychological Works of Sigmund Freud*, trans. James Strachey (London: Vintage Books, Hogarth Press,

and the Institute of Psychoanalysis, 2001), 239. Klein's recognition of infant sadism contradicted this benign conclusion. One of Klein's first papers, "Der Familienroman in statu nascendi" (1920) addressed the Freudian paradigm, discussing its manifestations in children's play. Frank, *Melanie Klein in Berlin*, 12.

77. Sarah Maier also understands Maggie's as a regressed Bildung for which the doll in the attic is an emblem; however, she reads the Fetish scene as acting out an incipient feminist rage: "Maggie's doll symbolises her inability to translate her silenced anger of childhood into a positive force in her adulthood that keeps her from succeeding in her progression," rather than the more psychically complicated envy and shame that I have traced here. Maier, "Female *Bildungsroman*," 329.

78. Klein, "Symbol-Formation," 220, 221.

79. Elizabeth A. Wilson, *Gut Feminism* (Durham, NC: Duke University Press, 2015), 71.

80. Klein, *Psycho-Analysis of Children*, 33, 38.

Conclusion: Toy Stories

1. This has been especially the case since the release of the first Pixar animation under that title.

2. Julie Gouraud, *Memoirs of a Doll: Written by Herself; A New Year's Gift: Adapted from the French by Mrs. Besset* (London: George Routledge, 1854), vi. Subsequent in-text references are to this edition.

3. Richard Henry Horne, *Memoirs of a London Doll, Written by Herself*, ed. Mrs. Fairstar, pseud. (Boston: Tocknor, Reed, and Fields, 1852), 2–3. Subsequent in-text references are to this edition.

4. Lois R. Kuznets notes that "in Latin and French, the words for doll are the same as those for puppet." *When Toys Come Alive: Narratives of Animation, Metamorphosis, and Development* (New Haven, CT: Yale University Press, 1994), 11–12.

5. Carlo Collodi, *Pinocchio*, trans. Geoffrey Brock (New York: New York Review Books, 2009), 3, 4, 6.

6. Collodi, *Pinocchio*, 10. Produced in the era of late literary modernism, post the development of psychoanalysis, we might expect the Disney cartoon to exemplify a knowingness lacking in the nineteenth-century tale. Yet the *Pinocchio* of 1940 is, as Kenneth Gross observes, a "saccharine retelling" of Collodi's tale. "The Madness of Puppets," *The Hopkins Review* 2, no. 2 (Spring 2009): 198. Disney's Pinocchio is a considerably more benign toy child than that of the 1880s, from the outset an innocent rather than a rascal. Apart from a moment on "Pleasure Island" where he briefly concedes that "being bad's a lot of fun," he is led astray by naivety rather than any kind of malice. His Bildung is underpinned by a clear morality, voiced by his externalized conscience Jiminy, the talking cricket. It is Collodi's original, like the other nineteenth-century toy stories discussed in this book, that depicts the kind of child that psychoanalysis had disclosed by the era of the Disney cartoon.

7. Collodi, *Pinocchio*, 159.

8. Collodi, *Pinocchio*, 50, 58.

9. Mrs. Alfred Gatty, *Aunt Sally's Life* (London: Bell and Daldy, 1865), 2, 3. Subsequent in-text references are to this edition.

10. Maria Edgeworth and Richard Lovell Edgeworth, *Practical Education* (London: J. Johnson, 1798), 15, 16.

11. Clara Bradford, *Ethel's Adventures in the Doll Country* (London: John F. Shaw, 1880), 2. Subsequent in-text references are to this edition.

12. Edgeworth and Edgeworth, *Practical Education*, 3.

13. Several critics have noticed Ethel's rejection of the domestic and social imperatives to understand her dolls as feeling subjects. Sharon Marcus regards Ethel's sadism as proto-sexualized. *Between Women: Friendship, Desire, and Marriage in Victorian England* (Princeton, NJ: Princeton University Press, 2007). This is an interpretation that Eugenia Gonzalez queries, arguing that "Certainly, Ethel derives pleasure from putting the doll through a number of punitive scenarios, but it is precisely because she does not attribute sentience to the doll." As she neatly expresses it: "Ethel puts dolls back in their place as objects." However, Gonzalez's focus is on the girl-child as accumulator: for her the object is the object of consumption, and explicitly not of psychoanalysis (Ethel, she emphasizes, is not "acting out of some unconscious source of anger"). "'I Sometimes Think She Is a Spy on All My Actions': Dolls, Girls, and Disciplinary Surveillance in the Nineteenth-Century Doll Tale," *Children's Literature* 39 (2011): 53. Victoria Ford Smith also observes that "For Ethel, dolls are not objects to coddle and nurse but instead opportunities for violence," although she castigates her behavior as "unforgiving [. . .] irrational and nearly always unjust." "Dolls and Imaginative Agency in Bradford, Pardoe, and Dickens," *Dickens Studies Annual* 40 (2009): 174–75, 174.

Works Cited

Ablow, Rachel. *Victorian Pain*. Princeton, NJ: Princeton University Press, 2017.

Adrian, Arthur A. *Dickens and the Parent-Child Relationship*. Athens: Ohio University Press, 1984.

Alexander, Christine. "Autobiography and Juvenilia: The Fractured Self in Charlotte Brontë's Early Manuscripts." In *The Child Writer from Austen to Woolf*. Edited by Christine Alexander and Juliet McMaster, 154–72. Cambridge: Cambridge University Press, 2005.

Allen, Amy, and Mari Ruti. *Critical Theory Between Klein and Lacan: A Dialogue*. London: Bloomsbury, 2019.

Amigoni, David. *Victorian Literature*. Edinburgh: Edinburgh University Press, 2011.

Anderson, Amanda. *Psyche and Ethos: Moral Life After Psychology*. Oxford: Oxford University Press, 2018.

Andrews, Malcolm. *Dickens and the Grown-Up Child*. Basingstoke, UK: Macmillan, 1994.

Ariès, Phillippe. *Centuries of Childhood: A Social History of Family Life*. Translated by Robert Baldick. New York: Knopf, 1962.

Armstrong, Frances. *Dickens and the Concept of Home*. Ann Arbor, MI: UMI Research Press, 1990.

Auerbach, Nina. "The Power of Hunger: Demonism and Maggie Tulliver." *Nineteenth-Century Fiction* 30, no. 2 (Sep 1975): 150–71.

Bach, Stefanie. "Musical Gypsies and Anti-Classical Aesthetics: The Romantic Reception of Goethe's Mignon Character in Brentano's *Die mehreren Wehmüller und ungarische Nationalgesichter*." In *Music and Literature in German Romanticism*. Edited by Siobhán Donovan and Robin Elliott, 105–20. Suffolk, UK: Camden House/Boydell and Brewer, 2004.

Badowska, Eva. "Choseville: Brontë's *Villette* and the Art of Bourgeois Interiority." *PMLA* 120, no. 5 (October 2005): 1509–23.

Baldridge, Cates. "'Agnes Grey': Brontë's 'Bildungsroman' That Isn't." *The Journal of Narrative Technique* 23, no. 1 (Winter 1993): 31–45.

Barker, Juliet. *The Brontës, Wild Genius on the Moors: The Story of a Literary Family.* New York: Pegasus, 2010.

Barossa, Julia, ed. *The New Klein-Lacan Dialogues.* Boca Raton, FL: Routledge, 2018.

Barthes, Roland. *Mythologies.* Translated Annette Lavers. London: Vintage, 1993.

Baudelaire, Charles. *The Painter of Modern Life and Other Essays.* Translated by Jonathan Mayne. London: Phaidon, 1964.

Bechdel, Alison. *Are You My Mother? A Comic Drama.* Boston: Houghton Mifflin Harcourt, 2012.

Beer, Gillian. *George Eliot.* Brighton, UK: Harvester Press, 1986.

Behler, Brianna. "The Doll's Gift: Ventriloquizing *Bleak House.*" *Nineteenth-Century Literature* 75, no. 1 (2020): 24–49.

Bell, Michael. *Open Secrets: Literature, Education and Authority from J. J. Rousseau to J. M. Coetzee.* Oxford: Oxford University Press, 2007.

Benjamin, Walter. *Illuminations.* Translated by Harry Zohn. New York: Schocken, 1986.

———. *Moscow Diary.* Edited by Gary Smith and translated by Richard Sieburth. Cambridge, MA: Harvard University Press, 1986.

Bennet, Rachel. "Punch versus Christian in *The Old Curiosity Shop.*" *The Review of English Studies* 22, no. 88 (November 1971): 423–34.

Berry, Laura C. *The Child, The State and the Victorian Novel.* Charlottesville: University of Virginia Press, 1999.

Best, Stephen, and Sharon Marcus. "Surface Reading: An Introduction." *Representations* 108 (Fall 2009): 1–21.

Blackwell, Bonnie. "War in the Nursery, 1798: The Persecuting Breast and the Melancholy Babe in Maria Edgeworth's *Ennui.*" *Women's Studies* 31, no. 3 (2002): 349–97.

Blackwell, Mark, ed. *The Secret Life of Things: Animals, Objects and It-Narratives in Eighteenth-Century England.* Lewisburg, PA: Bucknell University Press, 2007.

Blum, Virginia. *Hide and Seek: The Child Between Psychoanalysis and Fiction.* Urbana: University of Illinois Press, 1995.

Bock, Carol. "Authorship, the Brontës, and 'Fraser's Magazine': 'Coming Forward' as an Author on Early Victorian England." *Victorian Literature and Culture* 19, no. 2 (2001): 241–66.

———. "'Our Plays': The Brontë Juvenilia." In *The Cambridge Companion to the Brontës.* Edited by Heather Glen, 34–52. Cambridge: Cambridge University Press, 2002.

Bodenheimer, Rosemary. "Dickens and the Knowing Child," in *Dickens and the Imagined Child.* Edited by Peter Merchant and Catherine Waters, 13–26. Farnham: Ashgate Publishing, 2015.

Bott Spillius, Elizabeth, Jane Milton, Penelope Garvey, Cyril Couve, and Deborah Steiner. *The New Dictionary of Kleinian Thought.* London: Routledge, 2011.

Bradford, Clara. *Ethel's Adventures in the Doll Country.* London: John F. Shaw, 1880.

Braun, Gretchen. "'A Great Break in the Common Course of Confession': Narrating Loss in Charlotte Brontë's *Villette.*" *ELH* 78, no. 1 (Spring 2011): 189–212.

Bristow, Joseph. *Empire Boys.* London: Routledge, 2017.

Brontë, Anne. *Agnes Grey.* Oxford: Oxford World's Classics, 1988.

Brontë, Charlotte. "Biographical Notice of Ellis and Acton Bell (1850)." Reprinted in Emily Brontë, *Wuthering Heights,* 307–12.

———. "Editor's Preface to the New Edition of *Wuthering Heights* (1850)." Reprinted in Emily Brontë, *Wuthering Heights,* 313–16.

———. *The Glass Town Saga, 1826–1832.* In Vol. 1, *The Early Writings of Charlotte Brontë,* edited by Christine Alexander. Oxford: Blackwell, 1987.

———. *The Professor.* Edited by Heather Glen. London: Penguin, 1989.

———. "The Roe Head Journal." In *Tales of Glass Town, Angria, and Gondal: Selected Writings.* Edited by Christine Alexander, 158–74. Oxford: Oxford University Press, 2010.

———. "The Silver Cup: A Tale." Unpublished manuscript, Oct 1829. Houghton Library, MS Lowell 1 (5). https://iiif.lib.harvard.edu/manifests/view/drs:6131695$2i.

———. "To Sydney Dobell, 8 December 1850." Reprinted in Emily Brontë, *Wuthering Heights.*

———. *Villette.* London: Penguin, 2004.

Brontë, Emily. *Wuthering Heights.* Edited by Richard J. Dunn. New York: Norton, 2003.

Brontë, Emily, and Anne Brontë. "Appendix A: Diary Papers." In *Tales of Glass Town, Angria, and Gondal: Selected Writings.* Edited by Christine Alexander, 485–93. Oxford: Oxford University Press, 2010.

Brontë, Patrick Branwell. *The Works of Patrick Branwell Brontë.* Vol. 1, 1827–33, edited by Victor Neufeldt. London: Routledge, 1997.

Brooks, Peter. *Realist Vision.* New Haven, CT: Yale University Press, 2005.

Brown, Bill, ed. *Things.* Chicago: University of Chicago Press, 2004.

Brown, Kate E. "Beloved Objects: Mourning, Materiality, and Charlotte Brontë's 'Never-Ending Story.'" *ELH* 65 (1998): 395–421.

———. "Catastrophe and the City: Charlotte Brontë as Urban Novelist." *Nineteenth-Century Literature* 57, no. 3 (December 2002): 350–80.

Brown, Kenneth D. "Modelling for War? Toy Soldiers in Late Victorian and Edwardian Britain." *Journal of Social History* 24, no. 2 (Winter 1990): 237–54.

Buckmaster, Jonathan. *Dickens's Clowns: Charles Dickens, Joseph Grimaldi and the Pantomime of Life.* Edinburgh: Edinburgh University Press, 2019.

Butcher, Emma. *The Brontës and War: Fantasy and Conflict in Charlotte and Branwell Brontë's Youthful Writings.* Cham, Switzerland: Palgrave, 2019.

Butler, Janet. "Charlotte Brontë's Manuscripts: Two Sketches and Her Holograph Preface to *The Professor.*" *Studies in Bibliography* 40 (1987): 201–6.

Butler, Marilyn. "Edgeworth's Stern Father: Escaping Thomas Day, 1795–1801." In *Tradition in Transition: Women Writers, Marginal Texts, and the Eighteenth-*

Century Canon. Edited by Alvaro Ribiero and James G. Basker, 75–94. Oxford: Oxford University Press, 1996.

Byler, Lauren. "Dickens's Little Women; or, Cute as the Dickens." *Victorian Literature and Culture* 41 (2013): 219–50.

Cafarelli, Annette Wheeler. "Rousseau and British Romanticism: Women and British Romanticism." In *Cultural Interactions in the Romantic Age: Critical Essays in Comparative Literature*. Edited by Gregory Maertz, 125–56. Albany: State University of New York Press, 1998.

Cain, Lynn. *Dickens, Family, Authorship: Psychoanalytic Perspectives on Kinship and Creativity*. London: Routledge, 2016.

Carey, John. *The Violent Effigy: A Study of Dickens' Imagination*. London: Faber and Faber, 1973.

Carroll, David. *George Eliot: The Critical Heritage*. London: Routledge and Kegan Paul, 1971.

Carter, Sarah Anne. "An Object Lesson, or Don't Eat the Evidence." *The Journal of the History of Childhood and Youth* 3, no. 1 (2010): 7–12.

Cave, Terence. *Mignon's Afterlives: Crossing Cultures from Goethe to the Twenty-First Century*. Oxford: Oxford University Press, 2011.

Chandler, James. "Edgeworth and the Lunar Enlightenment." *Eighteenth-Century Studies* 45, no. 1 (2011): 87–104.

Chase, Karen, and Michael Levenson. *The Spectacle of Intimacy: A Public Life for the Victorian Family*. Princeton, NJ: Princeton University Press, 2000.

Chesterton, G. K. *Appreciations and Criticisms of the Works of Charles Dickens*. Boston, MA: E. P. Dutton, 1921.

Christoff, Alicia. *Novel Relations: Victorian Fiction and British Psychoanalysis*. Princeton, NJ: Princeton University Press, 2019.

Clement, Priscilla Ferguson. *Growing Pains: Children in the Industrial Age, 1850–1890*. New York: Twain, 1997.

Cohen, William. *Embodied: Victorian Literature and the Senses*. Minneapolis: University of Minnesota Press, 2009.

———. "Envy and Victorian Fiction." *NOVEL: A Forum on Fiction* 42, no. 2 (Summer 2009): 297–303.

Cohn, Elisha. *Still Life: Suspended Development in the Victorian Novel*. Oxford: Oxford University Press, 2016.

Collodi, Carlo. *Pinocchio*. Translated by Geoffrey Brock. New York: New York Review Books, 2009.

Conover, Robin St John. "Creating Angria: Charlotte and Branwell Brontë's Collaboration." *Brontë Society Transactions* 24, no. 1 (April 1999): 16–32.

Coveney, Peter. "The Child in Dickens." In *The Image of Childhood*. Rev. ed., 111–61. Baltimore: Penguin, 1967.

Cowper, William. "Hope." *Eighteenth-Century Poetry Archive*, lines 187–190. Accessed May 2022. https://www.eighteenthcenturypoetry.org/works/o3794-w0050.shtml.

Crone, Rosalind. *Violent Victorians: Popular Entertainment in Nineteenth-Century London*. Manchester: Manchester University Press, 2012.

Cross, Gary. *Kids' Stuff: Toys and the Changing World of American Childhood*. Cambridge, MA: Harvard University Press, 1997.

Cunningham, Hugh. *Children of the Poor: Representations of Childhood since the Seventeenth Century*. Oxford: Blackwell, 1991.

Cupelloni, Patrizia. "Anna and Her Father." *JEP: European Journal of Psychoanalysis* (Winter/Fall 2000): 10–11.

Currie, Richard A. "Surviving Maternal Loss: Transitional Relatedness in Dickens's Esther Summerson." *Dickens Quarterly* 6, no. 2 (June 1989): 60–66.

Dames, Nicholas. *Amnesiac Selves: Nostalgia, Forgetting, and British Fiction, 1810–1870*. Oxford: Oxford University Press, 2001.

Davies, Stevie. "'Three Distinct and Unconnected Tales': *The Professor, Agnes Grey* and *Wuthering Heights*," In *The Cambridge Companion to the Brontës*. Edited by Heather Glen, 72–98. Cambridge: Cambridge University Press, 2002.

Davis, Lennard J. *Factual Fictions: The Origins of the English Novel*. Philadelphia: University of Pennsylvania Press, 1996.

de Oliveira, Luiz Eduardo Prado. "The Nature of the Transference between Anna Freud and Melanie Klein: Learning from the Controversies." *International Forum of Psychoanalysis* 10 (2001): 247–58.

Derrida, Jacques. *Of Grammatology*. Translated by Gayatri Spivak. Baltimore: Johns Hopkins University Press, 1976.

Dever, Carolyn. *Death and the Mother from Dickens to Freud: Victorian Fiction and the Anxiety of Origins*. Cambridge: Cambridge University Press, 1998.

Dickens, Charles. *The British Academy/Pilgrim Edition of the Letters of Charles Dickens*, vol. 5, 1847–1849, edited by Graham Storey and K. J. Fielding. Oxford: Oxford University Press, 1980.

———. "The Cricket on the Hearth: A Fairy Tale of Home." In *A Christmas Carol and Other Christmas Books*, 163–244. Oxford: Oxford University Press, 2006.

———. *Great Expectations*. London: Penguin, 1996.

———. *Hard Times*. Oxford: Oxford World's Classics, 2008.

———. *Little Dorrit*. London: Penguin, 1985.

———. *Martin Chuzzlewit*. London: Penguin, 1999.

———. *The Old Curiosity Shop*. London: Penguin, 2000.

———. *Our Mutual Friend*. London: Penguin, 1997.

Dobell, Sydney. [Review of *Wuthering Heights*] *Palladium* (September 1850). Reprinted in Emily Brontë, *Wuthering Heights*, 293–98.

"Doll as Teacher, The" *The Londoner*, July 2, 1897.

Douthwaite, Julia. "Experimental Child-Rearing After Rousseau: Maria Edgeworth, *Practical Education* and *Belinda*." *Irish Journal of Feminist Studies* 2 (1997): 35–56.

Draper, R. P., ed. *George Eliot* The Mill on the Floss *and* Silas Marner: *A Casebook*. London: Macmillan, 1977.

Eagleton, Terry. *Myths of Power: A Marxist Study of the Brontës*. London: Macmillan, 1975.

Edelman, Lee. *No Future: Queer Theory and the Death Drive*. Durham, NC: Duke University Press, 2004.

Edgeworth, Maria. *Belinda*. Oxford University Press, 2008.

———. *Moral Tales: By Maria Edgeworth; With Original Designs by Darley*. Philadelphia: Ashmead and Evans, 1865.

Edgeworth, Maria, and Richard Lovell Edgeworth. *Practical Education*. London: J. Johnson, 1798.

Edgeworth, Richard Lovell. "Preface." In *Practical Education; Or, The History of Harry and Lucy*. Vol. 2. Honora Sneyd Edgeworth and Richard Lovell Edgeworth. Lichfield, UK: J. Jackson, 1780.

Edgeworth, Richard Lovell, and Maria Edgeworth. *Memoirs of Richard Lovell Edgeworth Esq. Begun by Himself and Concluded by his Daughter Maria Edgeworth*. London: Richard Bentley, 1844.

Eigner, Edwin M. *The Dickens Pantomime*. Berkeley: University of California Press, 1989.

Eliot, George. *The George Eliot Letters*, vol. 3, 1859–1861, edited by Gordon S Haight. New Haven, CT: Yale University Press, 1954.

———. *The Mill on the Floss*. London: Penguin, 1979.

Ericsson, Catarina. *A Child Is a Child, You Know: The Inversion of Father and Daughter in Dickens's Novels*. Stockholm: Almqvist and Wiksell, 1986.

Esty, Jed. *Unseasonable Youth: Modernism, Colonialism, and the Fiction of Development*. Oxford: Oxford University Press, 2012.

Festa, Lynn. "The Moral Ends of Eighteenth- and Nineteenth-Century Object Narratives." In *The Secret Life of Things: Animals, Objects and It-Narratives in Eighteenth-Century England*. Edited by Mark Blackwell, 309–28. Lewisburg, PA: Bucknell University Press, 2007.

Fraiman, Susan. "*The Mill on the Floss*, the Critics, and the Bildungsroman." *PMLA* 108, no. 1 (Jan 1993): 136–50.

Frank, Adam. *Transferential Poetics, from Poe to Warhol*. New York: Fordham University Press, 2014.

Frank, Claudia. *Melanie Klein in Berlin: Her First Psychoanalyses of Children*. New York: Routledge, 2009.

Franklin, Benjamin. *Experiments and Observations on Electricity, Made at Philadelphia in America, by Mr. Benjamin Franklin, and Communicated in Several Letters to Mr. P. Collinson, of London, F. R. S.* London: E. Cave, 1751.

Fraser, Antonia. *A History of Toys*. London: Spring Books, 1972.

Freud, Anna. "Beating Fantasies and Daydreams." In *Introduction to Psychoanalysis: Lectures for Child Analysts and Teachers 1922–1935*, 137–57. London: Hogarth Press and The Institute of Psycho-Analysis, 1974.

————. *The Ego and the Mechanisms of Defence.* Translated by Cecil Baines. London: Hogarth Press and the Institute of Psychoanalysis, 1966.

————. "Introduction to the Technique of the Analysis of Children." In *The Psycho-Analytical Treatment of Children: Technical Lectures and Essays.* Translated by Nancy Proctor-Gregg, 3–52. London: Imago Publishing, 1946.

————. "The Theory of Child Analysis." In *Introduction to Psychoanalysis: Lectures for Child Analysts and Teachers 1922–1935,* 162–75. London: Hogarth Press and The Institute of Psycho-Analysis, 1974.

Freud, Sigmund. "Analysis of a Phobia in a Five-Year-Old Boy." In *Case Histories 1. "Dora" and "Little Hans,"* vol. 8, *Pelican Freud Library,* 165–305. Translated by Alix and James Strachey. Edited by James Strachey and Angela Richards. Harmondsworth, UK: Penguin, 1977.

————. "Beyond the Pleasure Principle." In *Beyond the Pleasure Principle, Group Psychology and Other Works,* vol. 18, *The Standard Edition of the Complete Psychological Works of Sigmund Freud,* 1–64. Edited and translated by James Strachey. London: Vintage Books, Hogarth Press, and The Institute of Psychoanalysis, 2001.

————. "'A Child Is Being Beaten': A Contribution to the Study of the Origin of Sexual Perversions." In *An Infantile Neurosis and Other Works,* vol. 17, *The Standard Edition of the Complete Psychological Works of Sigmund Freud,* 175–204. Edited and translated by James Strachey. London: Vintage Books, Hogarth Press and The Institute of Psychoanalysis, 2001.

————. "Creative Writers and Daydreaming." In *Jensen's "Gradiva"; And Other Works,* vol. 9, *The Standard Edition of the Complete Psychological Works of Sigmund Freud,* 141–53. Edited and translated by James Strachey. London: Vintage Books, Hogarth Press, and The Institute of Psychoanalysis, 2001.

————. "Family Romances." In *Jensen's "Gradiva"; And Other Works,* vol. 9, *The Standard Edition of the Complete Psychological Works of Sigmund Freud,* 235–41. Edited and translated by James Strachey. London: Vintage Books, Hogarth Press, and The Institute of Psychoanalysis, 2001.

————. "The Uncanny." In *An Infantile Neurosis and Other Works.* Vol. 17, *The Standard Edition of the Complete Psychological Works of Sigmund Freud,* 217–56. Edited and translated by James Strachey. London: Vintage Books, Hogarth Press and The Institute of Psychoanalysis, 2001.

Frow, John. *Character and Person.* Oxford: Oxford University Press, 2014.

Gaskell, Elizabeth. *The Letters of Mrs Gaskell.* Edited by J. A. V. Chapple and Arthur Pollard. Manchester: Manchester University Press, 1997.

————. *The Life of Charlotte Brontë.* London: Penguin, 1997.

Gatty, Mrs. Alfred. *Aunt Sally's Life.* London: Bell and Daldy, 1865.

Gilbert, Sandra M., and Susan Gubar. *The Madwoman in the Attic: The Woman Writer and the Nineteenth-Century Literary Imagination.* 2nd ed. New Haven, CT: Yale University Press, 2000.

Gillis, John R. A *World of Their Own Making: Myth, Ritual and the Quest for Family Values*. Cambridge, MA: Harvard University Press, 1996.

Gitter, Elisabeth G. "The Blind Daughter in Dickens's 'Cricket on the Hearth.'" *Studies in English Literature, 1500–1900* 39, no. 4 (Autumn 1999): 675–89.

Glen, Heather. "Introduction." In Charlotte Brontê, *The Professor*. London: Penguin, 1989.

Goethe, Johann Wolfgang. *Wilhelm Meister's Apprenticeship*. Translated by Eleanor Grove. Leipzig: Tauchniz, 1873.

———. *Wilhelm Meister's Theatrical Mission*. Translated by Gregory A. Page. New York: Brentano, 1913.

Gonda, Caroline. *Reading Daughters' Fictions 1709–1834*. Cambridge: Cambridge University Press, 1996.

Gonzalez, Eugenia. "'I Sometimes Think She is a Spy on All My Actions': Dolls, Girls, and Disciplinary Surveillance in the Nineteenth-Century Doll Tale." *Children's Literature* 39 (2011): 33–57.

Goodman, Charlotte. "'The Lost Brother, the Twin': Women Novelists and the Male-Female Double Bildungsroman." *NOVEL: A Forum on Fiction* 17, no. 1 (Autumn 1983): 28–43.

Gordon, Jan B. "Gossip, Diary, Letter, Text: Anne Brontë's Narrative Tenant and the Problematic of the Gothic Sequel." *ELH* 51, no. 4 (Winter 1984): 719–45.

Gouraud, Julie. *Memoirs of a Doll: Written by Herself; A New Year's Gift: Adapted from the French by Mrs. Besset*. London: George Routledge, 1854.

Gray, Beryl. "Man and Dog: Text and Illustration in Dickens's *The Old Curiosity Shop*." In *The Lure of Illustration in the Nineteenth Century*. Edited by L. Brake, 97–118. London: Palgrave Macmillan, 2009.

Green, Martin. *Dreams of Adventure, Deeds of Empire*. New York: Basic Books, 1979.

Gross, Kenneth. "The Madness of Puppets." *The Hopkins Review* 2, no. 2 (Spring 2009): 182–205.

———. *Puppet: An Essay on Uncanny Life*. Chicago: University of Chicago Press, 2011.

Grosskurth, Phyllis. *Melanie Klein; Her World and Her Work*. London: Hodder and Stoughton, 1986.

Gubar, Marah. *Artful Dodgers: Reconceiving the Golden Age of Children's Literature*. Oxford: Oxford University Press, 2009.

Hallemeier, Katherine. "Anne Brontë's Shameful *Agnes Grey*." *Victorian Literature and Culture* 41 (2013): 251–60.

Han, Catherine Paula. "The Myth of Anne Brontë." *Brontë Studies* 42, no. 1 (2017): 48–59.

Harman, Claire. *Charlotte Brontë: A Fiery Heart*. Toronto: Alfred A. Knopf, 2015.

Heath, Michelle Beissel. *Nineteenth-Century Fictions of Childhood and the Politics of Play*. London, Routledge, 2017.

Hennelly, Mark M., Jr. "'Toy Wonders' in *Our Mutual Friend* (Part One)." *Dickens Quarterly* 12, no. 2 (1995): 60–72.

Hershinow, Stephanie Insley. *Born Yesterday: Inexperience and the Early Realist Novel*. Baltimore: Johns Hopkins University Press, 2019.

Hinshelwood, R. D. "Melanie Klein and Countertransference: A Note on Some Archival Material." *Psychoanalysis and History* 10, no. 1 (2008): 95–113.

Hoffmann, E. T. A. "The Sandman." In *Tales of Hoffman*. Translated by R. J. Hollingdale, with assistance by Stella Humphries, Vernon Humphries, and Sally Hayward. London: Penguin, 1982.

Holder, Alex. *Anna Freud, Melanie Klein, and the Psychoanalysis of Children and Adolescents*. London: Karnac, 2005.

Horne, Richard Henry. *Memoirs of a London Doll, Written by Herself*. Edited by Mrs. Fairstar, pseud. Boston: Tocknor, Reed, and Fields, 1852.

Inglis, Katherine. "Becoming Automatous: Automata in *The Old Curiousity Shop* and *Our Mutual Friend*." *19: Interdisciplinary Studies in the Long Nineteenth Century* 6 (2008). https://19.bbk.ac.uk/article/id/1726.

Jacobus, Mary. *First Things: The Maternal Imaginary in Literature, Art, and Psychoanalysis*. New York: Routledge, 1995.

———. *The Poetics of Psychoanalysis: In the Wake of Klein*. Oxford: Oxford University Press, 2005.

———. *Psychoanalysis and the Scene of Reading*. Oxford: Oxford University Press, 1999.

James, Henry. "Our Mutual Friend." *The Nation*, December 21, 1865.

Jenkins, Ruth Y. *Victorian Children's Literature: Experiencing Abjection, Empathy, and the Power of Love*. London: Palgrave, 2016.

Johnson, Barbara. *Persons and Things*. Cambridge, MA: Harvard University Press, 2008.

Johnstone, Peggy Fitzhugh. *The Transformation of Rage: Mourning and Creativity in George Eliot's Fiction*. New York: New York University Press, 1994.

Jordan, Thomas E. *Victorian Childhood: Themes and Variations*. Albany, NY: SUNY Press, 1987.

Kaiser, Matthew. *The World in Play: Portraits of a Victorian Concept*. Stanford, CA: Stanford University Press, 2012.

Kang, Minsoo. *Sublime Dreams of Living Machines: The Automaton in the European Imagination*. Cambridge, MA: Harvard University Press, 2011.

Kanwit, John Paul M. "'People Mutht be Amuthed': Work, Play, and the Dickensian Disabled Child." *Dickens Studies Annual* 47 (2016): 33–56.

Keefe, Robert. *Charlotte Brontë's World of Death*. Austin: University of Texas Press, 1979.

Ketabgian, Tamara. *The Lives of Machines: The Industrial Imaginary in Victorian Literature and Culture*. Ann Arbor: University of Michigan Press, 2011.

Kincaid, James. *Annoying the Victorians*. New York: Routledge, 2013.

————. *Child-Loving: The Erotic Child and Victorian Culture*. New York: Routledge, 1994.

King, Pearl. "Background and Development of the Freud-Klein Controversies in the British Psycho-Analytical Society." In *The Freud-Klein Controversies 1941–45*. Edited by Pearl King and Riccardo Steiner, 9–36. London: Routledge, 1991.

Klein, Melanie. "The Development of a Child (1921)." In *Love, Guilt and Reparation and Other Works 1921–1945*, 1–53. London: Vintage, 1998.

————. "Envy and Gratitude (1957)." In *Envy and Gratitude and Other Works 1946–1963*, 176–235. London: Vintage, 1997.

————. "The Importance of Symbol-Formation in the Development of the Ego (1930)." In *Love, Guilt and Reparation and Other Works 1921–1945*, 219–32. London: Vintage, 1998.

————. *Narrative of a Child Analysis: The Conduct of the Psycho-Analysis of Children as Seen in the Treatment of a Ten-Year-Old Boy*. London: Vintage, 1998.

————. "Personification in the Play of Children (1929)." In *Love, Guilt and Reparation and Other Works 1921–1945*, 199–209. London: Vintage, 1998.

————. *The Psycho-Analysis of Children*. Translated by Alix Strachey. London: Vintage, 1997.

————. "The Psycho-Analytic Play Technique; Its History and Significance (1955)." In *Envy and Gratitude and Other Works 1946–1963*, 122–39. London: Vintage, 1997.

————. "The Psychological Principles of Early Analysis (1926)." In *Love, Guilt and Reparation and Other Works 1921–1945*, 128–38. London: Vintage, 1998.

————. "Symposium on Child Analysis (1927)." In *Love, Guilt and Reparation and Other Works 1921–1945*, 139–69. London: Vintage, 1998.

————. "Weaning (1936)." In *Love, Guilt and Reparation and Other Works 1921–1945*, 290–305. London: Vintage, 1998.

Klein, Ula. "Bosom Friends and the Sapphic Breasts of *Belinda*." *Aphra Behn Online: Interactive Journal for Women in the Arts, 1640–1830* 3, no. 2 (2013). https://digitalcommons.usf.edu/abo/vol3/iss2/1/.

Kleist, Heinrich von. "On the Marionette Theatre." In *On Dolls*. Edited by Kenneth Gross, 1–10. London: Notting Hill Editions, 2012.

Komins, Brenton Jay. "Godaffiliation: Lucy Snowe's Thwarted Development in Charlotte Brontë's *Villette*." *Journal of Literary Studies* 16, no. 2 (2000): 38–49.

Kucich, John. *Repression in Victorian Fiction: Charlotte Brontë, George Eliot, and Charles Dickens*. Berkeley: University of California Press, 1987.

Kuznets, Lois R. *When Toys Come Alive: Narratives of Animation, Metamorphosis and Development*. New Haven, CT: Yale University Press, 1994.

Lacan, Jacques. *The Seminar, Book VII: The Ethics of Psychoanalysis, 1959–60*. Translated by Dennis Porter. London: Routledge, 1992.

Lamb, Edel. *Reading Children in Early Modern Culture*. London: Palgrave Macmillan, 2018.

Lane, Christopher. *Hatred and Civility: The Anti-Social Life in Victorian England*. New York: Columbia University Press, 2004.

Langbauer, Laurie. "Ethics and Theory: Suffering Children in Dickens, Dostoevsky, and Le Guin." *ELH* 75, no. 1 (Spring 2007): 89–108.
———. *The Juvenile Tradition: Young Writers and Prolepsis, 1750–1835*. Oxford: Oxford University Press, 2016.
———. "Marjorie Fleming and Child Authors: The Total Depravity of Inanimate Things." *Romanticism and Victorianism on the Net* 56 (November 2009).
Larson, Leah. "Breast Cancer and the 'Unnatural' Woman in Edgeworth's *Belinda.*" *The Explicator* 67, no. 3 (2009): 195–98.
Laubender, Carolyn. "Beyond Repair: Interpretation, Reparation, and Melanie Klein's Clinical Play-Technique." *Studies in Gender and Sexuality* 20, no. 1 (2019): 51–67.
———. "Empty Space: Creativity, Femininity, Reparation, Justice." *Free Associations: Psychoanalysis and Culture, Media, Groups, Politics* 75 (June 2019): 27–48.
Leach, Robert. *The Punch and Judy Show: History, Tradition and Meaning*. London: Batsford Academic and Educational, 1985.
Leavis, F. R. *The Great Tradition*. London: Chatto and Windus, 1948.
Lee, Yoon Sun. "Bad Plots and Objectivity in Maria Edgeworth." *Representations* 139 (2017): 35–59.
Likiermann, Meira. "The Debate between Anna Freud and Melanie Klein: An Historical Survey." *Journal of Child Psychotherapy* 21, no. 3 (1995): 313–25.
———. *Melanie Klein: Her Work in Context*. London: Continuum, 2001.
Litvak, Joseph. *Caught in the Act: Theatricality in the Nineteenth-Century English Novel*. Berkeley: University of California Press, 1992.
———. *Strange Gourmets: Sophistication, Theory, and the Novel*. Durham, NC: Duke University Press, 1997.
Locke, John. *Some Thoughts Concerning Education*. Mineola, NY: Dover, 2007.
Logan, Peter Melville. *Victorian Fetishism: Intellectuals and Primitives*. Albany: State University of New York Press, 2009.
Love, Heather. "Close but not Deep: Literary Ethics and the Descriptive Turn." *New Literary History* 41, no. 2 (Spring 2010): 371–91.
Lutz, Deborah. *The Brontë Cabinet: Three Lives in Nine Objects*. New York: Norton, 2015.
———. *The Dangerous Lover: Gothic Villains, Byronism, and the Nineteenth-Century Seduction Narrative*. Athens: Ohio University Press, 2006.
Lynch, Deidre Shauna. *The Economy of Character: Novels, Market Culture, and the Business of Inner Meaning*. Chicago: University of Chicago Press, 1998.
Lyons, Tony. "Play and Toys in the Educational Work of Richard Lovell Edgeworth 1744–1817." *Irish Educational Studies* 20, no. 1 (2001): 310–20.
Macaulay, Catharine. *Letters on Education. With Observations on Religious and Metaphysical Subjects. By Catharine Macaulay Graham*. London: C. Dilly, 1790.
Mackenzie, Henry. *The Man of Feeling*. Oxford: Oxford University Press, 1987.

Maier, Sarah E. "Portraits of the Girl-Child: Female *Bildungsroman* in Victorian Fiction." *Literature Compass* 4, no. 1 (2007): 317–35.

Malkovich, Amberyl. *Charles Dickens and the Victorian Child: Romanticizing and Socializing the Imperfect Child*. New York: Routledge, 2013.

Marcus, Sharon. *Between Women: Friendship, Desire, and Marriage in Victorian England*. Princeton, NJ: Princeton University Press, 2007.

Marin, Ileana. "Charlotte Brontë's Busy Scissors Revising *Villette*." *Brontë Studies* 39, no. 1 (2014): 42–53.

Matus, Jill. *Shock, Memory and the Unconscious in Victorian Fiction*. Cambridge: Cambridge University Press, 2011.

Mavor, Carol. *Reading Boyishly: Roland Barthes, J. M. Barrie, Jacques Henri Lartigue, Marcel Proust, and D. W. Winnicott*. Durham, NC: Duke University Press, 2007.

Mayhew, Henry. *London Labour and the London Poor*, vol. 3, *The London Street-Folk*. London: Griffin, Bohn, 1861.

McGrath, Brian. "Rousseau's Crusoe: Or, On Learning to Read as Not Myself." *Eighteenth-Century Fiction* 23, no. 1 (2010): 119–39.

Merchant, Peter, and Catherine Waters, eds. *Dickens and the Imagined Child*. Farnham: Ashgate, 2015.

Michals, Teresa. *Books for Children, Books for Adults: Age and the Novel from Defoe to James*. Cambridge: Cambridge University Press, 2014.

———. "Experiments before Breakfast: Toys, Education and Middle-Class Childhood." In *The Nineteenth-Century Child and Consumer Culture*. Edited by Dennis Denisoff, 29–42. Aldershot: Ashgate, 2008.

Michie, Helena. "'Who Is This in Pain?': Scarring, Disfigurement, and Female Identity in *Bleak House* and *Our Mutual Friend*." *NOVEL: A Forum on Fiction* 22, no. 2 (Winter 1989): 199–213.

Miller, J. Hillis. *Fiction and Repetition: Seven English Novels*. Cambridge, MA: Harvard University Press, 1982.

Moi, Toril. "Rethinking Character." In *Character: Three Inquiries in Literary Studies*. By Amanda Anderson, Rita Felski, and Toril Moi, 27–75. Chicago: University of Chicago Press, 2019.

Moon, Michael. *Darger's Resources*. Durham, NC: Duke University Press, 2012.

Moore, Ben. "The Doll's Dressmaker Re(ad)dressed: Jenny Wren's Critique of Childhood, Femininity, and Appearance." *Victorian Literature and Culture* 44 (2016): 473–90.

Moretti, Franco. *The Way of the World: The* Bildungsroman *and European Culture*. Translated by Albert Sbragia. London: Verso, 2000.

Morgenstern, Naomi. *Wild Child: Intensive Parenting and Posthumanist Ethics*. Minneapolis: University of Minnesota Press, 2018.

Myers, Mitzi. "'Anecdotes from the Nursery' in Maria Edgeworth's *Practical Education* (1798): Learning from Children 'Abroad and at Home.'" *The Princeton Library Chronical* 60, no. 2 (1999): 220–50.

Neufeldt, Victor. "The Child Is Parent to the Author: Branwell Brontë." In *The Child Writer from Austen to Woolf*. Edited by Christine Alexander and Juliet McMaster, 173–87. Cambridge: Cambridge University Press, 2005.

Newman, Beth. "Big Sister." *Victorian Review* 42, no. 2 (Fall 2016): 258–65.

Newsome, Robert. "Fictions of Childhood." In *The Cambridge Companion to Charles Dickens*. Edited by John O. Jordan. Cambridge: Cambridge University Press, 2001.

Norbelie, Barbro Almqvist. *"Oppressive Narrowness:" A Study of the Female Community in George Eliot's Early Writings*. Uppsala: Almqvist and Wiksell, 1992.

Nussbaum, Martha C. "Winnicott on the Surprises of the Self." *The Massachusetts Review* 47, no. 2 (Summer 2006): 375–93.

O'Farrell, Mary Ann. "Blindness Envy: Victorians in the Parlors of the Blind." *PMLA* (2012): 512–25.

O'Malley, Andrew. *The Making of the Modern Child: Children's Literature and Childhood in the Late Eighteenth Century*. Hove, UK: Psychology Press, 2003.

Orwell, George. "Charles Dickens." In *Essays*, 35–78. London: Penguin, 1994.

Park, Julie. *The Self and the It: Novel Objects in Eighteenth-Century England*. Stanford, CA: Stanford University Press, 2010.

Peters, Laura, ed. *Dickens and Childhood: A Library of Essays on Charles Dickens*. Aldershot, UK: Ashgate, 2012.

Phillips, Adam. *Winnicott*. London: Penguin, 2007.

Pick, Daniel. *Faces of Degeneration: A European Disorder, c. 1848–1918*. Cambridge: Cambridge University Press, 1989.

Pinchbeck, Ivy and Margaret Hewitt. *Children in English Society*. Vol. 1, *From Tudor Times to the Eighteenth Century*. London: Routledge and Kegan Paul, 1969.

———. *Children in English Society*. Vol. 2, *From the Eighteenth-Century to the Children's Act 1948*. London: Routledge and Kegan Paul, 1973.

Pittard, Christopher. "The Travelling Doll Wonder: Dickens, Secular Magic, and *Bleak House*." *Studies in the Novel* 48, no. 3 (Fall 2016): 279–300.

Plotz, John. *Portable Property: Victorian Culture on the Move*. Princeton, NJ: Princeton University Press, 2008.

Pontalis, J. B. *Frontiers in Psychoanalysis: Between the Dream and Psychic Pain*. Translated by Catherine and Phillip Cullen. London: Hogarth Press and The Institute of Psychoanalysis, 1981.

Ragussis, Michael. *Acts of Naming: The Family Plot in Fiction*. Oxford: Oxford University Press, 1986.

Raina, Badro. *Dickens and the Dialectic of Growth*. Madison: University of Wisconsin Press, 1986.

Ratchford, Fannie Elizabeth. *The Brontës' Web of Childhood*. New York: Columbia University Press, 1941.

Redfield, Marc. *Phantom Formations: Aesthetic Ideology and the Bildungsroman*. Ithaca, NY: Cornell University Press, 1996.

Riley, Denise. *War in the Nursery: Theories of the Child and the Mother*. London: Virago, 1983.

Riskind, Jessica. "The Defecating Duck, or, the Ambiguous Origins of Artificial Life." In *Things*. Edited by Bill Brown, 99–133. Chicago: University of Chicago Press, 2004.

Robson, Catherine. *Men in Wonderland: The Lost Girlhood of the Victorian Gentleman*. Princeton, NJ: Princeton University Press, 2001.

Rodas, Julia Miele. "Tiny Tim, Blind Bertha, and the Resistance of Mrs Mowcher: Charles Dickens and the Uses of Disability." *Dickens Studies Annual* 34 (2004): 51–97.

Rose, Jacqueline. *The Case of Peter Pan, or the Impossibility of Children's Fiction*. Philadelphia: University of Pennsylvania Press, 1984.

———. *Why War? Psychoanalysis, Politics and the Return to Melanie Klein*. Oxford: Blackwell, 1993.

Rose, Lionel. *The Erosion of Childhood: Child Oppression in Britain 1860–1918*. London: Routledge, 1991.

Rosenberg, Jordana. "The Bosom of the Bourgeoisie: Edgeworth's *Belinda*." *ELH* 70, no. 2 (2003): 575–96.

Rousseau, Jean-Jacques. *Émile or On Education*. Translated by Allan Bloom. London: Penguin, 1991.

Russell, David. *Tact: Aesthetic Liberalism and the Essay Form in Nineteenth-Century Britain*. Princeton, NJ: Princeton University Press, 2017.

Rylance, Rick. *Victorian Psychology and British Culture: 1850–1880*. Oxford: Oxford University Press, 2000.

Sanchez-Pardo, Esther. *Cultures of the Death Drive: Melanie Klein and Modernist Melancholia*. Durham, NC: Duke University Press, 2003.

Schaffer, Roy. "Wild Analysis." *Journal of the American Psychoanalytic Association* 33, no. 2 (1985): 275–99.

Schaffer, Simon. "Enlightened Automata." In *The Sciences in Enlightenment Europe*. Edited by William Clark, Jan Golinski, and Simon Schaffer, 125–65. Chicago: University of Chicago Press, 1999.

Schiffman, Robyn L. "Wax-Work, Clock-Work, and Puppet-Shews: *Bleak House* and the Uncanny." *Dickens Studies Annual* 30 (2001): 159–71.

Schlicke, Paul. *Dickens and Popular Entertainment*. London: Routledge, 2016.

Schor, Hilary M. *Dickens and the Daughter of the House*. Cambridge: Cambridge University Press, 1999.

Sedgwick, Eve Kosofsky. "Melanie Klein and the Difference Affect Makes." In *The Weather in Proust*. Edited by Jonathan Goldberg. Durham, NC: Duke University Press, 2011.

———. "Paranoid Reading and Reparative Reading; or, You're So Paranoid, You Probably Think This Essay Is About You." In *Touching Feeling: Affect, Pedagogy, Performativity*, 123–51. Durham, NC: Duke University Press, 2003.

Shuttleworth, Sally. *Charlotte Brontë and Victorian Psychology*. Cambridge: Cambridge University Press, 1996.

———. *The Mind of the Child: Child Development in Literature, Science, and Medicine, 1840–1900*. Oxford: Oxford University Press, 2010.

Smith, Victoria Ford. "Dolls and Imaginative Agency in Bradford, Pardoe, and Dickens." *Dickens Studies Annual* 40 (2009): 171–97.

Sotiropoulos, Carol Strauss. "Where Words Fail: Rational Education Unravels in Maria Edgeworth's "'The Good French Governess.'" *Children's Literature in Education* 32 (2001): 305–21.

Spilka, Mark. "Little Nell—Revisited." *Papers of the Michigan Academy of Science, Arts, and Letters* 45 (1960): 427–37.

Steedman, Carolyn. *Strange Dislocations: Childhood and the Idea of Interiority, 1780–1930.* Cambridge, MA: Harvard University Press, 1995.

Steig, Michael. "The Central Action of *The Old Curiosity Shop*; or, Little Nell Revisited Again." *Literature and Psychology* 13, no. 3 (Summer 1965): 163–70.

Stewart, Susan. *On Longing: Narratives of the Miniature, the Gigantic, the Souvenir, the Collection.* Durham, NC: Duke University Press, 1992.

Stiles, Anne. "Victorian Psychology and the Novel." *Literature Compass* 5, no. 3 (2008): 668–80.

Stoler, John A. "Affection and Lust in *The Old Curiosity Shop*: Dickens and Mary—Again." *McNeese Review* 53 (1997): 90–102.

Stone, Lawrence. *The Family, Sex and Marriage in England 1500–1800.* London: Weidenfeld and Nicolson, 1977.

Stonebridge, Lyndsey. *The Destructive Element: British Psychoanalysis and Modernism.* New York: Routledge, 1998.

Strange, Julie-Marie. "Fairy Tales of Fertility: Bodies, Sex and the Life-Cycle, c. 1750–2000." In *The Routledge History of Sex and the Body 1500 to the Present.* Edited by Sarah Toulalin and Kate Fisher, 296–309. Abingdon: Routledge, 2013.

Sussman, Herbert, and Gerhard Joseph. "Prefiguring the Posthuman: Dickens and Prosthesis." *Victorian Literature and Culture* (2004): 617–28.

Swinburne, Algernon Charles. "The Greatness of Dickens." In *Charles Dickens: A Bookman Extra Number, 1914.* London: Hodder and Stoughton, 1914.

Taylor, Jenny Bourne, and Sally Shuttleworth, eds. *Embodied Selves: An Anthology of Psychological Texts 1830–1890.* Oxford: Oxford University Press, 1998.

Thackeray, William Makepeace. *Vanity Fair: A Novel Without a Hero.* London: Penguin 2001.

Thiel, Elisabeth. *The Fantasy of Family: Nineteenth-Century Literature and the Myth of the Domestic Ideal.* London: Routledge, 2008.

Thormählen, Marianne, ed. *The Brontës in Context.* Cambridge: Cambridge University Press, 2012.

———. *The Brontës and Education.* Cambridge: Cambridge University Press, 2007.

Tiffany, Daniel. *Toy Medium: Materialism and Modern Lyric.* Berkeley: University of California Press, 2000.

Tilley, Heather. *Blindness and Writing: From Wordsworth to Gissing.* Cambridge: Cambridge University Press, 2018.

Toal, Catherine. "Control Experiment: Edgeworth's Critique of Rousseau's Educational Theory." In *An Uncomfortable Authority: Maria Edgeworth and her*

Contexts. Edited by Heidi Kaufman and Chris Fauske, 212–31. Cranbury, NJ: Associated University Presses, 2004.

Tressler, Beth. "Illegible Minds: Charlotte Brontë's Early Writings and the Psychology or Moral Management in *Jane Eyre* and *Villette*." *Studies in the Novel* 47, no. 1 (Spring 2015): 1–19.

Trumpener, Katie. "Actors, Puppets, *Girls*: Little Women and the Collective Bildungsroman." In *The Bildungsroman: Form and Transformations*. Edited by John Frow, Melissa Hardie, and Vanessa Smith. Special issue, *Textual Practice* 34, no. 12 (2020): 1911–31.

———. *Bardic Nationalism: The Romantic Novel and the British Empire*. Princeton, NJ: Princeton University Press, 1997.

———. "The Making of Child Readers." In *The Cambridge History of British Romanticism*. Edited by James Chandler. Cambridge: Cambridge University Press, 2009.

Vale, Brenda, and Robert Vale. *Architecture on the Carpet: The Curious Tale of Construction Toys and the Genesis of Modern Buildings*. London: Thames and Hudson, 2013.

Van Ghent, Dorothy. "The Dickens World: A View from Todgers's." *Sewanee Review* 58, no. 3 (1950): 419–38.

Vanneufville, Monique. "The Theme of Writing in the Letters between Lou Andreas, Anna Freud, and Sigmund Freud." *Savoirs et Clinique* 15, no. 1 (2012): 118–27.

Waters, Catherine. *Dickens and the Politics of the Family*. Cambridge: Cambridge University Press, 1997.

Wiegman, Robyn. "The Times We're In: Queer Feminist Criticism and the Reparative 'Turn.'" *Feminist Theory* 15, no. 1 (2014): 4–25.

Williams, Meg Harris. "Book Magic: Aesthetic Conflicts in Charlotte Brontë's Juvenilia." *Nineteenth-Century Literature* 42, no. 1 (June 1987): 29–45.

Wilson, Elizabeth A. *Gut Feminism*. Durham, NC: Duke University Press, 2015.

Wiltshire, Irene. "Speech in *Wuthering Heights*: Joseph's Dialect and Charlotte's Emendations." *Brontë Studies Journal* 30, no. 1 (2005): 19–29.

Winnicott, Donald. *Playing and Reality*. Abingdon: Routledge, 2005.

Wollstonecraft, Mary. *Vindication of the Rights of Woman: With Strictures on Moral and Political Subjects*. Auckland: The Floating Press, 2010.

Woloch, Alex. *The One vs. the Many: Minor Characters and the Space of the Protagonist in the Novel*. Princeton, NJ: Princeton University Press, 2004.

Young-Bruehl, Elisabeth. *Anna Freud*. 2nd ed. New Haven, CT: Yale University Press, 2008.

———. "Anna Freud and Dorothy Burlingham at Hempstead [*sic*]: The Origins of Psychoanalytic Parent-Infant Observation." *Annual of Psychoanalysis* 32 (2004): 185–97.

Zieger, Susan. "Dickens's Queer Children." *Literature, Interpretation, Theory* 20, nos. 1–2 (2009): 141–57.

Index

Page numbers in italics refer to illustrations.

Vanessa Smith is Professor of English at the University of Sydney, Australia. Her books include *Intimate Strangers: Friendship, Exchange and Pacific Encounters* (2010) and *Literary Culture and the Pacific: Nineteenth-Century Textual Encounters* (1998/2005).

www.ingramcontent.com/pod-product-compliance
Lightning Source LLC
Chambersburg PA
CBHW020252030426
42336CB00010B/727